LIVING IN FEAR

LIVING IN FEAR

A History of Horror in the Mass Media

BY LES DANIELS

A DA CAPO PAPERBACK

ACKNOWLEDGMENTS

To Edward Arnold Ltd., for "Rats" by M. R. James, from *The Collected Ghost Stories*; to Alfred A. Knopf, Inc., for "Novel of the White Powder" by Arthur Machen, from *The Three Impostors*; to Arkham House Publishers, for "The Outsider" by H. P. Lovecraft, from *The Outsider and Others*; to Scott Meredith Literary Agency, Inc., for "Slime" by Joseph Payne Brennan, from *Weird Tales*; and to Harold Matson Co., Inc., for "Blood Son" by Richard Matheson, from *The Shores of Space*.

The author also wishes to express his gratitude to the following individuals, whose cooperation, advice, and encouragement contributed to the completion of this book: Norma Asbornsen, H. L. P. Beckwith, Jr., Syd Blazar, Alec Chalmers, Desi De Simone, Harris Dienstfrey; William Gaines, Al Feldstein, and Jerry De Fuccio; Donald Grant, John King, Ellen Mayer, Mad Peck Studios, Barry Smith, Robert Somma, Barton L. St. Armand, Flo Steinberg, James Warren, Kenny Weinstein, and Marshall Wyatt. Special thanks also to two people who have spent a long time living in fear: my agent, Max Gartenberg, and my editor, Patricia Cristol.

Library of Congress Cataloging in Publication Data

Daniels, Les, 1943–
    Living in fear.

    (A Da Capo paperback)
    Reprint. Originally published: New York: Scribner, [1975]
    Includes index.
    1. Horror in mass media. 2. Horror tales, American—History and criticism. 3. Horror tales, English—History and criticism. I. Title.
[P96.H65D3 1983]   809.3'872   82-25261
    ISBN 0-306-80193-0 (pbk.)

This Da Capo Press paperback edition of *Living in Fear: A History of Horror in the Mass Media* is an unabridged republication of the first edition published in New York in 1975. It is reprinted by arrangement with Charles Scribner's & Sons.

Copyright © 1975 by Les Daniels

Published by Da Capo Press, Inc.
A Subsidiary of Plenum Publishing Corporation
233 Spring Street, New York, N.Y. 10013

CONTENTS

LIVING
IN
FEAR

·1·

THE PLAGUE YEARS: A BACKGROUND OF BELIEF

It might seem that there are enough things to be afraid of in real life. Poverty and pain, crime and corruption, oppression and depression, disease and death—all these lurk in the shadows, and sooner or later they pounce on everybody. And yet, for a substantial audience, purely imaginary terrors represent an authentic attraction. A fondness for fabricated fright is almost a universal human characteristic, although there are those who reject it, either because they find expressions of this impulse too terrifying or because they consider the whole genre crude and degrading. A possibility exists that the latter sort of disdain actually conceals the former sort of distress, but most people at least occasionally overcome both attitudes enough to experience some enjoyment from fictitious fears. There is an almost irresistible impulse to speculate on what may lie beyond our mortal miseries; this inclination may count for more than the wish to be terrified, since devotees of the macabre often continue to indulge their interest long after they are too jaded to be authentically unnerved.

Innumerable essays have been written attempting to explain the fascination for terror tales; there are enough theories to fill a book, but none of them are completely convincing. The fact is that the muse of the macabre has inspired more variations in style and subject than many glib commentators have encountered. It is commonplace to picture prehistoric people huddled in the darkness, making up stories to explain the bewildering world around them. This is an interesting image, but it fails to acknowledge that primitive myths were as likely to involve benevolent forces as brutal ones. It also ignores the fact that stories of the sinister supernatural really began to come into their own after belief in the uncanny had been almost extinguished. The myths and legends of ancient days are often full of horrors, but these are presented in a context where marvels are commonplace, so much so that virtually all of the narratives that have survived from the distant past have some fantastic element. The horror story as a distinct entity is a relatively recent invention, only a few centuries old, and it developed almost simultaneously with the idea of fiction. Modern audiences are so accustomed to tales which are obvious inventions that they fail to realize the extent to which their ancestors expected and believed their stories to be gospel truth. Even the terrifying tragedies of the relatively sophisticated Elizabethan era were usually presented as biographies of historical characters, and the pioneering novelists of the seventeenth and eighteenth centuries took great pains to disguise their fictions as fact so that they would not be accused of spreading lies.

So interest in fearsome fantasies cannot be completely explained as the result of a desire to understand the unknown. Still, the legends of the past provided many of the monsters that haunt the literature of the present, and part of the modern enthusiasm for the macabre may be attributed to ancestral memories of the days when demons were almost expected to put in an occasional appearance. The theory that ancient ideas survive in modern minds is one of the explanations that psychologists offer for the present prevalence of occult entertainments, but this interpretation is not as widespread as the psychoanalytical one which asserts that supernatural events symbolize neurotic personal problems. Sigmund Freud, in his essay "The Uncanny," calls it "that class of the terrifying which leads us back to something long known to us, once very familiar"; these, he asserts, are not recollections of primitive cultural attitudes but of "repressed infantile complexes." Thus, for instance, the hungry fiends that haunt so many horror tales may be taken to represent the oral stage of infant development, and many menaces have been analyzed as embodiments of maladjusted sexuality. Such suggestions may have some validity, but they fail to account for the intensity of the audience's vicarious experience. A skillful presentation is engrossing enough to create a sense of participation, and the imaginary horrors produce something like the dismay they would elicit if they were real, regardless of their symbolic value. An attack by a werewolf would be sufficient cause for alarm, even without the victim pausing to contemplate a misspent youth. The Freudian theory offers some insights, but is insufficient as a complete explanation, like the "collective unconscious" theory of Freud's disciple Carl Jung, which might account for the continued validity of motifs based on superstition but not for the effect of the new science fiction concepts which have demonstrated their chilling power in recent decades.

A quasi-psychological theory frequently offered by less knowledgeable commentators than Freud or Jung suggests that the appeal of the macabre exists primarily for masochists, or, alternatively, for sadists. In brief, this is an accusation that devotees take a depraved pleasure either in their own painful emotions or in the suffering of various imaginary victims. These assertions represent an obvious oversimplification, since sadism and masochism are diametrically opposed states of mind. The two explanations largely cancel out each other, and attempts to reconcile them through the use of the fatuous phrase "sadomasochism" can only further muddy the waters. Some works may appeal to one attitude or the other, but many more do not. The terms when properly used refer to states of sexual excitement caused by inflicting or experiencing pain; most suffering has more obvious motivation and does not include these special emotions. Ascribing exclusively sexual interests of a debatable nature to the artists and audiences who appreciate the awesome is primarily a tactic to discredit the genre by those who find it distressing.

Arguments about the relative tastefulness of various approaches have often been based on questions of terminology. Such important contributors as actors Boris Karloff and Christopher Lee have insisted that the word *terror* should be employed, since its strict definition implies a spiritual state of fear, whereas *horror* suggests a physical revulsion bordering on nausea. They may well be correct in designating the ideal description, but this semantic issue is largely technical: phrases like *horror film* and *horror story* have gained such popular acceptance that quibbling is irrelevant. The attempt to differentiate derives from a desire to distinguish between acceptable and unacceptable entries in the field, but such classifications are inevitably a matter of taste. Each individual has an opinion regarding the limits of taste, yet it must be acknowledged that the appeal of the macabre is dependent in large measure on the way in which it violates decorum. Discretion is one of the genre's minor virtues, and while it is possible to feel that certain episodes are excessively grim, no rigid code of restrictions could be devised that would be anything less than ludicrous.

Some aesthetic justification for the portrayal of terrifying events was offered by the ancient Greek philosopher Aristotle, whose *Poetics* includes the theory of catharsis. Aristotle held that the frequently frightening tragedies written and performed by his contemporaries served to purge the emotions through pity and terror, leaving the audience less likely to behave horribly because they had experienced the results vicariously. Perhaps the most gruesome of the classic Greek tragedies were the work of Aeschylus, whose masterpiece is the *Oresteia* (458 B.C.). This series of three plays chronicles the bloody history of the House of Atreus in the aftermath of the Trojan War. King Agamemnon has sacrificed his daughter's life to ensure victory; upon his return he is murdered by his wife Clytemnestra, and she in turn is slain by their son Orestes. As punishment, he is haunted by the Furies, hideous female spirits with serpents in their hair who weep bloody tears. While the traditions of the formalized Greek theater dictated that the murders, and indeed all action, should take place offstage, the Furies themselves were permitted to tread the boards; they are among the earliest examples of the vengeful spirits that have reappeared in literature ever since.

An even earlier narrative form than the drama is the epic poem. The legendary blind bard Homer produced the two great Greek epics; *The Iliad* is a tale of war, but *The Odyssey* includes many uncanny creatures and incidents in its hero's ten-year voyage home: the one-eyed giant cannibal Polyphemus, the seductive Sirens whose songs drive men to destruction, the sorceress Circe who turns sailors into swine, and the descent of Odysseus into Hades, where he converses with the spirits of the dead, feeding them with the blood of rams. Like the early tragedies, epics were considered to be historical records. They survive as literature because of the brilliant interpreters who set them down; but the lore of ancient Greece contains a myriad of memorable monsters, usually provided to prove a hero's prowess, but not so often blessed by the touch of a literary luminary.

That part of Western culture not derived from the Greeks owes most to the Judeo-Christian tradition represented by the Holy Bible, which contains many incidents involving sinister manifestations of the supernatural, most obviously in the person of the fallen angel Lucifer, who is credited with controlling most of the malignant entities that have infested literature since the dawn of time. Also worth noting are the stories of Enoch and the Witch of Endor, not to mention the awesome visions described in the Book of Revelation. The Bible offers glimpses of the Assyrian and Egyptian civilizations which were storehouses of the occult; little survives in the form of melodramatic narratives, but the lore of Egypt especially has proved an inspiration to modern authors in search of an idea. It seems a pity that comparatively few writers have drawn material from the equally fascinating American cultures of the Aztecs and the Mayas; not much more has been done than a couple of poor films.

The arts in ancient Rome followed the lead of the Greeks; Virgil's epic *The Aeneid* contains several weird scenes based on Homer's example. The Roman drama made some innovations, involving more action on stage, in the lurid tragedies of Seneca. The real development, though, was in the appearance of comparatively casual prose tales, like the werewolf story written by Petronius and the tale of a haunted house from Pliny's *Letters*, both fascinating in that they are full of stock incidents (such as clanking chains) that have survived two thousand years without alteration.

The whole world is full of tales like these; but it is impossible to recount them all, and it seems wisest to concentrate on what has proved to be the most flourishing branch of this universal tree. A powerful and persuasive tradition of terror tales has grown up among English-speaking people, first in Britain and later in America. Many of the creations conjured up in this milieu have spread to other nations with a thoroughness that no other culture has been able to duplicate. Even essentially alien concepts such as the vampire legend have received their definitive treatment in Anglo-American hands. This ability to assimilate the uncanny lore of all nations is exemplified by indefatigable researchers like the eccentric twentieth-century Englishman Montague Summers who, clad in a black cloak and buckled shoes, ravaged the archives of Europe to produce purportedly factual compilations like *The History of Witchcraft and Demonology* (1926) and *The Vampire, His Kith and Kin* (1928). Such efforts helped to preserve traditions of the past that had yet to be presented in artistic form.

The first great appearance of the uncanny in English literature is the epic adventure *Beowulf*. This poem, written down over a thousand years ago and presumably composed even earlier, recounts the adventures of Beowulf, a fighter of monsters who slays Grendel, a terrible troll, and is then drawn into combat with the creature's even more menacing mother. He survives this struggle but gives his life to defeat a dragon. This tale of heroism and horror is told in Old English, a form of the language so archaic that it is impossible for the modern reader to understand it.

Old English was succeeded by the comparatively intelligible Middle English, the development of which coincided with the period when printing became feasible. The greatest work of this era is Geoffrey Chaucer's *Canterbury Tales*, written over several years near the end of the fourteenth century (the precise dates of composition for works of this period are uncertain). This narrative poem includes many tales told by religious pilgrims to relieve the tedium of their journey; several of the stories are supernatural. "The Prioress's Tale" describes a murdered boy who sings his favorite hymn after his throat has been cut, leading to the discovery of his corpse and the punishment of his killers; "The Nun's Priest's Tale" includes uncanny anecdotes on the power of dreams. In one of them, a man has a nightmare in which his traveling companion reveals the facts of his murder, and in another a nightmare saves the life of a man who envisions a shipwreck.

This was also the era when the legends of King Arthur and his knights began to achieve literary permanence. The anonymous poem *Sir Gawain and the Green Knight* recounts the strange bargain between Sir Gawain and his grotesque green adversary, who offers the hero three opportunities to strike him in exchange for submission to the same conditions a year later. Although Sir Gawain beheads his opponent, the Green Knight gathers up his head and rides away, leaving Gawain in an agony of suspense for a year before the Green Knight decides to spare him. Sir Thomas Malory's definitive collection of Arthurian lore, *Le Morte d'Arthur*, is full of supernatural sequences; but they are submerged in an essentially heroic narrative and frequently involve benevolent entities. Malory's prose romance was published in 1485, several years after the author's death, by William Caxton, who had set up England's first printing press in 1476. Caxton was also responsible for the first edition of the *Canterbury Tales*, and his pioneering efforts marked the beginning of mass media in the English-speaking world. Ironically, the press came into being at a period when the best writers were moving toward the theater, so

Divers kinds of Tortures exercised on the Primitive Martyrs during the 10.ᵗʰ Roman Persecution.

Cruelties inflicted on the Primitive Christians, their Bodies being tied to Stakes, thrust through with Spears, & others thrust under their nails with Thorns.

B. Tanner Sc.

An eighteenth-century illustration for John Foxe's *Book of Martyrs*, popular for centuries after its original appearance in 1563.

The Tragicall Historie of the Life and Death of Doctor Faustus.

With new Additions.

Written by C H. M A R.

Printed at London for *John Wright*, and are to be sold at his shop without Newgate. 1631.

This 1631 title page includes the oldest known illustration for Christopher Marlowe's play about a tragic deal with devils, *Doctor Faustus* (1588).

that books provided less of the important literature of succeeding centuries than might have been expected. Still, most of the important plays were preserved for posterity by the press.

English drama began with "mystery plays," religious spectacles performed under church auspices and based on Bible stories. These gave way to "morality plays," allegorical dramas portraying personified vices and virtues. These culminated around 1500 with the anonymous masterpiece *Everyman*, in which the title character is visited by Death and discovers how little of his life he can bring with him to the grave. This short, stark piece is still a disturbing drama, perhaps the only work of its era that can still be performed effectively.

Everyman remained the greatest English play for nearly a century, until it was superseded by the robust and realistic drama of the Elizabethans. The tragedies of this period are full of violence, villains, and visions. The first important innovator in the field was Thomas Kyd, whose *Spanish Tragedy* was first produced around 1585. It proved to be the biggest hit of its day and was revived for decades. Kyd's most influential idea was to abandon the technique of ancient drama, in which all important action took place out of sight while the stage was occupied by static figures who discussed the situation. His sensational approach included the presentation of eight death scenes, along with assorted maniacs, ghosts, and such gory details as the removal of a man's tongue. The plot, in which a spirit incites the hero Hieronimo to punish his murderer, inspired the Elizabethan tradition of "revenge tragedy"; in fact, Revenge is one of the characters, a relic from the morality plays. Historical perspective and discreet scholarship have caused modern audiences to regard the drama of this age as something elegant and effete, but in truth it was an age of lurid thrillers. Actors wore bladders of sheep's blood under their clothing to make the slaughter more convincing; real weapons were used, and a performer would sometimes be so carried away that he would actually kill a colleague or even a member of the audience.

Surpassing Kyd in both style and substance was Christopher Marlowe, whose *Doctor Faustus*, even in the faulty transcriptions that have survived, is a masterpiece of the macabre. Marlowe transformed fragmentary legends into the definitive treatment on the subject of selling one's soul to Satan; he also created archetypal characters in the mocking Mephistopheles and his victim Faust, who trades eternity for youth, knowledge, power, and passion. Doctor Faustus, who as an alchemist is a cross between a scientist and a magician, is the model for the hero of hundreds of horror stories, not only because he deals with devils, but because his thirst for achievement leaves him blind to its chilling consequences.

Of course, William Shakespeare overshadows all his contemporaries. Many of his supernatural scenes are familiar, but his first tragedy, written under the influence of Kyd, is not so well known. *Titus Andronicus* (1594) contains so many ghastly incidents that some scholars have labored, in vain, to prove that Shakespeare did not write it. Titus is a conquering general of ancient Rome whose daughter is raped by the sons of the queen he has defeated. Her tongue and hands are removed to prevent accusation, but Titus discovers the culprits regardless. Insane with rage, he butchers the sons and feeds them to their mother, who discovers the nature of the feast just before Titus stabs her. He also kills his daughter at the same banquet of blood and is slaughtered himself along with several other characters, one of them by being buried up to his neck in an anthill. There are no scenes involving the uncanny, but the play is certainly horrifying enough without them.

Vicemq̃ noſtris:redde me inferis precor
Vmbris reductum meq̃ ſubiectum tuis
Reſtitue uinclis:ille me abſcondet locus
Sed & ille nouit. The. Nr̃a te tellus manet
Illic ſolutam cede gradiuus manum
Reſtituit armis.illa te alcide uocat.
Facere inocétes terra quæ ſuperos ſolet.

Tragœdia ſecunda. Thyeſtes.
Act⁹.i. Tāta.& Mege. Tātalus loq̃t̃
Vis me furor nūc ſedab iſauſtaabſtra
Auido ſugaces orecaptāté cibos(hit
Quis male deorum tantalo uias domos
Oſtendit iterum peius eſt inuentum ſiti
Arente in undis aliquid. & peius fame
Hiante ſemper ſiſyphi nunquid lapis
Geſtandus humeris lubricus noſtris uenit
Aut membra celeri deferens curſu rota
Aut pœna Tytiiſe per accreſcens iecur

A woodcut, ca. 1510, illustrating *Thiestes*, by the ancient Roman dramatist Seneca, whose scenes of cannibalism influenced Shakespeare's *Titus Andronicus*.

Lucifer, improbably dressed in the garb of a Roman soldier, rakes over damned souls in John Baptist Medina's 1688 illustration for John Milton's *Paradise Lost*.

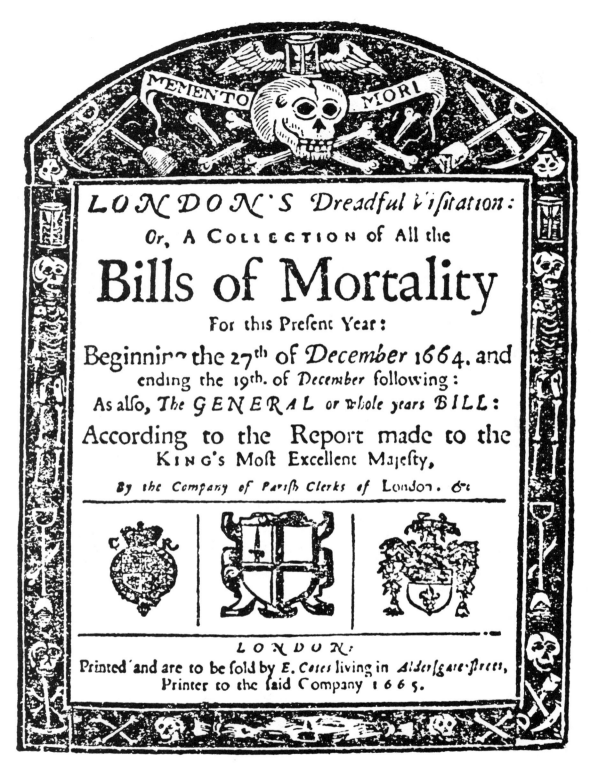

MEMENTO MORI

LONDON'S Dreadful Visitation:

Or, A COLLECTION of All the

Bills of Mortality

For this Present Year:

Beginning the 27th of December 1664. and
ending the 19th. of December following:
As also, The GENERAL or whole years BILL:

According to the Report made to the
KING's Most Excellent Majesty,

By the Company of Parish Clerks of London. &c

LONDON:
Printed and are to be sold by E. Cotes living in Aldersgate-street,
Printer to the said Company 1665.

Gravestones inspired the design for the title page of this report to royalty on the plague of 1665, immortalized in Daniel Defoe's *Journal of the Plague Year*.

Most of Shakespeare's succeeding tragedies contain some elements of terror, if nothing as intense as *Titus Andronicus*. Even *Romeo and Juliet* (1596) has its macabre moments as Juliet imagines and then experiences her awakening among the corpses in her family crypt. In *Julius Caesar* (1599), the emperor appears as a ghost who helps drive his killers to suicide, and it is the spirit of his father that drives Hamlet to madness and murder in Shakespeare's finest and final revenge tragedy, the ultimate refinement of Kyd's theme. The later tragedies are free from such fantastic elements, with the notable exception of *Macbeth* (1606). His tragedy is precipitated by the enigmatic prophecies and visions provided by three witches, and he is haunted by the ghost of his victim, Banquo.

It was inevitable that the theater should decline somewhat from the heights attained by its greatest genius, but the stage and indeed all the arts in England suffered a terrible setback from the civil war which brought the Puritans to power. In 1642, a scant quarter of a century after Shakespeare's death, a grim and narrow-minded Puritan Parliament banned the performance of plays "to appease and avert the wrath of God." The greatest author of this gray period was the blind poet John Milton, whose *Paradise Lost* (1667) contains a portrait of a defiant Lucifer so powerful that Milton unwittingly inspired devilish sentiments in the poets of a less devout age more than a century later.

Literature recovered slowly from the effects of repression, and the trend for decades, even after the defeat of the Puritans, was away from extravagant tales of the marvelous and the macabre. Fantasy would find a foothold only after the idea of fiction had been firmly established. The turning point proved to be the birth of the novel, which evolved slowly from embellished accounts of actual events, or at least of reasonable facsimiles. Daniel Defoe has perhaps the best claim to the title of first English novelist, yet all his works were presented to the public as statements of fact. His nervousness about the new form was expressed in a piece he wrote debating whether or not the perusal of fiction was sinful. Originally a journalist, Defoe published a pamphlet in 1706 now known as "The Apparition of Mrs. Veal." It was purportedly a true ghost story, and research has indicated that the characters were real persons; but the idea persists that it was written to help the sales of a treatise on the afterlife prominently mentioned in the text. Defoe's most powerful work in the vein of terror is *A Journal of the Plague Year* (1722), a grippingly convincing eyewitness account of the London plague of 1665. It seems almost impossible to believe that it is a work of the imagination, loaded as it is with vivid details and exhausting documentation. The scenes of carts full of victims rolling away to mass graves amid the awful command "Bring out your dead!" are truly grim, all the more so because although the story was concocted, the plague was real.

These years, and the ones before them, were the years when diseases did destroy multitudes, when executions were public spectacles, when accusations of sorcery were commonplace. It is customary to regard our times as the most violent and dangerous of all, not without some justice; but modern civilization, for all its faults, has built a buffer between the average individual and the brutal realities of death and destruction. Perhaps it is because there has been less and less horror to confront face to face that we have embraced it more and more in synthetic forms. The root of many contemporary problems may be buried in the recent centuries of spiritual skepticism, yet the left-handed religious sentiments that inspire tales of demons and doom have survived.

Perhaps it is more than a coincidence that 1717, the year of England's last witchcraft trial, saw the birth of Horace Walpole, the man whose nostalgia for the bad old days of tyranny and terror ushered in the modern method of living in fear.

·2·

STRAWBERRY HILL: GOTHIC GHOSTS

The first modern horror story, like so many of its successors, was inspired by a dream. Its author wrote: "I waked one morning, in the beginning of last June, from a dream, of which all I could recover was, that I had thought myself in an ancient castle (a very natural dream for a head like mine filled with Gothic story) and that on the uppermost banister of a great staircase I saw a gigantic hand in armour. In the evening I sat down, and began to write, without knowing in the least what I intended to say or relate. The work grew on my hands and I grew so fond of it that one evening, I wrote from the time I had drunk my tea, about six o'clock, till half an hour after one in the morning, when my hands and fingers were so weary that I could not hold the pen to finish the sentence."

The dreamer was Horace Walpole, describing in a letter to a friend how he came to write *The Castle of Otranto*. It may seem strange to describe this short novel, now over two centuries old, as the beginning of the "modern" mainstream of macabre imaginings; but it marked a distinct departure from the tales of supernatural doings that had been told in the past centuries. By 1764, when Walpole made a book out of his nightmare, belief in forces beyond man's control or understanding had begun to fade away. The eighteenth century was the Age of Reason, and the best minds in the most influential circles were dismissing the idea of the supernatural as nonsense. Even those who stopped short of atheism held that creation had been so perfectly planned as to exclude the intervention of forces from beyond, whether they represented light or darkness. Of course, this skepticism was far from universal; but it represented a cultural attitude that has continued to expand its influence, so that stories like *Otranto* are now classified as fantasies, to be enjoyed rather than believed.

In this sense, the whole field of macabre fantasy is reactionary, basing its appeal on subjects that were still compelling, even if they had ceased to be convincing. Walpole, whose tale of ghostly vengeance in medieval days was based on his personal interests, discovered a large audience who, if they did not believe in ghosts, could still be frightened by them and could find the fright enjoyable. The wealthy and eccentric English aristocrat was doubtless surprised at his book's popularity. Who would have thought so many people were willing to spend even an imaginary night in a Gothic castle—especially since Walpole was the only man in England who had built one for centuries?

No present-day nostalgia buff can compare with Walpole, who devoted two decades and a considerable fortune to the construction of archaic architecture on his estate, Strawberry Hill. In this strange sort of private Disneyland he was free to indulge his passion for the romance of bygone days, and the unusual atmosphere finally inspired his novel, whose setting was patterned after Walpole's bizarre home. *The Castle of Otranto* proved to be so successful and influential that it gave birth to countless imitators over the next half-century—so many, in fact, that it inaugurated an entire school of English literature: the Gothic novel.

A handful of these Gothic novels are still remembered as part of the history of English literature, and more specifically as landmarks in the field of fantasy. Most have been completely forgotten, despite their status as the most widely read works of their era. They were the eighteenth century's best sellers, and they achieved that status despite a general lack of critical acclaim. Indeed, the Gothic novel might be said to have brought in its wake the whole concept of mass culture, of works of art that have won great popularity despite their lack of official sanction. What they failed to produce in the way of serious themes or elegant style was replaced by their sensational effects.

Walpole established the formula with his tale of madness, murder, and family intrigue. His principal character is Manfred, master of the Castle of Otranto, who has gained his position by poisoning the former prince, Alfonso. Although this crime is not revealed

Horace Walpole, the originator of the Gothic novel, built this imitation medieval castle on his estate, Strawberry Hill.

until the end of the tale, it is Alfonso's ghost, clad in armor and grown to enormous stature, who perpetrates most of the story's eerie events. Manfred's son is crushed to death on his wedding day by a gigantic helmet, and Manfred decides to provide himself with a new heir by pursuing Isabella, the disappointed bride. She succeeds in keeping him at arm's length with the help of Manfred's distressed wife Hippolita and their daughter, Matilda. Further obstructions are provided by a mysterious young man named Theodore and by the ghost, who continues to appear piecemeal, once as the hand of Walpole's dream and most ludicrously as an overgrown, ironclad foot. There is also a fairly ridiculous incident in which a statue of Alfonso expresses its indignation by developing a bloody nose.

Such are the horrors of *The Castle of Otranto*, climaxing when the ghost finally collects itself into a titanic figure and bursts out of the walls of its dwelling, leaving only ruins. Declaring the stranger Theodore to be the true heir to the castle it has so thoughtlessly destroyed, the spirit rises slowly into the clouds and disappears. Manfred, who has just mistakenly murdered his daughter in an attempt on Theodore, confesses and repents. The usurper and his luckless wife join religious orders, and Theodore weds Isabella, on the less than gallant grounds that she may console him in his grief over his true love, the murdered Matilda.

The ghost is perhaps the most believable character in this conglomeration of quaint dialogue and stilted action, which is filled with sentiments and motivations of the most naïve and melodramatic type. Walpole's intentions provide an explanation if not an excuse: the book was originally published not as his own work, but as a translation of an Italian manuscript from the twelfth century. He even invented a pseudonym for the translator and wrote a tongue-in-cheek introduction, praising the work for "the piety that reigns throughout, the lessons of virtue that are inculcated, and the rigid purity of the sentiments." These were offered as compensation for the supernatural events, "exploded now even from romances." Thus Walpole continued to work in the tradition of the early English novelists who claimed historical accuracy and uplifting morality in order to justify their excursions into the suspicious field of fiction. His anonymity may also have been motivated by doubts about the reception that might be given to such an excursion into the archaic. Yet Walpole's interest in the antique and the uncanny struck a responsive chord in thousands of readers, so that he was ready to acknowledge his authorship for the second edition. The book was published abroad in several languages and freely adapted as a play, *The Count of Narbonne*, by Robert Jephson.

The Castle of Otranto was a deliberate reaction to the realistic and detailed books that are the classic examples of the eighteenth-century novel. In his preface to the first edition, Walpole praised the book for its adherence to the rules of drama, which traditionally prescribed a single setting and a concentrated passage of time. This contrasts his book with the famous novels of the preceding quarter-century, which ranged over wide stretches of geography and allowed for the passage of many years. The resulting tight construction is most obviously seen in the length of his story, which runs barely a hundred pages, while many of his predecessors come closer to a thousand. His low opinion of those considered to be his superiors is a matter of record: he called Richardson "deplorably tedious," Fielding "perpetually disgusting," and Sterne "tiresome."

Such judgments put Walpole at odds with the serious literary historians of today, but there is little doubt that he spoke for many of his contemporaries. His "Gothic" formula gradually attracted more and more followers, while realistic fiction suffered a serious

"The sleep of reason breeds monsters," the title of this work by Francisco de Goya, sums up the Gothic reaction to Rationalism. The artist, whose productions became increasingly morbid, spent his last years studying magic.

decline. For over a generation, novels based on *Otranto* were to dominate English literature, and their preeminence continued well into the nineteenth century. The public gleefully abandoned the sensible for the sensational, and the result was an apparently endless wave of "trash," of works that were despised by critics but were nevertheless enjoyed by huge audiences.

Yet the triumph of the Gothic novel was a gradual process. The world of eighteenth-century letters was a leisurely one, and it was thirteen years before Walpole's first disciple got into print. This was Clara Reeve, whose novel *The Old English Baron* was published in 1777 under the less atmospheric title *The Champion of Virtue*. Again, it was published anonymously; the author's name appeared with the new title in 1780. Somewhat longer and far more restrained than *The Castle of Otranto*, this novel retained the Gothic setting but reduced the uncanny occurrences to three consecutive "dismal hollow" groans heard as the hero uncovers evidence of a murder committed years before. Stripped to its essentials, the plot is virtually the same as Walpole's, involving a young man, Edmund, who recovers his birthright and deposes a murderous usurper. Poorly constructed, so that it trails off in a monotonous discussion of claims to the estate, this novel is hardly worth considering as an example of macabre literature. Yet it is important as a transition between Walpole's early effort and the flood that was to follow.

The author declared that it was her purpose to create a "literary offspring" of *Otranto*, "written upon the same plan" but devoid of the fantastic elements that "instead of attention, excite laughter." The result is something like the historical novel of today, not even especially mysterious or suspenseful within its naturalistic framework. All in all, *The Old English Baron* surpasses its predecessor only in the exaggerated priggishness of its virtuous characters. A disgusted Horace Walpole wrote, "The work is a professed imitation of mine, only stripped of the marvellous, and so entirely stripped, except in the one awkward attempt at a ghost or two, that it is the most insipid dull thing you can read. It certainly does not make me laugh; for what makes one doze, seldom makes one merry."

The problem of providing thrills while maintaining plausibility found a solution of sorts in the work of Ann Radcliffe, the most widely read of all the Gothic novelists. Her technique involved describing weird events that were explained at the end of the book as villainous tricks which, however contrived and unlikely, were definitely not supernatural. This recipe allowed skeptical readers to have their cake and eat it too, a fact that may have helped account for Mrs. Radcliffe's popularity, as well as for her comparatively high standing with the more serious-minded critics. Yet such devices are likely to exasperate the present-day enthusiast of macabre fiction. Similarly, her considerable gifts as a stylist are more likely to irritate than to entertain, since she employed them in elaborate descriptions of largely irrelevant landscapes or in conjuring up mysterious atmospheres in which, ultimately, nothing much happens. She was, in short, the mistress of anticlimax, and all the more annoying because her books are very long. Her major contribution was to shift the focus of her tales so that villains and spooks were pushed into the background. Instead, her novels are presented largely through the eyes of terror's intended victim. In all of Mrs. Radcliffe's novels, the heroine stands at the center of the stage. She may be threatened, pursued, harassed, or imprisoned, but no real harm ever comes to her, so that the plots are sequences of events that almost happen.

Born in the same year the first Gothic novel appeared, Ann Radcliffe had five novels published during her lifetime: *The Castles of Athlin and Dunbayne* (1789), *A Sicilian Romance* (1790), *The Romance of the Forest* (1792), *The Mysteries of Udolpho* (1794), and *The Italian*

(1797). The last two are generally considered her best, but *Udolpho* represents the apex of her career. This is the story of Emily de St. Aubert, who is persecuted by her aunt's sinister spouse, Montoni. (Mrs. Radcliffe's insistence on Italian villains, if duplicated today, would doubtless inspire action from an antidefamation league.) A classic example of Radcliffean terror occurs when Emily, having worked herself up into a highly nervous condition, pulls aside a tapestry and promptly swoons. A healthy chunk of the novel must be perused before the reader discovers that Emily saw a corpse, and another decent interval elapses before said corpse is exposed as a wax dummy, left lying around on a flimsy pretext.

This sort of hemming and hawing apparently provided thrills aplenty for Ann Radcliffe's predominantly female, middle-class, middlebrow followers, who were delighted to imagine themselves as persecuted aristocrats of exquisite beauty and unsullied virtue, fleeing from ambiguous dangers that might have been death or the fate worse than death. The genteel paranoia of maiden ladies dreaming of demon lovers pervades these works, driving such a literary luminary as Jane Austen to parody them in her earliest novel, *Northanger Abbey.* Yet even she excepted the Radcliffe sagas from her general mockery of such works, reinforcing the opinion that these were the best of a bad lot, most of them mercifully forgotten.

If some of the Gothic novels seem a trifle insipid, there were others of a more colorful cast, less concerned with the tribulations of the innocent than with the transgressions of the depraved. One such volume is *Vathek.* Written by an Englishman, William Beckford, it was originally composed in French and only later translated into the author's native tongue. This unique and delightful book virtually defies classification. Witches, demons, and ghouls wander through its pages; yet it is far from frightening, and not because Beckford lacks skill. His book is a fantasy with an Arabian Nights flavor, describing the sins and damnation of Vathek, ninth caliph of the race of the Abassides. Although such a theme is appropriate to the Gothic tradition, Beckford's luxuriant imagery and sly humor create a mood totally antithetical to that suggested by the gray castles and black deeds of medieval Europe.

Much of the action of *Vathek* takes place in a gigantic tower, eleven thousand steps high, where the caliph's wicked mother casts spells and performs human sacrifices to guide him on a pilgrimage to an underworld of demons. There he seeks power and glory, but he finds only the torture of a heart set eternally aflame. William Beckford was to build a tower too, though the results were less spectacular. Perhaps inspired by Horace Walpole's success with Strawberry Hill, Beckford personally designed a huge and elaborate structure which, upon completion, promptly fell over. Undaunted, Beckford tried again with somewhat better results, only at tremendous expense. Indeed, his life's work was the dissipation of the fortune he had inherited from his father, who had been Lord Mayor of London. It took him most of his eighty-four years to spend the money; but he did it, and he declared that he was never bored for a moment of his life.

Vathek included enough entertaining Oriental outrages to make Beckford a prime contender for the title of most decadent artist in eighteenth-century England; but the crown was snatched away from him in 1796 by one Matthew Gregory Lewis, who also took Beckford's seat in Parliament. The sensational Lewis novel, *The Monk,* which appeared with its author's government credentials firmly affixed, was the most morbidly erotic and morally exotic product of the Gothic period. *The Monk* also defined the archetypal horror hero, half-saint and half-Satanist, in the person of its protagonist, who runs amok in an orgy of rape and murder.

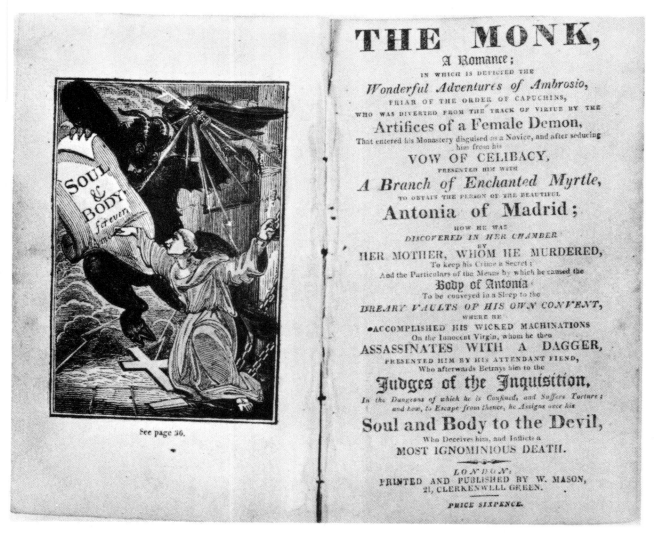

See page 36.

The frontispiece and title page for an abridged edition of the controversial Gothic novel *The Monk* by Matthew Gregory Lewis.

Ambrosio, the abbot of the Capuchins, is a foundling raised by the monks, whose extraordinary piety has made him the leader of his order and the most respected clergyman in Madrid at the time of the Spanish Inquisition. He meets temptation in the form of the beautiful Matilda, a young woman who, disguised as the novice Rosario, enters the monastery to seduce the abbot. Ambrosio breaks his vow of chastity and is led by Matilda into a whirlpool of greater and greater sin. When he tires of her charms, he conceives a passion for an innocent girl, Antonia, and attempts to force himself upon her, encouraged and aided by Matilda, who reveals herself as a sorceress. His first attempt to rape Antonia is frustrated by her mother, whom Ambrosio murders while the girl, under a spell, is unconscious. Later, he succeeds in kidnapping Antonia, rapes her, then murders her in a vain effort to avoid discovery. He and Matilda are finally taken prisoner by the Inquisition. Employing black arts to escape, Matilda appears to Ambrosio in his cell and convinces him to sell his soul in order to avoid execution. A devil transports Ambrosio from prison, as agreed, but then callously hurls the monk from a precipice, after revealing to him the terrible truth that Antonia had been his sister and her mother, his own.

This was stronger stuff than any of Lewis's predecessors had attempted, and the book created a scandal, aggravated by the fact that the author was identified on the title page as a member of Parliament. An organization called the Society for the Suppression of Vice succeeded in having the book banned, and later editions were printed with some of the more lurid scenes of sex and violence removed, as well as certain passages smacking of blasphemy. While there is nothing in *The Monk* that would be censored today, its overall tone is still sufficient to disturb a sensitive reader. In fact, Lewis has been accused of most of Ambrosio's mental attitudes, although there is nothing in his biography to support such charges. On the contrary, it seems clear that Lewis had made a clever and calculated attempt to shock the public, and in that he did not fail.

He also carried many of the themes of the Gothic novel to their logical conclusions. If writers of the Radcliffe school could titillate their readers with the prospect of dastardly crimes, why not go all the way and show what they constantly suggested? If the mere suggestion of the supernatural could thrill an audience, why not present it as a tangible reality? This direct approach makes *The Monk* the most dramatic and readable product of its school, and its vivid details were to become standard fare in subsequent tales of the macabre. Lewis even influenced Ann Radcliffe, whose *Mysteries of Udolpho* had inspired him to try his hand at Gothic fiction. Her novel *The Italian*, which appeared a year after *The Monk*, is about a girl-chasing monk, Schedoni, who ends up in the hands of the Inquisition.

The Monk's exaggerated treatment of conventional material helps to explain the Age of Reason's fascination with Gothic novels; it also anticipated the ideas that were to prevail among creative artists in the Romantic movement. In fact, Lewis is a pivotal figure in the transition between these two antithetical views of life and art; he employed a standard fictional formula to promote the causes of liberty and libertinism. The dark, forbidding edifices in which horrors were perpetrated came to symbolize established corruption, while the authoritarian figure of the monk took on the colors of rebellion by releasing his passions in defiance of reason and propriety. Drawn larger than life, Ambrosio's self-indulgence and damnation influenced the melancholy, posturing heroes of the great Romantic poet Lord Byron. Unchecked emotions in conflict with absolute power were not merely literary concerns, as the French Revolution had so recently demonstrated, and *The Monk* includes a scene in which a furious mob storms a stronghold of the Inquisition to tear its proprietors limb from limb.

The book made Lewis an overnight celebrity at the age of twenty, and for the rest of his life he was known as "Monk" Lewis. He was never to have comparable success with a work of fiction, although he adapted a number of German stories whose explicit horrors had influenced his approach to the Gothic novel. Yet he was to create a few more sensations before he stopped writing at thirty-three by writing a series of spectacular works for the stage. Some of his plays were tragedies and comedies of the standard type; but he made his reputation as a dramatist with supernatural melodramas which were, in effect, the horror movies of their era. As such, they were distinguished less by ingenious plotting or effective dialogue than by clever staging. Lewis excelled in the use of lighting, music, and mechanical devices which, in combination, produced uncanny scenes of real power. It appears that he supervised such technical effects personally and that they accounted for most of his reputation as a playwright.

His most popular play was *The Castle Spectre* (1797). This featured a strangely familiar plot revolving around the treacherous Osmond who murders his brother and sister-in-law in order to become an earl. He has lecherous designs on his niece but is frustrated by her mother's ghost. Lewis had to struggle with his producers, who wanted to keep the ghost offstage; but he finally had his way, and the apparition in his fourth act had a suitably chilling effect on the audience. In fact, it is generally credited with making *The Castle Spectre* a hit. Some credit may also be due to the author's sister, Maria. Fearing a recurrence of the legal problems that had plagued *The Monk* just a year before, he had employed her to censor the play.

Lewis seems to have saved some of his most outlandish ideas for one of his last dramatic efforts, *The Wood Daemon* (1807). A window flies open in the midst of a thunderstorm to reveal a witch flying through flames in a dragon-powered chariot. Later, a magician's cave—complete with two huge snakes breathing blue fire, four demons, and a bloodstained altar—is suddenly transformed into a castle's barren hall. Such special effects kept audiences enthralled; but Lewis had had enough, and he gave up literature the next year, confessing that he was bored and convinced that his work would never improve.

Two decades after *The Monk* appeared, Lewis undertook a new project which some of his contemporaries must have found even more shocking. He had inherited a family plantation in Jamaica, and he embarked on a series of hazardous ocean voyages to examine his estate. He was shocked by the desperate condition under which his slaves were struggling, and he embarked on a series of reforms that scandalized his neighbors. Such changes as he made may seem inadequate today (decently fed and clothed slaves are slaves nonetheless); but his humanitarian policies were far ahead of their time and gave him more satisfaction than his fame as an author. The strain of traveling from Europe to the tropics finally proved too much for him, however, and he died of a fever on a ship bound for Jamaica. His funeral was grotesque enough to have appeared in one of his stories: he was buried at sea, but his coffin refused to sink and was last seen floating off across the Atlantic.

Lewis's last visit to Europe found him exchanging ghost stories with a group of expatriate English writers that included the great Romantic poets Byron and Shelley. Thus he was coincidentally present during the composition of the most famous and influential Gothic novel, *Frankenstein*. This classic horror novel was the best entry in a four-way contest. The losers included Percy Bysshe Shelley, Lord Byron, and Byron's physician, Dr. John Polidori; the winner was Mary Wollstonecraft Shelley, whose prize was literary immortality. Indeed, nothing written by either of her more respected competitors is more widely known or recognized today. There are few fictional characters whose names so readily conjure an image and a plot summary in the average person's mind—perhaps only *Romeo and Juliet* or *Robinson Crusoe* can be compared to *Frankenstein* as "household words."

When it was proposed at Geneva in 1816 that each member of the ingenious quartet write a ghost story, only Mrs. Shelley found herself at a loss. The others began in earnest but soon abandoned their projects. The germ of her plot finally appeared in a nightmare, which seems to have been inspired by discussions between Byron and her husband about the possibility of creating or restoring life through the use of galvanic batteries.

That night, as she wrote in her introduction, "I saw—with shut eyes, but acute mental vision—I saw the pale student of unhallowed arts kneeling beside the thing he had put together. I saw the hideous phantasm of a man stretched out, and then, on the working of some powerful engine, show signs of life, and stir with an uneasy, half vital motion. . . .

Frankenstein at work on his monster's ill-fated mate, as depicted by the twentieth-century American artist Lynd Ward.

His success would terrify the artist; he would rush away from his odious handiwork, horror-stricken. He would hope that, left to itself, the slight spark of life which he had communicated would fade; that this thing, which had received such imperfect animation, would subside into dead matter; and he might sleep in the belief that the silence of the grave would quench forever the transient existence of the hideous corpse which he had looked upon as the cradle of life. He sleeps; but he is awakened; he opens his eyes; behold the horrid thing stands at his bedside, opening his curtains, and looking on him with yellow, watery, but speculative eyes."

This is the story in a nutshell; in the experimenter's dismay is foreshadowed all the terrors that will follow. In fact, it was some version of this brief sketch that Mary Shelley originally wrote; her enthusiastic husband convinced her to expand it into a novel. In the process, it was changed from a vivid thriller into an elaborate, sometimes clumsy discussion of problems involving education and morality. *Frankenstein* is perhaps the most serious and high-minded horror story ever written, and the monster is no inarticulate brute, but a literate, introspective individual, fond of debate and given to long-winded philosophical discourses. No popular adaptation has captured the flavor of this bizarre character, who narrates a large portion of the book in the best oratorical fashion.

The novel is the story of Victor Frankenstein, a young Swiss student who leaves his family to attend the university at Ingolstadt. His mother dies of scarlet fever just before his departure, and a later dream suggests that this loss may have helped inspire his determination to conquer death. Surviving are his father, two younger brothers—Ernest and William—and Elizabeth Lavena, ward of the family, who is engaged to Frankenstein. After two years of intense study and effort, the young scientist succeeds in fulfilling his ambition by discovering the secret of life. The result is a gigantic and grotesque monster, which escapes from his creator's quarters while the young man suffers a nervous collapse.

As Frankenstein is being nursed back to health by his devoted friend Henry Clerval, the monster attempts to find companionship and sympathy but is rebuffed and mistreated by the horrified human beings he encounters. He flees to a forest, where he has his most significant experience with the De Laceys, a family of cottagers on whom he spies for over a year, attempting to learn their language and their ways. He finally attempts to approach them; however, his appearance disgusts everyone but the father, who is blind, and he is driven away by violence.

Embittered and enraged, the monster decides to seek out his creator and demand some sort of release from his lonely torment. He first encounters Frankenstein's little brother William and murders him, infuriated by the child's fear. The family's servant Justine is executed for the crime. The monster finally meets his maker, and after telling his story, he demands that a mate be created for him. Guilty and fearful, Frankenstein attempts the task in the hope of placating the monster but is finally unwilling to continue, fearing that he may unleash an entire race of loathsome creatures.

The monster, who has threatened revenge for the destruction of his half-completed mate, murders Clerval and, on their wedding night, Frankenstein's bride, Elizabeth. Frankenstein's father dies of shock, and the young man takes it upon himself to pursue the monster and destroy him. After a protracted chase in which the monster leads his creator into the icy regions of the north, the exhausted and half-mad Frankenstein is taken aboard the ship of an Arctic explorer, Robert Walton. He describes his adventures to Walton and dies. The monster finds his body aboard the ship and vows to burn himself alive, his life purposeless now that his vengeance is complete.

Boris Karloff as the Frankenstein monster in a scene from the 1931 film that comes close to capturing the Gothic mood of the original novel. From *Frankenstein* (1931). *Courtesy of Universal Pictures.*

When the book was published in 1818, Percy Bysshe Shelley published an anonymous review declaring that the book had a moral, "and it is perhaps the most important, and of the most universal application of any moral that can be enforced by example. Treat a person ill, and he will become wicked." This is something of a simplification, since the monster can scarcely be considered a person. His appearance makes it obvious that he is something unnatural: "His yellow skin scarcely covered the work of muscles and arteries beneath; his hair was of a lustrous black, and flowing; his teeth of a pearly whiteness; but these luxuriances only formed a more horrid contrast with his watery eyes, that seemed almost of the same colour as the dun white sockets in which they were set, his shrivelled complexion and straight black lips."

Nevertheless the attempts of this walking corpse to become human do strike a genuine note of pathos that make him something unique in the history of the Gothic novel. The best villains have a certain ambiguity about them; but if the monster's predecessors inspire sympathy, it is only because the reader can identify with the lusts for power, wealth, and passion which they embody. Mary Shelley created a new mood, one that would be frequently imitated, by imagining a character who could excite pity and terror in equal proportions.

She has also been credited with writing the first science fiction novel. This seems a fair claim, despite the lack of any significant scientific details in the story. Frankenstein, who narrates the section of the book dealing with the life-giving process, reveals nothing of his technique because he wants to discourage imitators; but there are hints in the second chapter that lightning may have supplied the spark of life. Yet this reticence does not invalidate the book's status as science fiction, since its horrors spring from an experiment and not from the demons or deceptions that characterize the Gothic novel. Thus it stands apart from its predecessors and is traditionally included among them only because of its publication date.

The era in which *Frankenstein* appeared was one in which scientific advancement had hardly made a dent in the solid traditions of the past. Yet technological advances were in the wind, and the Industrial Revolution was working permanent changes in the fabric of society. On one level, the story mirrors the transformations that were to create displaced, dehumanized people in the name of progress. More to the point, *Frankenstein* is prophetic in symbolizing modern problems like pollution and nuclear power, which demonstrate the drawbacks inherent in scientific achievements. The book has yet to lose its relevance as a fable of human fallibility.

Mrs. Shelley's concern with social issues came to her naturally. Her father, William Godwin, was a radical political theorist and writer whose novel *The Adventures of Caleb Williams* (1794) includes a long chase after a murderer which may have inspired the protracted pursuit at the end of *Frankenstein*. Her mother, Mary Wollstonecraft, was an early feminist, the author of a tract called *Vindication of the Rights of Women*. Both of Mrs. Shelley's parents, however, were surpassed by her husband, whose ideas about changing the world took some remarkably bizarre forms. He once distributed copies of a political pamphlet by attaching them to small balloons and releasing them over a city, and on another occasion he demonstrated his distress over cruelty to animals by sneaking out one night and slaughtering his neighbor's entire flock of sheep. Especially in the light of Mrs. Shelley's dream, there seems little doubt that this eccentric idealist was the model for Victor Frankenstein.

With this character, Mrs. Shelley inaugurated another important tradition in nightmarish narratives, that of the "mad scientist." Most of those who followed

Frankenstein into this line of work were considerably more unscrupulous but continued to share his obsessiveness and shortsightedness. The theme of an experimenter whose work destroys him degenerated into a melodrama in which the scientist "deserves" his punishment because he has been wicked; his well-intentioned counterpart usually succeeds in rectifying his errors and emerging more or less unscathed. Only a few of Frankenstein's more distinguished colleagues, like Stevenson's Dr. Jekyll, take on the tinge of tragedy. They have more than a little in common with the medieval Faust, who destroys himself in a search for forbidden knowledge. In fact, Frankenstein confesses that he devoted much of his study to the ancient alchemists, which gives his story supernatural overtones and at the same time suggests the dark and mysterious sources from which modern science has grown.

If *Frankenstein* is immortal because of its compelling theme, it is still readable largely because of the strange relationship between the man and his monster. Both are rebels; the creator defies nature, and his creature defies society. They represent diametrically opposed causes of antisocial behavior: the monster, desperate because his condition is so miserable; his maker, arrogant because he has had every advantage. When mass murder has reduced Frankenstein to a suitable degree of desperation, a strange feeling of fellowship grows between the two, so that the monster even leaves food for Frankenstein to prolong their chase through the wilderness. Before death overtakes them, each has become the other's only reason for living.

Mary Shelley wrote one other novel in a fantastic vein, *The Last Man* (1826). This is even further than *Frankenstein* from the Gothic tradition and even closer to modern concepts of science fiction. It depicts the end of the human race in a futuristic world complete with airships and other imaginary devices that have since become real. *The Last Man* may have been the first book to describe the end of civilization, with the exception of religious works predicting an apocalypse. It is less frightening than melancholic, however, and seems intended less to thrill the reader than to describe allegorically the author's distress at the death of so many of her contemporaries, including her husband. She had been less than twenty when she composed her first novel; when *The Last Man* appeared a decade later, most of the brilliant poets of the Romantic era had died prematurely: Shelley by drowning, Keats from consumption, and Byron in a Greek revolution. Wildly praised and condemned in their time, these men were labeled "The Satanic School" by England's conservative poet laureate Robert Southey, because of the self-indulgent quality of their characters and work and more specifically because of the sympathy they expressed for Satan as portrayed in Milton's *Paradise Lost*. Not too coincidentally, this was one of the few books read by Frankenstein's monster, who also counted himself among the devil's party.

Lord Byron's misanthropic, occasionally incestuous heroes show the strongest influence of the Gothic attitude on any of these poets; but it was Samuel Taylor Coleridge who penned the undisputed masterpiece among macabre poems of the era, *The Rime of the Ancient Mariner* (1798). The story of the sailor who cursed himself and his ship by defying superstition still remains one of the most powerful and popular poems in the English language. Coleridge was equally important as a critic, and his suggestion that readers should approach works of the imagination with a "willing suspension of disbelief" is particularly relevant to tales with supernatural themes. To those who remain completely locked in the world of rationality against which Gothic and Romantic artists revolted, the realm of fantasy is a closed book.

The Gothic novel had pretty well played itself out as a literary form by the time

Frankenstein appeared; its innovations might be said to be the death knell of a type that had already begun to repeat itself shamelessly, as such imitative titles as the anonymous *Monks of Otranto* indicate. The last gasp came in 1820 when an Irish clergyman named Charles Robert Maturin produced the ponderous but powerful *Melmoth the Wanderer*. It was wildly praised by literary titans like Poe, Balzac, and Baudelaire, who saw the legend of the Wandering Jew submerged beneath the author's shifting subplots. Maturin's high critical reputation rests on his compilation and renovation of many stock devices that characterized the Gothic novel, set in a new framework that gave them a unique perspective. Melmoth is a man who has sold his soul to the devil in exchange for prolonged life and forbidden knowledge. Unlike the standard document, his contract contains an escape clause: Melmoth can avoid damnation if he can induce someone else to take his place. It seems to be an unusually bad bargain even for this sort of thing, since Melmoth uses his long life and magical powers almost exclusively to search for the substitute, as if he has made his deal with the devil only to help himself in backing out of it. The novel consists of a number of episodes in which the immortal wanderer seeks out wretched individuals in situations so grim that they will welcome temporary relief at whatever cost. Yet none of them accepts his offer, and he disappears over the edge of a cliff after a last visit to his ancestral home.

This most ambitious and complicated of the Gothic novels is clumsily constructed in a series of interlocking flashbacks, so that each episode is interrupted by the next. Only an unusually alert and patient reader can encounter such a structure without annoyance, and persons of this type were doubtless more common in the nineteenth century than they are today. Although the novel as a whole is somewhat tedious, many of the incidents are handled with superior skill. Melmoth's most likely prospects are discovered in typical Gothic predicaments: one is trapped in a primitive insane asylum; another, almost inevitably, is a victim of the Inquisition. But the most eerie and unusual scene occurs when the wanderer takes time out from temptations to woo and win an innocent young woman; their wedding is performed and witnessed by reanimated corpses.

Melmoth the Wanderer was not Maturin's only work in the Gothic vein; in addition to a number of conventional plays and novels, he had previously produced a derivative tale of treachery and parricide called *The Fatal Revenge*, or *The Family of Montorio* (1807). The villain, Orazio, makes his intentions clear to even the dullest reader by disguising himself as a monk named Schemoli. *Melmoth* was quite a bit more original, especially in the treatment of its grim, tormented hero-villain who, although he tries his damnedest, never really manages to destroy anyone but himself. Forced by his quest to seek out the most tragic victims of injustice and inhumanity, he is more a witness to horrors than a perpetrator of them, conscious all the time that something worse is in store for him. Balzac was so moved by his plight that he wrote a frivolous sequel, *Melmoth Reconciled*, in which the curse is passed on to an embezzler.

Although the Gothic novel had run its course by the second decade of the nineteenth century, it continued to influence the mainstream literature of the years to come, most obviously in the case of Emily Brontë's *Wuthering Heights* and her sister Charlotte's *Jane Eyre*, both published as late as 1847. Of course, the influence of this style on future tales of the macabre is incalculable. Never again, though, would studies in terror so completely dominate the imagination of a mass audience.

The twentieth century has seen a resurrection of the term "Gothic" applied to works quite distinct from the horror stories that it originally inspired. The term has been adopted by Mrs. Radcliffe's sorority of successors, generally to its discredit, although

This vision of angels and corpses was created by Gustave Doré to illustrate Samuel Taylor Coleridge's classic macabre poem *The Rime of the Ancient Mariner*.

there are tasteful exceptions like Daphne Du Maurier, author of *Rebecca*. In general, these books, now accounting for a considerable share of the paperback market, concern an unlikely multitude of young ladies married to men who seem bent on murdering them. The so-called Gothic novel of the twentieth century is debased currency, with the menaced heroine (always rescued) at the center of the stage, the supernatural (always explained away) in the background, and the damned soul of the defiant villain who inspired these stories imprisoned in the body of a cheap cad.

·3·

IMPS OF THE PERVERSE: AFRAID IN AMERICA

If the British horror tradition was a reaction against widespread rationalism, expressing itself in a nostalgic and somewhat frivolous attitude toward traditional religious beliefs, the situation in colonial America was considerably less sophisticated. The grim Puritan philosophy, which proved to be little more than a brief phase in the progress of English history, became the bedrock upon which colonial culture was based. The earliest American publications were fundamentalist religious tracts that treated witches and devils as tangible threats. In 1693, the year after the accused Salem witches had been executed, the immensely powerful clergyman Cotton Mather published his most hair-raising work, *The Wonders of the Invisible World*, describing a supernatural conspiracy abroad in the land. He explained that Satan was particularly anxious to cause trouble in the colonies, because the land had been, until a few years before, a heathen stronghold under the dominion of hell.

As Mather explained the situation, "We have been advised by some Credible Christians yet alive, that a Malefactor, accused of *Witchcraft* as well as *Murder*, and Executed in this place more than Forty Years ago, did then give Notice, of *An Horrible* PLOT *against the Country by* WITCHCRAFT, *and a Foundation of* WITCHCRAFT *then Laid, which if it were not seasonably Discovered, would probably Blow up, and pull down all the Churches in the Country.* And we have now with Horror seen the *Discovery* of such a *Witchcraft!* An Army of *Devils* is horribly broke in upon the place which is the *Center,* and after a sort, the *First-born* of our *English* Settlements: and the Houses of the Good People there, are fill'd with the doleful Shrieks of their Children and Servants, Tormented by Invisible Hands, with Tortures altogether preternatural."

With this sort of thing available to give them nightmares, early Americans had no need to fall back on fiction. And for generations, there would be none to fall back on. Political and historical documents began to pour off the printing presses along with the sermons, but literature designed to entertain as well as edify was still a long way off. The first American play was produced in 1767, and the first novel in 1789. Meanwhile, readers in search of morbid thrills did the best they could with Cotton Mather's later works like the quaintly titled *Death Made Easy and Happy* (1701). Hell-fire and damnation found another expert witness in Jonathan Edwards, who achieved his first great success in 1741 with *Sinners in the Hands of an Angry God*. Of course, works like these were appearing simultaneously in Europe, which also had its share of witchcraft trials; but there they were counterbalanced by a wide range of opinions and entertainments that served to create a more humane atmosphere.

Given such a background, it is not too surprising that America's first major novelist had a bit of a morbid streak and made a murderous religious fanatic the title character of his most famous novel. The author was Charles Brockden Brown, who transferred the mood and tone of the British Gothic novels to a new continent. By setting his stories in his own country, Brown abandoned the ready-made air of medieval mystery on which his English contemporaries depended so much. Instead, he dwelt on the fragility of the new civilization, threatened as it was by the wilderness it had so recently replaced and by the strange personalities drifting through an infant society. Although his efforts are better remembered by historians than by the general public, the books had a definite influence on writers who followed him.

Wieland; or, The Transformation (1798) is generally considered to be his best work; it is also his most effective excursion into the domain of the macabre. Wieland is a farmer living with his wife, children, and sister near a grotesque temple constructed by his father, a retired missionary. Old Wieland, who had invented his own religion, died mysteriously after an unexplained incident in the temple that left him delirious, with his clothing burned away. Wieland and his sister Clara are never able to forget this puzzling tragedy, especially when disembodied voices are heard near the scene. At first the voices warn people to stay away from the temple; later they speak in the house to terrify Clara and then to alienate the affections of her fiancé. There are enough witnesses to convince Wieland that the voices represent a genuine supernatural manifestation, and when they finally order him to kill his wife and their four children, he does so. He is arrested, but he escapes and returns to the farm to murder Clara. There he is confronted with the all-too-human source of the instructions which he had interpreted as divine. They have been produced by Carwin, a wandering stranger who has been visiting the family. Unknown to the others, Carwin is a ventriloquist, or, in the author's terminology, a biloquist. This seems to be a typical explanation in the style of Ann Radcliffe, but Brown introduces a significant variation. Carwin, although mischievous and even malicious, is not a murderous character. He had warned the family away from the temple because he had been using it as a lovers' rendezvous, and he had interfered with Clara's romance just to see how much more he could get away with; but he had never ordered the killings. What he had done was to drive Wieland, already haunted by the memory of his father, into a form of madness in which the orders he received came from his own troubled mind. Confronted with the proof that what had seemed to be indisputably divine inspiration was actually inherited insanity, Wieland commits suicide.

Brown's use of mental aberration as the cause of frightening incidents was to be repeated in the works of many American authors, most notably Poe, who praised Brown's novels highly. Brown returned to the theme in *Edgar Huntly; or, Memoirs of a Sleep-Walker* (1799). This book is narrated by the title character, whose mind fails after the death of a friend and the loss of a fortune. His illness first takes the form of bouts of somnambulism; at one point he blacks out and wakes up trapped in a cave which is also the den of a panther. For a long nightmarish portion of the novel, Huntly is lost in the wilderness, delirious, fighting off wild animals and hostile Indians, and simultaneously suffering from the delusion that his entire family is dead. He finally recovers his reason, but another sleepwalker whom Huntly has attempted to help is less fortunate: he goes completely mad and, after an attempted murder, kills himself.

A third novel, *Arthur Mervyn*, has a more ordinary plot involving the career of a young man seeking his fortune; but the first half contains some gruesome incidents based on Brown's personal experiences during the yellow fever epidemic of 1773. Much of the material indicates that Brown was familiar with Defoe's *Journal of the Plague Year*, but he achieves an intimacy his predecessor had not even attempted. His details were the result of his own observation rather than historical records, and he intensified his effectiveness by letting his hero fall victim to the dread disease, which nearly kills him. Perhaps the most horrible scenes occur in the hospitals staffed by desperate and greedy men who ignore their patients to avoid infection, leaving the dead and the dying together in dark and desolate wards. Arthur Mervyn also witnesses the brutality of hardened corpse collectors who do not even wait until men are dead to load them onto their carrion carts; he barely escapes being buried alive himself, regaining consciousness just before he is put in a coffin.

Charles Brockden Brown published several other books and countless articles or pamphlets on political and historical subjects; but his fame rests on these three novels, all written in the space of one year. They established him as the first American master of frightening fiction. A considerably larger reputation in this field was achieved with a much smaller output by Washington Irving, the first American author to achieve wide fame abroad as well as at home. Like Brown, Irving was trained as a lawyer; but he soon abandoned that profession to pursue a career in literature. He did, however, have the distinct advantage of a wealthy background which permitted him to work without haste or distraction. His sophistication and sense of humor make his spectral tales unique and have endeared them to a wider audience than can be found for the grim narratives he sometimes seemed to be mocking.

Although he published books on geographical and historical subjects, including a biography of George Washington, most of Irving's reputation came from the short pieces collected in *The Sketch Book of Geoffrey Crayon, Gent.* (1819), more commonly known simply as *The Sketch Book*. This included his most celebrated stories, "Rip Van Winkle" and "The Legend of Sleepy Hollow," as well as "The Spectre Bridegroom," about a man who did not let his death interfere with his forthcoming wedding.

Irving, who toured the capitals of Europe as a traveler and a diplomat, treats terror and the supernatural from a comfortable distance, as quaint relics of an almost forgotten folklore. In "The Legend of Sleepy Hollow," he describes Ichabod Crane, the foolish schoolmaster who is scared out of town by the imaginary ghost of the Headless Horseman, as a devoted reader of Cotton Mather. In fact, it is Ichabod's fondness for repeating the old preacher's spook stories that inspires his rival in love to impersonate Sleepy Hollow's legendary horror. The fact that the Horseman's dreaded head turns out to be a humble pumpkin is perhaps a Radcliffean echo, but it is primarily a piece of comic relief and represents an implied attack on the naïve credulity of the Puritan era. In spite of this, the "galloping Hessian of the Hollow" remains a splendid vision, a relic of overthrown authority which is no longer a cause for alarm.

The idea that the Headless Horseman represents the regime defeated by the American Revolution is reinforced by "Rip Van Winkle." It can hardly be a coincidence that Rip's twenty-year nap encompasses the struggle to remove a government and replace it with another, so that he wakes up pledging his loyalty to King George instead of President George. That Rip misses the bloody conflict and finds life very much the same under the

Ichabod Crane is pursued by the Headless Horseman in this scene from Washington Irving's "The Legend of Sleepy Hollow," drawn during the author's lifetime by Felix O. C. Darley.

new order serves only to reinforce the impression that his enchanted sleep has been enchanting as well. Even the picture of the president over Rip's favorite inn is indistinguishable from the old one of the king. Losing two decades of one's life, which should be a shocking experience, is treated as a blessing, especially since it separates the hero from his nagging wife. Thus Irving helped to inaugurate the literary tradition of solving domestic difficulties by bizarre if not bloodcurdling methods. And the drunken, bowling ghosts who offer Rip the magic brew are predominately figures of fun, further establishing Irving's reputation as the man who made foolish phantoms fashionable.

At least one more of Irving's stories is worth mentioning: "The Devil and Tom Walker," from the later collection *Tales of a Traveller* (1824). Tom trades his soul to Satan for success in business and enjoys a brilliant career as a moneylender until he is dragged away screaming. The usual light, mocking tone predominates; but Irving has some telling points to make about crooked commercial practices and strikes even closer to home when the devil describes his special interests in America: "Since the red men have been exterminated by you white savages, I amuse myself by presiding at the persecutions of Quakers and Anabaptists; I am the great patron and prompter of slave dealers, and the grand-master of the Salem witches."

Growing up in America when Irving was publishing his best work was Edgar Allan Poe, without doubt the most important author to make his name as a delineator of the demonic. Many great writers have touched on terrifying themes, but Poe stands alone as one who achieved worldwide recognition while concentrating almost entirely on the inhuman side of human nature. It was an uphill struggle.

Although he is arguably the most significant writer, critic, and literary theorist in the history of the United States, Poe has been almost consistently under attack since he first set pen to paper. Engaged in controversies with powerful and influential figures like Longfellow, whom he accused of plagiarism, during his lifetime Poe suffered from bad luck compounded by his own irascibility and intemperance. His worst mistake in this vein came when he put his posthumous literary affairs in the hands of one Rufus

The dwarfish spirits who cast a spell on Rip Van Winkle, as imagined by the modern English illustrator Arthur Rackham.

Griswold, who used his position to blacken Poe's reputation in every possible way. Griswold obviously never forgot that Poe had attacked him years before in a critical article. His authorized edition of Poe's work contained a maliciously distorted biography, and he even altered the text of Poe's letters to create a convincingly ugly portrait of the man who had entrusted him with his life's work.

It took the best part of a century for responsible scholars to undo the damage Griswold had done, but Poe had hardly been cleared of these charges when he was subjected to a new sort of slander. Certain psychological critics, more familiar with Freudian analysis than literary artifice, treated his tales as if they were the unconsidered outpourings of a subconsciousness run wild, rather than the carefully crafted products of a skillful technician. Starting with Marie Bonaparte, who published a huge volume called *The Life and Works of Edgar Allan Poe: A Psycho-Analytic Interpretation*, it became fashionable to use his artistic symbols to construct theories about his private life and personal behavior that were unsupported by any convincing historical evidence. Poe was accused of most of the sins of which his characters were guilty, or at least of having wished to commit them, and he had shortcomings ascribed to him that he had never even mentioned in his stories. All this was done on the apparent assumption that the writer did not really know what he was talking about, that his work was somehow over his own head. And this happened to a man who was unusually self-conscious about what went into his writing and who even published a group of essays explaining how all the incidents and details in his tales and poems were calculated to produce deliberate effects.

There can be little doubt that Poe was a troubled individual. Indeed, he once described himself as "insane, with long intervals of horrible sanity." Nevertheless, his published works do not constitute a case history, nor should they be considered as such. Neither can the impact of his writing be explained in terms of hypothetical abnormalities. Freudian critics might be well advised to consider these lines from his "Sonnet—To Science":

> *Science! true daughter of Old Time thou art!*
> *Who alterest all things with thy peering eyes.*
> *Why preyest thou thus upon the poet's heart,*
> *Vulture, whose wings are dull realities?*

Poe began his career as a poet, although his most famous poem, "The Raven" (1845), did not appear until four years before his death. But, strangely enough, the earliest prose efforts of this master of the macabre were in a humorous vein. These were the "Tales of the Folio Club," a collection of parodies and satires which he hoped to publish as a book. Although this ambition was never realized, several of these stories were printed separately in *The Philadelphia Saturday Courier* in 1832. Throughout his career Poe continued to produce comic sketches; many of them made light of the same themes that were treated seriously in his more famous tales. He demonstrated an awareness of the ludicrous side of horror tales, as well as a knowledge of his era's requirements for popular entertainment, in a pair of pieces entitled "How to Write a *Blackwood's* Article" and "A Predicament." *Blackwood's* was a popular British magazine which increased its circulation with a series of sensational stories of the hair-raising variety. Poe mocked the convention of a narrator who continues to record impressions while involved in the most perilous situations by describing the plight of Psyche Zenobia. Seeking atmosphere in an old clock tower, she gets caught in the works and finally is decapitated by the "huge, glittering, scimitar-like minute-hand of the clock." Even this does not dissuade her from taking elaborate notes on her condition, her head watching her body from the street below.

This sort of black humor occurs in many of Poe's lesser-known tales, such as "The Man That Was Used Up," describing a war hero turned political candidate. He has sustained so many injuries in becoming a celebrity that his body is almost completely destroyed, and he can appear in public only with the help of four false limbs, a wig, false teeth, and an unbelievable variety of artificial devices. Apparently the "manufactured" political candidate was invented before the twentieth century. In "Some Words with a Mummy," an ancient Egyptian named Count Allamistakeo is revived with an electric shock (possibly the first use of this popular resurrected-mummy theme) and proves to be a genial fellow with a low opinion of certain American political practices. When Poe was not having fun with his readers, he might be making fun of them instead, as in the case of the piece now known as "The Balloon Hoax," in which he managed to convince the *New York Sun* and its readers that a pair of Welsh balloonists had flown across the Atlantic almost a century before the feat was actually to be accomplished.

Even his grimmest tales were sometimes inspired by apparently frivolous motives. For instance, "Berenice" (1835) is often cited as an example of Poe's bad taste and of his personal obsessions. The hero of this tale blacks out after his sweetheart's death and wakes up to discover that he has broken open her tomb and removed all of her teeth. Those who search for deep meaning or even common sense in this wildly overwritten little epic are apparently unaware of the commonplace explanation: the author claimed to have written it on a bet with an acquaintance who was convinced that it would be impossible to write a story on such a theme and get it published. Poe won.

Dead ladies of one sort or another are, it must be admitted, among Poe's most common themes. The reason is not much of a mystery. His mother, a traveling actress who had been deserted by her husband, died in her son's presence just before he turned three. He was almost immediately adopted by Mr. and Mrs. John Allan of Richmond, Virginia, largely on the insistence of Mrs. Allan. She died when he was twenty, thus dissolving the somewhat shaky relationship between John Allan and Edgar Allan Poe, who was finally disowned and disinherited. He married his cousin, Virginia Clemm, who came down with tuberculosis, the same disease that had killed Mrs. Poe and Mrs. Allan. She lingered between life and death, constantly recovering and relapsing, for five years. And finally she died, too.

The impact of these three tragic coincidences permanently colored Poe's view of life and had considerable influence on his art as well. Many of his tales and most of his poems deal with the loss of a beloved woman; he even argues in "The Philosophy of Composition" that the death of a beautiful woman "is, unquestionably, the most poetical topic in the world." This conclusion is drawn from the premise that tragedy produces the greatest emotional effects, but it still seems debatable at best. Nevertheless, Poe almost makes it convincing, at least in his poems. Even the bald statement of policy was probably not too shocking to the readers of his era, who were well versed in a tradition of sentimental sadness. Their willingness to go along with the idea made "The Raven" his most popular work, the one that made his reputation. In fact, "The Philosophy of Composition" was an article about how he came to write the poem, an effort to get a little more mileage out of his greatest success, for which he was paid the lordly sum of twenty-five dollars. Poe did at least have the satisfaction of selling the article to a former employer who had rejected the poem while slipping its author a few dollars as an act of kindness.

No doubt Poe needed the money. Raised in the expectation of becoming a wealthy southern gentleman, he spent his entire adult life in poverty. It was next to impossible for an American in the first half of the nineteenth century to make a living with a pen; most of his contemporaries had other sources of income, but the best Poe ever got was a few short-lived, ill-paying editorial positions, terminated by clashes over policy, his occasional bouts of alcoholism, or the collapse of the business. His principal ambition was to start his own magazine, but he could never raise the capital. None of his books realized any profit—he was lucky when he didn't have to finance the printing, and received a few free copies for his trouble. One collection of poems that he couldn't give away is now a rare item valued at fifty thousand dollars; but Poe isn't getting any of the money.

Perhaps it was because of Poe's precarious financial position, coupled with his disappointment at not inheriting a fortune, that he decided to place so many of his characters in the idle aristocracy. Yet they are rarely happy in their lot, and more likely to be the tormented, dissolute remnants of a once proud family. A case in point is Roderick Usher, protagonist of the story that is generally regarded as Poe's best, "The Fall of the House of Usher" (1839). Usher's senses have become so unnaturally acute that ordinary sounds, smells, textures, tastes, and lights have become intolerable to him. He has been refined almost completely out of existence, perhaps symbolizing a class whose days, like his own, were numbered. The collapsing "house" is, of course, not only the building but Roderick and his dying sister Madeline as well, all inextricably linked together so that the end of one means the end of all and of the dynasty they represent. Thus, Roderick's apparently unmotivated decision to bury Madeline alive is, in effect, a kind of suicide. He dies when she returns from the tomb to confront him, and their ancestral mansion disintegrates almost immediately, the result of a fissure in its walls which is a visual emblem of personalities hopelessly split or, in common parlance, "cracked."

The hint of the supernatural in this coincidental collapse is relatively rare in Poe's tales, which characteristically find their frightening aspects in madness and murder. The major stories in which uncanny events play a significant part include "Morella" (1835), "Ligeia" (1838), "William Wilson" (1839), "The Masque of the Red Death" (1842), and "The Facts in the Case of M. Valdemar" (1845). Even in most of these, the ghostly elements are sufficiently subtle to be open to interpretation. In "Morella," the narrator's wife dies, but her spirit apparently returns to possess the body of their dying daughter. A variation on this theme occurs in Poe's favorite of his tales, "Ligeia," in which a widower remarries, only to discover that his fatally ill second wife has somehow been replaced by her predecessor. Both stories are written so that it is possible to suspect that the narrator is hallucinating, haunted by his own mind rather than by the spirits of the dead. A sentimental counterpoint to "Ligeia" appears in the story "Eleonora" (1842). The heroine returns not to demand a love that transcends the grave but to whisper approval of her husband's new marriage.

"William Wilson" is the story of a man haunted by his double, who has been with him since childhood and even bears the same name. At first it seems no more than a grotesque coincidence, but the double has an intimate knowledge of all Wilson's actions, especially the deplorable ones. He is so intent upon detecting and frustrating vice that he appears to be an embodied conscience; when Wilson finally murders him, he destroys himself as well. Indeed, the censorious superego seems to be the source for most of Poe's horrors, especially when coupled with a senseless desire to do wrong. This even seems to

The most intense and terrifying illustrations for the tales of Edgar Allan
Poe were done seventy years after the author's death by Harry Clarke;
this drawing is for "The Masque of the Red Death."

Another Harry Clarke drawing, depicting the climax of Poe's putrescent
"Facts in the Case of M. Valdemar."

be true of the extravagant Gothic fantasy "The Masque of the Red Death," in which Prince Prospero and his aristocratic friends revel in a locked abbey while awaiting the passing of a terrible plague. Their masquerade ball is invaded by the personification of the pestilence, whose presence seems to reprimand their selfish seclusion and their special privileges as well.

A very different sort of fear is at issue in "The Facts in the Case of M. Valdemar." On the point of dying from tuberculosis (Poe calls it "phthisis"), Valdemar is hypnotized and remains in the trance for seven months after he announces his own death. The documentary style of the narrative, complete with clinical descriptions of the patient's condition and the hypnotist's techniques, makes Valdemar's living death truly awe inspiring. The climax of the story, in which the trance is broken and Valdemar instantly decays, is perhaps the most gruesome Poe ever conceived.

If Poe was fascinated with the mystery of what might lie beyond the life we know, he could do no more than hint at its solution. He had better luck with mysteries of his own devising, and he became known as the father of the detective story because of his stories of "ratiocination." The first of these, "The Murders in the Rue Morgue" (1841), contains the terrifying image of a razor-wielding, homicidal "Ourang-Outang"; but the rest are more restrained or, in the case of the treasure-hunting "Gold-Bug," almost idyllic. Poe wrote of these tales that "people think them more ingenious than they are—on account of their method and air of method. In the 'Murders in the Rue Morgue,' for instance, where is the ingenuity of unravelling a web which you (the author) have woven for the express purpose of unravelling?"

Such stories did, however, lend themselves to Poe's critical theory on the construction of short fiction, which demanded that every word be calculated to produce a climactic effect, a "pre-established design." The involuted structure of the detective story, putting first things last, is the logical result of this theory; but Poe's real triumph was living up to his criteria in tales told in a more straightforward manner. His delvings into the minds of detectives were comparatively easy for others to imitate, but his compelling explorations of the criminal mind have rarely been duplicated.

Deranged murderers had been a commonplace in Gothic fiction, but Poe offered a new perspective on such characters by making them the narrators of their own adventures. This first-person technique caused readers to identify so completely with the killers that they were less likely to be shocked by the crime than by the subsequent capture. And the realization that insanity could be so infectious was most frightening of all. By making his audience aware of the darker side of their own natures, Poe added a different dimension to the literature of fear.

Poe's major works in this vein include "The Black Cat" (1843), "The Tell-Tale Heart" (1843), and "The Cask of Amontillado" (1846). The last tale is a bit different in that the narrator seems to be getting away with murder; but then again the story itself is a confession, delivered by a man who is still reliving his crime fifty years later. Here again the victim is buried alive; this was a fate that Poe apparently considered the most horrible imaginable; he even wrote a piece on the subject, "The Premature Burial" (1844), which is really an essay giving factual accounts of "the ultimate woe," with a fictional tag in which the narrator is cured of his obsessive fear. Amusingly enough, one aspect of the cure involved giving up the reading of "bugaboo tales—*such as this.*"

The narrator of "The Cask of Amontillado" claims revenge as a motive, although no details of his injuries are provided; but the killer in "The Tell-Tale Heart" says his morbid distaste for the appearance of his victim's blind eye is reason enough. When the

Clarke's ornate illustration for the final scene of "The Black Cat" contrasts strongly with a starker scene by Aubrey Beardsley (opposite page), whose techniques were nonetheless a discernible influence on the later artist.

old man has been buried beneath the floorboards, his murderer places his chair on the spot while being interviewed by the police and is driven to confession by a sound that he takes to be his victim's heartbeat but is surely his own. Similarly, "The Black Cat" describes a man who reveals his wife's corpse to the police when he raps on the cellar wall that hides her, driven by "the mere phrenzy of bravado." His knock is answered by the cat he had meant to kill and had inadvertently walled up alive. The hysterical self-assurance with which these characters seal their own dooms suggests that they subconsciously desire to be found out and that their crimes, like Roderick Usher's, are more than half-suicidal.

"The Black Cat" contains a passage that gives a clue to the psychology at work in these stories. "Perverseness," the killer claims, "is one of the primitive impulses of the human heart," and the realization that an act is senseless or dangerous can in fact become a compelling reason for committing it. This idea, which anticipates Freud's theory of the "death wish," receives its fullest discussion in one of Poe's lesser-known tales, "The Imp of the Perverse." This story, reprinted here, first appeared in the July 1845 issue of *Graham's Magazine*, a publication that Poe had edited for a year in 1841–42. It may have been Poe's own "imp" that caused him to lose the position, probably the best he ever had, by too much drinking and arguing with the publisher. Nevertheless, *Graham's* continued to be one of his best markets, although it was George Graham who rejected "The Raven" and was later forced to eat crow by publishing the spin-off "Philosophy of Composition."

Although it is far from his best efforts as an artistically finished work of fiction, "The Imp of the Perverse" is significant for the light it casts on the major tales. Like "The Premature Burial" and many other minor Poe tales, this begins with a long essay to which a much shorter narrative is attached. The psychological theorizing has its basis in the now discarded system of phrenology, which attempted to analyze character on the basis of the head's shape. Certain traits were assigned to various portions of the skull, and their comparative prominence was purportedly a key to the subject's personality. It has been reported that Poe had a particular fondness for this system (then considered perfectly scientific) because the dimensions of his own dome reportedly indicated a man of unusual talent and intelligence. Maybe there was something to it after all.

The contrast between the verbose theorizing and the terse narrative is readily apparent; each successive paragraph moves at a quicker pace, so that the story steadily accelerates. Poe even includes a passage about the perversity of circumlocution, suggesting that the long-winded opening to his tale may have been written tongue in cheek. Those critics who have discussed this story generally attribute these opening remarks directly to Poe rather than to the fictional character he created to deliver them. Yet the confession that the Imp forces from the criminal is not exactly the equivalent of the foolish or wicked acts the narrator discusses so glibly. The Imp here is the conscience, and all the murderer's rationalizations cannot disguise the moral blindness of a man who sees harmony in homicide and cacophony in confession. The man who wrote this story may have been aware of his own weaknesses, but that does not make him wicked. The fact is that in this story, as in most of these tales of madness and murder, Poe-etic justice has struck again.

Unfortunately, life is not often as just as art. Poe's crimes were all imaginary, but his punishment was painfully real. His wife's inevitable death finally came in 1847, when he was at the peak of his powers. He never really recovered from the shock of losing her; two years later, after increasingly heavy drinking and at least one attempted suicide, he gave

Odilon Redon's "Mask Tolling the Hour of Death" is one of a series of lithographs which the French Symbolist attributed to the influence of Poe, who was recognized abroad before he was appreciated in his native land.

up the ghost under mysterious circumstances. He was found unconscious in the streets of Baltimore and died four days later without ever really coming around. Although it can never be proved beyond doubt, it seems likely that he was the victim of dirty work at the ballot box. It was not uncommon for ward heelers to round up inebriated individuals and drive them from poll to poll until they collapsed, after racking up as many votes as possible. The fact that Poe was found in such poor condition on an election day suggests that he may have given his all for the democracy he professed to despise. Baltimore's most bizarre tribute to Poe's memory is a school for unwed mothers which, inexplicably, bears his name.

Poe had only one contemporary with a comparable talent for the construction of macabre fiction: the gloomy New Englander Nathaniel Hawthorne. Poe's review of Hawthorne's *Twice-Told Tales* gave him the opportunity to expound his famous theory on the construction of the short story; he also saw fit to describe Hawthorne as "a man of the truest genius." There was undoubtedly a distinct sympathy between the two men; Hawthorne's subjects are often bizarre or uncanny, although his tone is very different from Poe's. Hawthorne is primarily a moralist, and his stories inevitably tend toward allegory. His themes and characters never entirely lose their abstract quality, and they never achieve the breathless terror that is characteristic of Poe at his best. There is something cold and calculating about Hawthorne's approach; the author and his attitudes are always very much in the foreground, and the reader is more likely to contemplate the meaning of the fiction than to be swept along by its dramatic intensity.

A trio of his best tales exemplify Hawthorne's approach to the macabre: "Young Goodman Brown" (1835), "Rappaccini's Daughter" (1844), and "Ethan Brand" (1851). Young Goodman Brown is a colonist who comes upon a meeting of devil worshipers while traveling through a forest. He discovers to his dismay that they include friends and neighbors from his village, which is the notorious Salem. There is no melodramatic climax; rather, Brown returns home and resumes his life, not knowing whether or not his experience was a dream. Nevertheless, his values have been so shattered that he becomes hostile and suspicious, and he remains miserable until his death many years later. The story is not really about Satanism but rather about the dangers of hypocrisy and self-righteousness: Brown destroys himself when he is unable to accept the idea that all mortals are touched by sin.

"Rappaccini's Daughter" is the story of an Italian scientist who specializes in the cultivation of exquisitely beautiful but poisonous plants. His zeal and possessiveness have caused him to raise his daughter Beatrice among his other creations, so that she is equally deadly. When an aspiring lover administers an antidote in an attempt to restore her to a normal condition, the cure proves fatal. The story in synopsis seems like a scenario for dozens of twentieth-century "mad scientist" epics; but Hawthorne's style makes it clear that this is another moral fable, with both the poisons and the antidote representing the selfishness of those who attempt to manipulate innocence for their own ends.

Perhaps Hawthorne's most typically Gothic effort is "Ethan Brand," which he subtitled "A Chapter from an Abortive Romance." It would appear to be the last chapter of this nonexistent novel, since it ends with the death of the hero, who has returned home after a long and successful search for the "Unpardonable Sin." This sin is never identified, but Ethan Brand's pride and isolation are emphasized in such exaggerated terms that his story almost seems to be a spoof of works like Maturin's

Melmoth the Wanderer. Vague allusions to the events in previous "chapters" are so instantly identifiable that further details are unnecessary; in fact, Hawthorne has created a miniature Gothic novel through a compendium of the genre's most typical clichés. Brand burns himself alive in a limekiln, and the taciturn tender is pleased to discover that the skeleton left behind will increase his haul of lime by half a bushel. Such are the practical results of a romantic quest for exotic damnation.

Hawthorne wrote many more tales with supernatural subjects. Some are serious, and many are almost whimsical; but the author's apparent intention to create moral fables generally overcomes the eerie atmosphere. His novels also contain some supernatural overtones. *The House of the Seven Gables* (1851) seems to be slightly haunted, and *The Marble Faun* (1860) hints at revenants from classical mythology, but both books are principally concerned with other topics. The innate idealism in his apparently irresistible tendency toward allegory had a counterpart in real life when Hawthorne joined an early experiment in communal living at Brook Farm. The community was not a success, but at least it provided material for another novel.

Herman Melville, the third great figure in mid-nineteenth-century American literature, is even further than Hawthorne from the dark, demonic world of Poe; but his great novel *Moby Dick* (1851) is in many respects a Gothic story all at sea. The obsessed tyrant Captain Ahab would have been right at home in a medieval castle, and the giant white whale he pursues so feverishly looks at times like a monster from hell. The book is many other things, but it is at least half a horror story. It has more than a few features in common with Poe's only novel, *The Narrative of Arthur Gordon Pym* (1838), in which a shipwrecked sailor is driven to cannibalism before drifting to the South Pole, where he is confronted, as the book ends, by a huge figure whose skin is "of the perfect whiteness of the snow."

Several of Melville's shorter pieces have terrifying aspects. His *Billy Budd*, with its personifications of good and evil, has the grim tone of an old morality play. A more typical horror tale is "The Bell-Tower," in which a master workman murders one of his assistants in his enthusiasm to complete work on a gigantic clock and is killed in turn by his own mechanism, flawed as it is by the blood of his victim, which has weakened the metal he had cast. Melville also envisioned some stranger menaces drawn from the burgeoning American free enterprise system. One was "Bartleby the Scrivener," who creates chaos and despair in an office full of go-getters by being the one man there who, whatever is proposed to him, "would prefer not to." At the opposite end of the spectrum is "The Lightning-Rod Man," a traveling salesman who roams the country deliberately instilling paranoia in his customers so that he can drum up a little business.

One writer of this period who concentrated almost exclusively on the macabre was Fitz-James O'Brien, an Irish immigrant to the United States who concocted some surprisingly original concepts during a tragically short career. "The Diamond Lens" describes a miniature world discovered through a microscopic device, and "The Wondersmith" depicts a menacing mannequin who may as well be a robot. Both of these stories anticipated themes that were to become stock devices in a later era, as did O'Brien's most famous tale, "What Was It?" This compelling piece concerns the discovery of a mute, invisible man who dies in captivity, leaving no clue to his origin. "The Lost Room" disappears when its tenant gambles for possession of it with a band of spirits and loses. O'Brien's ingenuity might have brought him greater fame if he had lived long enough to write even a few more stories. As it was, poverty induced him to hire himself out as a military substitute for the sentimental writer Thomas Bailey Aldrich, whose success had made it possible for him to fulfill his military obligation with cash (this was perfectly legal at the time). The result was O'Brien's death in a Civil War skirmish.

One writer who lived through this conflict was Ambrose Bierce, who was to make an even more impressive contribution to the literature of the uncanny. He wrote *The Devil's Dictionary* at the top of his voice; everybody quotes him, but few know his name. And nobody knows how he died.

THE IMP OF THE PERVERSE
By Edgar Allan Poe

In the consideration of the faculties and impulses—of the *prima mobilia* of the human soul, the phrenologists have failed to make room for a propensity which, although obviously existing as a radical, primitive, irreducible sentiment, has been equally overlooked by all the moralists who have preceded them. In the pure arrogance of the reason, we have all overlooked it. We have suffered its existence to escape our senses solely through want of belief—of faith;—whether it be faith in Revelation, or faith in the Kabbala. The idea of it has never occurred to us, simply because of its supererogation. We saw no *need* of impulse—for the propensity. We could not perceive its necessity. We could not understand, that is to say, we could not have understood, had the notion of this *primum mobile* ever obtruded itself;—we could not have understood in what manner it might be made to further the objects of humanity, either temporal or eternal. It cannot be denied that phrenology and, in great measure, all metaphysicianism have been concocted *a priori*. The intellectual or logical man, rather than the understanding or observant man, set himself to imagine designs—to dictate purposes to God. Having thus fathomed, to his satisfaction, the intentions of Jehovah, out of these intentions he built his innumerable systems of mind. In the matter of phrenology, for example, we first determined, naturally enough, that it was the design of the Deity that man should eat. We then assigned to man an organ of alimentiveness, and this organ is the scourge with which the Deity compels man, will-I nill-I, into eating. Secondly, having settled it to be God's will that man should continue his species, we discovered an organ of amativeness, forthwith. And so with combativeness, with ideality, with causality, with constructiveness,—so, in short, with every organ, whether representing a propensity, a moral sentiment, or a faculty of the pure intellect. And in these arrangements of the *principia* of human action, the Spurzheimites, whether right or wrong, in part, or upon the whole, have but followed, in principle, the footsteps of their predecessors; deducing and establishing everything from the preconceived destiny of man, and upon the ground of the objects of his Creator.

It would have been wiser, it would have been safer, to classify (if classify we must) upon the basis of what man usually or occasionally did, and was always occasionally doing, rather than upon the basis of what we took it for granted the Deity intended him to do. If we cannot comprehend God in his visible works, how then in his inconceivable thoughts, that call the works into being? If we cannot understand him in his objective creatures, how then in his substantive moods and phases of creation?

Induction, *a posteriori*, would have brought phrenology to admit, as an innate and primitive principle of human action, a paradoxical something, which we may call *perverseness*, for want of a more characteristic term. In the sense I intend, it is, in fact, a *mobile* without motive, a motive not *motivirt*. Through its promptings we act without comprehensible object; or, if this shall be understood as a contradiction in terms, we may so far modify the proposition as to say, that through its promptings we act, for the reason that we should *not*. In theory, no reason can be more unreasonable; but, in fact, there is none more strong. With certain minds, under certain conditions it becomes absolutely irresistible. I am not more certain that I breathe, than that the assurance of the wrong or error of any action is often the one unconquerable *force* which impels us, and alone impels us to its prosecution. Nor will this overwhelming tendency to do wrong for the wrong's sake, admit of analysis, or resolution into ulterior elements. It is radical, a primitive impulse—elementary. It will be said, I am aware, that when we persist in acts because we feel we should *not* persist in them, our conduct is but a modification of that which ordinarily springs from the *combativeness* of phrenology. But a glance will show the fallacy of this idea. The phrenological combativeness has, for its essence, the necessity of self-defence. It is our safeguard against injury. Its principle regards our well-being; and thus the desire to be well is excited simultaneously with its development. It follows, that the desire to be well must be excited simultaneously with any principle which shall be merely a modification of combativeness, but in the case of that something which I term *perverseness*, the desire to be well is not only not aroused, but a strongly antagonistical sentiment exists.

An appeal to one's own heart is, after all, the best reply to the sophistry just noticed. No one who trustingly consults and thoroughly questions his own soul will be disposed to deny the entire radicalness of the propensity in question. It is not more incomprehensible than distinctive. There lives no man who at some period has not been tormented, for example, by an earnest desire to tantalise a listener by circumlocution. The speaker is aware that he displeases; he has every intention to please; he is usually curt, precise, and clear; the most laconic and luminous language is struggling for utterance upon his tongue; it is only with difficulty that he restrains himself from giving it flow; he dreads and deprecates the anger of him whom he addresses; yet, the thought strikes him, that by certain involutions and parentheses this anger may be engendered. That single thought is enough. The impulse increases to a wish, the wish to a desire, the desire to an uncontrollable longing, and the longing (to the deep regret and mortification of the speaker, and in defiance of all consequences) is indulged.

We have a task before us which must be speedily performed. We know that it will be ruinous to make delay. The most important crisis of our life calls, trumpet-tongued, for immediate energy and action. We glow, we are consumed with eagerness to commence the work, with the anticipation of whose glorious result our whole souls are on fire. It must, it shall be undertaken to-day, and yet we put it off until to-morrow; and why? There is no answer, except that we feel *perverse*, using the word with no comprehension of the principle. To-morrow arrives, and with it a more impatient anxiety to do our duty, but with this very increase of anxiety arrives, also, a nameless, a positively fearful, because unfathomable, craving for delay. This craving gathers strength as the moments fly. The last hour for action is at hand. We tremble with the violence of the conflict within us,—of the definite with the indefinite—of the substance with the shadow. But, if the contest has proceeded thus far, it is the shadow which prevails,—we struggle in vain. The clock strikes, and is the knell of our welfare. At the same time, it is the chanticleer-note to the ghost that has so long overawed us. It flies—it disappears—we are free. The old energy returns. We will labour *now*. Alas, it is *too late!*

We stand upon the brink of a precipice. We peer into the abyss—we grow sick and dizzy. Our first impulse is to shrink from the danger. Unaccountably we remain. By slow degrees our sickness and dizziness and horror become merged in a cloud of unnamable feeling. By gradations, still more imperceptible, this cloud assumes shape, as did the vapour from the bottle out of which arose the genius in the *Arabian Nights*. But out of this *our* cloud upon the precipice's edge, there grows into palpability, a shape, far more terrible than any genius or any demon of a tale, and yet it is but a thought, although a fearful one, and one which chills the very marrow of our bones with the fierceness of the delight of its horror. It is merely the idea of what would be our sensations during the sweeping precipitancy of a fall from such a height. And this fall—this rushing annihilation—for the very reason that it involves that one most ghastly and loathsome of all the most ghastly and loathsome images of death and suffering which have ever presented themselves to our imagination—for this very cause do we now the most vividly desire it. And because our reason violently deters us from the brink, *therefore* do we the most impetuously approach it. There is no passion in nature so demoniacally impatient as that of him who, shuddering upon the edge of a precipice, thus meditates a plunge. To indulge, for a moment, in any attempt at *thought,* is to be inevitably lost; for reflection but urges us to forbear, and *therefore* it is, I say, that we *cannot*. If there be no friendly arm to check us, or if we fail in a sudden effort to prostrate ourselves backward from the abyss, we plunge, and are destroyed.

Examine these and similar actions as we will, we shall find them resulting solely from the spirit of the *Perverse*. We perpetrate them merely because we feel that we should *not.* Beyond or behind this there is no intelligible principle; and we might, indeed, deem this perverseness a direct instigation of the arch-fiend, were it not occasionally known to operate in furtherance of good.

I have said thus much, that in some measure I may answer your question—that I may explain to you why I am here—that I may assign to you something that shall have at least the faint aspect of a cause for my wearing these fetters, and for my tenanting this cell of the condemned. Had I not been thus prolix, you might either have misunderstood me altogether, or, with the rabble, have fancied me mad. As it is, you will easily perceive that I am one of the many uncounted victims of the Imp of the Perverse.

It is impossible that any deed could have been wrought with a more thorough deliberation. For weeks, for months, I pondered upon the means of the murder. I rejected a thousand schemes, because their accomplishment involved a *chance* of detection. At length, in reading some French memoirs, I found an account of a nearly fatal illness that occurred to Madame Pilau, through the agency of a candle accidentally poisoned. The idea struck my fancy at once. I knew my victim's habit of reading in bed. I knew, too, that his apartment was narrow and ill-ventilated. But I need not vex you with impertinent details. I need not describe the easy artifices by which I substituted, in his bed-room candle stand, a wax-light of my own making for the one which I there found. The next morning he was discovered dead in his bed, and the coroner's verdict was—"Death by the visitation of God."

Having inherited his estate, all went well with me for years. The idea of detection never once entered my brain. Of the remains of the fatal taper I had myself carefully disposed. I had left no shadow of a clue by which it would be possible to convict, or even suspect, me of the crime. It is inconceivable how rich a sentiment of satisfaction arose in my bosom as I reflected upon my absolute security. For a very long period of time I was accustomed to revel in this sentiment. It afforded me more real delight than all the mere worldly advantages accruing from my sin. But there arrived at length an epoch, from which the pleasurable feeling grew, by scarcely perceptible gradations, into a haunting and harassing thought. It harassed me because it haunted. I could scarcely get rid of it for an instant. It is quite a common thing to be thus annoyed with the ringing in our ears, or rather in our memories, of the burthen of some ordinary song, or some unimpressive snatches from an opera. Nor will we be the less tormented if the song in itself be good, or the opera air meritorious. In this manner, at last, I would perpetually catch myself pondering upon my security, and repeating, in a low under-tone, the phrase, "I am safe."

One day, whilst sauntering along the streets, I arrested myself in the act of murmuring, half aloud, these customary syllables. In a fit of petulance I re-modelled them thus: "I am safe—I am safe—yes—if I be not fool enough to make open confession."

No sooner had I spoken these words, than I felt an icy chill creep to my heart. I had had some experience in these fits of perversity (whose nature I have been at some trouble to explain), and I remembered well that in no instance I had successfully resisted their attacks. And now my own casual self-suggestion, that I might possibly be fool enough to confess the murder of which I had been guilty, confronted me, as if the very ghost of him whom I had murdered—and beckoned me on to death.

At first, I made an effort to shake off this nightmare of the soul. I walked vigorously—faster—still faster—at length I ran. I felt a maddening desire to shriek aloud. Every succeeding wave of thought overwhelmed me with new terror, for, alas! I well, too well, understood that to *think*, in my situation, was to be lost. I still quickened my pace. I bounded like a madman through the crowded thoroughfares. At length, the populace took the alarm and pursued me. I felt *then* the consummation of my fate. Could I have torn out my tongue, I would have done it—but a rough voice resounded in my ears—a rougher grasp seized me by the shoulder. I turned—I gasped for breath. For a moment I experienced all the pangs of suffocation; I became blind, and deaf, and giddy; and then some invisible fiend, I thought, struck me with his broad palm upon the back. The long-imprisoned secret burst forth from my soul.

They say that I spoke with a distinct enunciation, but with marked emphasis and passionate hurry, as if in dread of interruption before concluding the brief but pregnant sentences that consigned me to the hangman and to hell.

Having related all that was necessary for the fullest judicial conviction, I fell prostrate in a swoon.

But why shall I say more? To-day I wear these chains, and am *here!* To-morrow I shall be fetterless!—*but where?*

·4·

MY FAVORITE MURDER: VICTORIAN VILLAINY

The second half of the nineteenth century was an era in which ghostly tales flourished. A growing number of writers achieved success as specialists in the spectral, and many serious "mainstream" novelists took an occasional stab at the supernatural. Yet what Poe's followers produced were not exactly, in his phrase, "Tales of the Grotesque and the Arabesque." His dreamworld of mysterious madness was engulfed by a rising tide of restraint called Victorianism in Britain and industrialism in the United States. The era of romantics and revolutionaries was over, passions had cooled, and finance became the principal motive for the use of force, in fact and in fiction. Poe's more frankly morbid stories were ultimately to have less effect on his followers than his studies in ratiocination, which became increasingly popular as bloodthirsty individuals took to the printed page and created murder for fun and profit. The intellectual air of the detective story, with its inverted logic and deductive substructure, brought all sorts of lurid details to light that previously might have been considered illegitimate, at least in respectable literature. "Mysteries" seemed more intelligent and uplifting than tales of terror, even though their subject matter was often as grim as that of the more despised genre. By the beginning of the twentieth century, there were hordes of mystery fans who would never be caught dead with anything as tasteless as a horror story.

On the other side of the coin, it became possible for at least one man to construct a humor of homicide. This was Ambrose Bierce, who employed an ironic tone and some outrageous incidents to create the cruel comedy of stories like "My Favorite Murder," which in its title alone is a commentary on the growing popularity of literary crimes. Born in 1842, Bierce fought on the Union side in the Civil War and wrote what may well be the best war stories in American literature, although they will never be recognized as such by those who imagine that battles are anything but brutal and bloody. He also wrote some brilliant tales of psychic phenomena, including such famous works as "An Occurrence at Owl Creek Bridge" and "The Damned Thing." In addition he was a gifted wit and satirist, author of the sardonic *Fantastic Fables* (1899) and *The Devil's Dictionary* (originally *The Cynic's Word Book*), a series of sarcastic definitions that more or less inaugurated this popular form. Many of Bierce's grim wisecracks, now almost a century old, are still current among people who may have no idea of their source.

The apparent contrast between the two fields in which Bierce gained his reputation becomes less striking when his works are read. His humor is cold and cutting, and it exhibits the same hostility toward humanity to be found in his short stories. Bierce is beyond melancholy or even morbidity; his characteristic attitude is misanthropy, born of an idealism outraged by people's failure to live up to their professed principles. His wartime experiences demonstrated the hollowness of conventions about the glory of war, and his innocent involvement in some shady business deals made him skeptical about the sources of financial success. Many of his tales reflect the vicious behavior prevalent during the settlement of the West, which he experienced firsthand as a surveyor and a miner.

Although he lived for a few years in England, Bierce spent most of his literary career in San Francisco, where he was associated with several regional periodicals. Book publication and widespread recognition did not come until years after he had begun to write fiction. His first book in the vein of the macabre appeared in 1892; it was unfortunately *The Monk and the Hangman's Daughter*, a tired Gothic novel translated by G. A. Danziger from a German text and rendered into proper English by Bierce. Danziger, whose literary ambitions would involve him, decades later, after he had changed his name to Adolphe de Castro, in collaborations with the twentieth-century spine chiller H. P. Lovecraft, proved very troublesome about dividing the profits, and the matter was not really settled until their publisher went bankrupt. Both men ended up with nothing, though the book was not as bad as all that.

Luckily for Bierce, the same year also saw the publication of his fine collection of Civil War stories, *Tales of Soldiers and Civilians*, now better known under its British title, *In the Midst of Life*. This book is so much better than *The Monk and the Hangman's Daughter* that it almost justifies Bierce's definition of a novel, in *The Devil's Dictionary*, as "a short story padded." Bierce went on to defend short fiction in a manner very reminiscent of Poe, and there seems little doubt that their arguments are justified, at least with regard to tales of terror. After the decline of the Gothic novel, few of the best stories in the graveyard genre were of book length. It is not inappropriate to consider *In the Midst of Life* in this context; some of the tales in the volume are as harrowing as anything in English. Bierce's grim realism demonstrates by misdirection that the appeal of the horror tale depends on an understanding between reader and writer that they are playing a frivolous game and that too much truth makes for the wrong sort of mood. Such is the case with stories like "Chickamauga," in which a deaf child, too young to comprehend his situation, wanders through a battlefield and rides on the backs of hideously wounded men who are crawling away to die. The collection also includes the celebrated tour de force "An Occurrence at Owl Creek Bridge," in which a spy about to be hanged seems to escape when the rope breaks and has almost made his way to safety when he suddenly dies of a broken neck; all his adventures are revealed as hallucinations experienced in the second before his execution.

The "Civilians" section of this volume features a pair of tales on the psychology of fear, "A Watcher by the Dead" and "The Suitable Surroundings." Both treat wagers based on a character's avowed ability to withstand scary situations, and both men end up dead of fright. In "A Watcher by the Dead," a man bets that he can spend a night locked in an empty house with a corpse. He expires when the "corpse," actually a friend of his opponent, comes to life; and the unfortunate practical joker, now trapped with the man he has killed, proceeds to go mad. In "The Suitable Surroundings," a writer of ghost stories challenges an acquaintance to read some of his work in a supposedly haunted house. The story contains the information that the author intends to kill himself and then visit his victim. When a frightened boy looking for ghosts peers through the window at the appalled reader, nature takes its course.

A year later, in 1893, Bierce published his ghostly tales under the title *Can Such Things Be?* Among them is "The Damned Thing," about an invisible monster that terrorizes and finally kills a lonely farmer. Speculation that the creature is of a color outside the spectrum visible to the human eye gives the story a science fiction flavor. Like many of Bierce's best efforts, "The Damned Thing" has a complicated structure. Although only a few pages long, it is divided into four sections, narrated from different points of view and not in chronological order. The first section describes a coroner's inquest on the dead man, the second is an eyewitness account of his fatal encounter with the unseen beast, the third relates the jury's rejection of the testimony, and the fourth is an excerpt from the victim's diary in which he discusses the nature of his killer. This elaborate technique serves to create an air of mystery and enables Bierce to withhold his most shocking material until the end of the story, so that by roundabout means he follows Poe's advice about building to a final climax of horror. The breakdown into "chapters" also allows Bierce to slip a bit of cruel comedy into his serious work; the sections frequently have facetious titles like "One Does Not Always Eat What Is on the Table," used to introduce the description of a corpse laid out for the coroner's inspection.

Bierce's convoluted construction sometimes invokes a supernatural aura only to dispel it with an interpretation that is more plausible and equally unpleasant. In "The Death of Halpin Frayser," a man long separated from his family falls asleep unwittingly on the grave of his mother and has a nightmare in which her ghost attacks him. He is found strangled the next morning; but he has actually been murdered not by his mother's ghost but by her second husband, a maniac who guards her grave. Ingenious arrangement and the powerful symbolism of the nightmare join to make this combination of coincidences more effective than they should be, and in fact the coincidences become uncanny rather than merely unbelievable. Several of Bierce's tales employ spectral vengeance as an antidote to racial prejudice; both "The Haunted Valley" and "The Night-Doings at 'Deadman's'" describe murdered Chinese immigrants who rise to destroy their bigoted butchers. Bierce also gave the Frankenstein theme a wry rehash in "Moxon's Master," the story of a mechanical chess player driven to homicide by his creator's plot to win the game by cheating. "A Psychological Shipwreck" is perhaps the best fictional treatment of the wraith, the spirit of a living person released to provide a warning of impending disaster.

Bierce's tales of morbid mirth were not published as separate books, but they appear in his collected works under the titles *Negligible Tales* and *The Parenticide Club*. They are to some extent offshoots of pioneer America's fondness for "tall tales"; by combining perfectly outrageous descriptions of villainy with ironic understatement he anticipated the twentieth century's fondness for "sick" comedy. The fact that these stories so often involve interfamilial infamies need not provide a field day for Freudians; Bierce was obviously making a calculated effort to be as offensive as possible. A hint of his method can be found in the first sentence of "An Imperfect Conflagration": "Early one June morning in 1872 I murdered my father—an act which made a deep impression on me at the time." No summary can do justice to tales like "A Bottomless Grave" or "Oil of Dog"; but "My Favorite Murder," reprinted at the end of this chapter, shows Bierce at his most hideously hilarious.

In 1913, the seventy-one-year-old writer took it into his head to visit Mexico, where a revolution was in progress. He disappeared without a trace. More than one author has been tempted into imagining an appropriate end for this colorful character, but nothing could really improve on the mystery he himself left behind him. A man who could describe a hearse as "Death's baby-carriage" should be entitled to have the last laugh on his readers.

He had a successor of sorts in the person of Stephen Crane, who spiritualized Bierce's war stories into *The Red Badge of Courage* (1895). Most of Crane's tales deal with men facing fear in a variety of situations. He rarely touches on the uncanny, but several pieces describe men adrift in the wilderness who are driven to regard their bleak surroundings as omens of supernatural malignancy. Perhaps his most shocking story is "The Monster" (1898) in which a black servant is hideously mutilated while rescuing a white child from a burning building. His injury also leaves him slightly if not dangerously insane, so that he does not acknowledge his deformity and insists on attempting to socialize with people who find his appearance horrifying. His employer is morally obligated to retain his services and finds his business ruined and his family ostracized as a result. "The Monster" ends on a note of despair; there is no solution to what is presented as an intolerable situation. All the more frightening because it seems so perfectly plausible, the story is at once a powerful piece of realism and a parable on the pernicious effects of prejudice.

Bierce really stands alone in this period as the major American master of the macabre, but the British Isles seemed to be teeming with ghost stories. One of the most important figures in the development of a British tradition was Joseph Sheridan Le Fanu, whose influence on later writers was so great that some have compared him to Poe. He is certainly not as fine an artist, but his work defined a tradition that many of his followers found invaluable in the construction of their own tales. His major achievement was to make a transition between the ponderous Gothic novel and the short story, which is now generally regarded as the most appropriate form for frightening fiction.

Born in 1814, Le Fanu was, like Bierce, a successful journalist. He wrote several novels, all pervaded with a gloomy Gothic atmosphere, of which the most impressive is *Uncle Silas*. They were very popular in their time but today are almost completely overshadowed by his briefer works, which are more concentrated and more frankly supernatural. The majority of these were composed during the last few years of his life when, after the death of his wife, he became a recluse and an invalid. He began to retire early and wake after midnight, writing in bed by candlelight until dawn, fortified with strong tea. This habit became the subject of one of his finest tales, "Green Tea," the story of a clergyman whose use of that stimulant induces horrible visions of a monkey-demon which torments him until he is driven to suicide. The tale is an early example of what has been called the "psychological" ghost story, one in which apparitions can be interpreted either as genuine spirits or as the products of disordered minds. A third explanation is offered by one of the characters: abnormal mental states may produce a susceptibility to dangerous spiritual forces whose existence normally goes undetected. This theory is propounded by a Dr. Hesselius, who represents another of Le Fanu's innovations: that of the psychic investigator who is consulted in cases involving supernatural manifestations. Such figures became increasingly popular as ghost stories began to compete with detective fiction; Hesselius is the father of such characters as Algernon Blackwood's Dr. John Silence, William Hope Hodgson's Carnacki, Dennis Wheatley's Duke de Richleau, Seabury Quinn's Jules de Grandin, and Joseph Payne Brennan's Lucius Leffing.

Le Fanu's work is distinguished by a leisurely pace and a certain subtlety in the introduction of his uncanny effects. His tone is not as feverish as Poe's nor as grim as

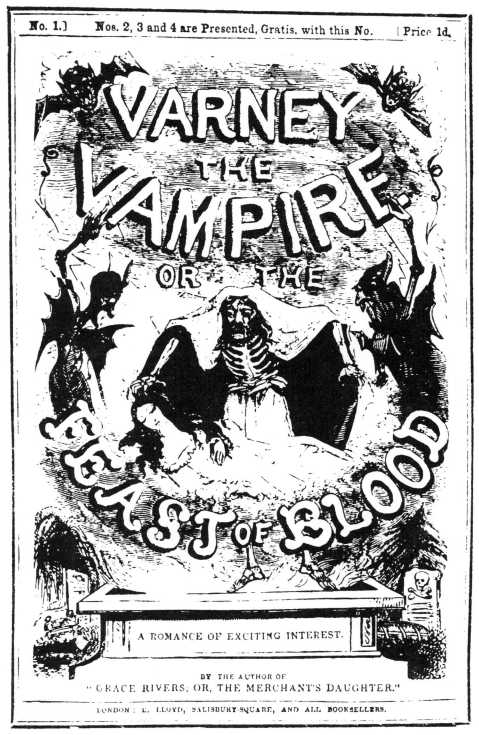

An anonymous artist designed this cover for the anonymously published *Varney the Vampire*, usually ascribed to Thomas Peckett Prest but more recently attributed by some authorities to James Malcolm Rymer.

Bierce's, and he usually begins by describing normal events in the lives of his protagonists, only gradually allowing the nature of his story to emerge. Often the ghostly manifestations are preceded by some disturbing but natural event that throws the characters off balance and leaves them open to the forces described by Dr. Hesselius. He used many stock situations like the vengeful ghost and the deal with the devil, but he told them better than they had ever been told before. And many of his stories inaugurated traditions, like "Narrative of the Ghost of a Hand," an incident from a novel, whose title should be self-explanatory.

The imaginative Irish author's most impressive tale may well be "Carmilla" (1871), a vampire story, which its proponents suggest is the most outstanding presentation of its theme, although it has been overshadowed by the enormous success of Bram Stoker's *Dracula*. The legend of the reanimated corpse that feeds on the blood of the living had been exposed before in two markedly inferior literary productions by John Polidori and Thomas Peckett Prest. Polidori, who had failed to produce anything for the contest that inspired Mary Shelley to write *Frankenstein*, abandoned his first idea and adapted one of Lord Byron's to produce "The Vampyre," originally published under Byron's name, in 1819. An improbable plot, in which the hero allows his sister to marry the vampire rather than break a promise to keep the fiend's identity a secret, pretty well destroys whatever effect the story might have had. Prest's novel, *Varney the Vampire*, or *The Feast of Blood* (1847) was one of a series of melodramatic potboilers with which Prest entertained vast audiences before sinking into well-deserved obscurity. This book, recently reprinted, has a reputation that a perusal of the text will not sustain. Even a dedicated devotee would be hard pressed to wade through its eight hundred pages of thinly connected incidents to watch Varney fling himself into the mouth of Mount Vesuvius. Prest is perhaps best remembered by the extravagant title of one of his forgotten epics: *The Skeleton Clutch*, or *The Goblet of Gore*.

"Carmilla" is far superior to either of these earlier efforts. Le Fanu takes great pains with the character of his vampire, a beautiful young woman who prefers seduction to violence and makes a specialty of becoming the houseguest of her victims. A note of perversity is struck by her preference for female conquests, a contravention of the literary convention that vampires prefer to inflict themselves on the opposite sex. An atmosphere of barely subdued eroticism pervades the relationship between Carmilla and the lady who narrates the story, creating a mood that has few parallels in Victorian literature. The fact that the scenes of stifled passion occur before Carmilla's bloodthirsty motives are exposed only serves to make them more remarkable.

Le Fanu died in 1873 after a prolonged illness that was characterized by terrible nightmares, many of which may have worked their way into his fiction. He was particularly upset by a recurrent dream in which an old house collapsed on him, so much so that the doctor who pronounced him dead said only, "I feared this; that house fell at last."

The "Green Tea" theme of a drug that produces horror received its most famous treatment at the hands of Robert Louis Stevenson, whose *Strange Case of Dr. Jekyll and Mr. Hyde* was published in 1886. This short novel, about a doctor whose potion transforms him into a being with all his worst traits intensified, is unfortunately a victim of its own notoriety. There can hardly be a person alive who does not know the outline of the plot; but Stevenson shrouds it in mystery, introducing Jekyll and Hyde as separate characters and withholding the secret of their single identity and origin until the last few pages. As a result of the story's success, Stevenson's carefully contrived air of confusion and suspense is lost, and it is virtually impossible to give it a fair reading. Such is the price of fame.

A magazine illustration by D. H. Friston for the first publication of Joseph Sheridan Le Fanu's classic tale of a female vampire, "Carmilla."

Nevertheless, the tale is a classic, and Stevenson, for all his brilliant romances, is probably best remembered as its author. The circumstances of its composition are almost as remarkable as the story itself. Stevenson, never in the best of health, was seriously ill when the germ of the plot came to him in the form of a dream. "All I dreamt of *Dr. Jekyll and Mr. Hyde,*" he wrote later, "was that a man was being pressed into a cabinet, where he swallowed a drug and changed into another being." Inspired by this visionary fragment, he wrote the entire book in three days, all the while suffering from severe hemorrhages. When he read it to his wife, she criticized him for neglecting the plot's moral implications, insisting that what he had treated as a thriller was really a powerful allegory. Furious, the writer stormed out of the room. He returned a moment later, cried "You are right!" and threw the manuscript into the fire. He then proceeded to write another version from scratch, again taking a mere three days to complete the task.

A few critics have bemoaned the loss of the first version, which they imagine to have been more exciting if less edifying; but such speculations can never be proved. In its final form the book created a sensation and still contained enough moral sentiment to become the subject for numerous sermons. It was immediately adapted for the stage and later became one of the most frequently filmed stories in the history of motion pictures. These popularized versions have obscured many of the details of the original, giving rise, for instance, to the notion that Hyde is a hideous monster, complete with fangs and claws. In fact, he is perfectly human and not at all deformed physically, distinguished from Jekyll by being smaller and younger. The characters who describe him as horrible admit that it is his attitude, rather than his appearance, which frightens them. The idea of a hideous Hyde seems to be an unconscious recognition that the story is a science fiction version of

Mr. Hyde was described by Stevenson as an individual of comparatively presentable appearance; the concept that he was a monster seems to derive from Frederic March's Oscar-winning film performance in 1932. From *Dr. Jekyll and Mr. Hyde* (1932). *Courtesy of MGM.*

the werewolf legend. It is also worth noting that Jekyll is not quite the noble seeker after truth usually portrayed on the screen but rather a man fully aware of his sinful side and rather fond of it. His confessed intention was to embody his evil impulses so that they could be expressed without guilt or shame. Of course, Hyde overpowers Jekyll and begins to appear without chemical aid, and it is Hyde who commits suicide when he runs out of the ingredient that permits him to disguise himself.

Stevenson created almost a mirror image of Jekyll and Hyde in his short story "Markheim," concerning a murderer haunted by his double, who seems at first to be a devil but is ultimately portrayed as a guardian angel, driving Markheim to despair so that he will repent and confess. A powerful portrayal of the criminal's growing panic makes this slightly strained parable palatable. Stevenson also incited quite a bit of late-blooming controversy with "The Body Snatcher," which has been cited as the definitive example of supernatural elements introduced too abruptly into a basically straightforward story. Yet his is the best treatment of the grim "resurrection" trade, which provided stolen corpses for purposes of medical instruction during the nineteenth century. The criminal who had serviced the doctors is murdered to seal his lips, but his dissected body inexplicably ends up among their spoils when they begin grave robbing on their own. Those who find the first part of the tale unnerving will scarcely be put off by its uncanny resolution.

Stevenson was just one of the many successful authors whose fiction included sinister sidelines. Sir Walter Scott had been a serious student of the occult and wrote a factual history of the subject, as well as fictional efforts like "Wandering Willie's Tale" and "The Tapestried Chamber." Charles Dickens, well known for his whimsical Christmas ghost stories like "A Christmas Carol" (1843) and for chilling scenes in novels like *Oliver Twist* and *Great Expectations*, wrote a pair of fine out-and-out chillers in "The Signal-Man" and "To Be Taken with a Grain of Salt" (or "Trial for Murder"), both describing premonitions of death. These stories were published in *All the Year Round*, a magazine Dickens edited in a manner that revealed his lively interest in spooky stories. Among his contributors was Edward Bulwer-Lytton, best remembered today for *The Last Days of Pompeii*. A true believer in worlds beyond our ken, Bulwer-Lytton infused most of his popular novels with weird atmosphere and produced one of the finest accounts of a haunted house in "The Haunted and the Haunters, or the House and the Brain" (1857), which suggested that ghosts are the revenants not of personalities but of their powerful thoughts and emotions, which have taken on an independent existence. Wilkie Collins, who occasionally collaborated with Dickens, undercut the tradition of uncanny fiction with the first major detective novel, *The Moonstone* (1868), which nevertheless inspired many eerie tales with its theme of a desecrated Oriental idol whose worshipers demand vengeance. Some of his shorter works, like "The Dream Woman" and "A Terribly Strange Bed," are still effective tales of terror.

In later decades, Rudyard Kipling, who chronicled the rise of British imperialism in India, used the same exotic setting for "The Phantom 'Rickshaw" (1888), in which a faithless lover is haunted by the ghost of the woman he has betrayed; and "The Mark of the Beast," in which a soldier is cursed for defiling a sacred statue. And the subtle and brilliant Henry James, an American expatriate who settled in England, took time off from his more serious work to concoct several eerie tales, including one that may outlive everything else he wrote, *The Turn of the Screw* (1898). Told from the viewpoint of a young governess who is convinced that her young charges are influenced by the spirits of two sinister servants, it is fashioned so that it is impossible to tell whether the ghosts are genuine or merely a product of the lady's overworked imagination. Both interpretations

Edward Bulwer-Lytton's novel of a magician's quest for eternal life, *Zanoni* (1842), was illustrated by C. T. Deblois.

are equally unnerving, since one of the children is finally scared to death; but the popularity of Freudian criticism has given the psychological theory the upper hand in recent years, despite the author's clear intention to leave the point ambiguous. Elaborately written, *The Turn of the Screw* has the dubious distinction of being the favorite ghost story of people who dislike ghost stories.

A few writers have suffered the irony of having their major efforts virtually forgotten, while the thrillers they have tossed off in idle moments have brought them a small measure of immortality. Such is the case with F. Marion Crawford, whose novels made him the best-selling author in turn-of-the-century America. Hardly anyone reads them today, but the stories collected in *Wandering Ghosts* (1894) include some minor classics in the domain of the weird that seem likely to survive as long as such things are read. "The Upper Berth" is a chilling account of a drowned man whose clammy presence fills the stateroom in which he made his last voyage, and "The Screaming Skull" is the skillfully presented monologue of a man haunted by a skull found in his house in a hatbox. This tale seems to have inaugurated the now popular tradition of a doomed character whose

An impressionistic illustration for Robert W. Chambers's "The Yellow Sign," done decades after the story's original appearance by the popular pulp magazine artist Hannes Bok. *Courtesy of Sisu Publishers.*

narration points to an inevitable climax supplied by a newspaper account of his death. A depraved old man who arranges for a brother and sister to marry is the owner of "The Dead Smile"; his plot is foiled only when a document is removed from his coffin in an exceptionally gruesome scene.

Crawford's career is paralleled by that of Robert W. Chambers, a popular and prolific novelist who specialized in fashionable love stories. His reputation today rests almost entirely on one of his earliest books, *The King in Yellow* (1895). This macabre collection included a few trivial and sentimental pieces; but the best selections were not only effective but also extremely influential on his successors in the United States. Chambers dropped fascinating hints of a new kind of horror, not based on fear of death or the devil, but rather on a vague awareness of other worlds and dimensions threatening to overwhelm our own. More suggested than specified, the menace of *The King in Yellow* fascinated many later writers like H. P. Lovecraft, who attempted to detail the nameless forces lurking in the background of this book. The most famous Chambers story is "The Yellow Sign," describing an artist who innocently acquires a talisman of strange design, then finds it is a symbol of the evil lore described in a blasphemous book called *The King in Yellow*. Already shocked to the point of madness by the secrets of the forbidden volume, he is hardly even surprised when a living corpse comes to reclaim the talisman, leaving death in its wake. More fascinating, if more clumsily told, is "The Repairer of Reputations," whose hero has also read the deadly book. He encounters an agent of the King in Yellow, a deformed old man with a pointed head, missing fingers, and wax ears, whose uncanny sources of information make him a master blackmailer. He promises to make the maddened narrator ruler of the earth; but the plan is frustrated when the blackmailer's cat, which has a great fondness for scratching him, finally tears his throat out. It almost seems that the visions of power are no more than the plans of lunatics, but evidence of the old man's powers reveals that the world has narrowly escaped a catastrophe. The story is set in a futuristic 1920, overshadowed by the presence of a government "lethal chamber" in which legal suicides are permitted.

More traditional, and far more popular, were the menaces imagined by the Anglo-Irish author Bram Stoker, who made himself immortal with *Dracula* (1897). Not a professional writer, Stoker made his living as the manager of the distinguished actor Sir Henry Irving. His interest in the macabre, however, may have been encouraged in part by Irving's roof-raising performance in his production of *The Bells*, a play about a murderer haunted by the sound of his victim's sleigh bells who is finally brought to justice by an ingenious hypnotist. Irving's other eerie efforts on the stage included a version of Faust and a treatment of the legend of a haunted ship, The Flying Dutchman.

Stoker claimed that *Dracula*, in the grand tradition, had been inspired by a nightmare. It had also entailed a fair amount of research. Stoker based his vampire character on a historical personage, a fifteenth-century Romanian warlord named Vlad Tepes, notorious for his acts of wanton cruelty. The nickname Dracula meant "son of the dragon." The author picked up historical and geographical details from Arminius Vambery of Budapest University; but his references to the medieval character are slight, and Dracula might as well have been the fictional character he was generally assumed to be.

The book has been frequently condemned without a fair reading (often with none at all); but it is nevertheless a vivid and gripping melodrama, on an epic scale never suggested by the hastily contrived stage version or the many film adaptations, all apparently based on the play's confined settings. An irresistible combination of

John Carradine, with his gray hair and moustache, came closer than most actors to Bram Stoker's description of Dracula. From *The House of Dracula* (1945). *Courtesy of Universal Pictures.*

repression and mayhem, rife with sexual and religious symbolism, *Dracula* is probably the best out-and-out horror novel ever written.

Narrated by various characters in their letters and diaries, the novel tells the now familiar tale of the "undead" nobleman from Transylvania who travels to London in search of new blood but is finally destroyed by a band of men with the knowledge and courage to oppose him. The early scenes are set in Dracula's mountain castle, where the vampire-count is visited by Jonathan Harker, who has come to sell him a home in England. This section, in which Harker gradually realizes what a strange household he is in, is probably the best part of the book. In the closing chapters, Dracula is pursued across Europe and killed outside the castle after a wild battle with his Gypsy servants. In the contrast between these medieval scenes and the main action in Victorian London, Stoker devised a method for bringing the Gothic novel up to date. The malevolent aristocrat who literally feeds upon the people of his domain is a more powerful symbol of predatory privilege than anything devised by Stoker's eighteenth-century predecessors, and his attempt to emigrate has all the implications of a foreign invasion.

The story is so well known that it has become the authoritative source on the care and feeding of vampires; Stoker's decisions regarding the legendary attributes of these lecherous leeches have been accepted as gospel truth. Unlike most of the vampires described in the purportedly factual manuscripts of olden days, Dracula can transform himself into a mist, a wolf, or a bat. He has a marked aversion for symbols of Christianity and a chauvinistic fondness for female victims. Other debatable points include Stoker's declaration that this cursed condition is contagious and that the proper cure is a wooden stake through the monster's heart (vampires were most commonly burned by those who believed in them). At any rate, Stoker's deviations from tradition were dramatically sound, and they helped ensure his book's success.

Dracula is a particularly fascinating monster because, unlike the equally famous creations of Dr. Frankenstein and Dr. Jekyll, he is almost completely remorseless. Rich, immortal, irresistible, and nearly omnipotent, he is the embodiment of an unleashed id, sleeping all day and spending his nights creeping into bedrooms. The sexual side of his ungentlemanly behavior undoubtedly titillated Victorian readers; this is particularly evident in the incident of his first English victim, Lucy Westerna, who keeps three suitors at arm's length while Dracula is turning her into a lustful fiend like himself. The highly charged scene in which her frustrated admirers converge on her coffin to hammer a stake into her has overtones of a symbolic rape.

Dracula is not the only colorful character in the book; some effectively eerie moments are provided by Renfield, a lunatic with a fondness for eating insects who hopes to work up to bigger things with the count's cooperation. Unaccountably forgotten in virtually every adaptation of the novel is Quincey Morris, a visiting American cowboy with an incredible vocabulary who sacrifices his life to kill Dracula and save the heroine, Harker's wife, Mina. Stoker also contributed to the growing tradition of psychic detectives with Dr. Abraham Van Helsing, the wily old Dutch physician who provides the necessary expertise to defeat the Transylvanian terror.

The author of *Dracula* produced several other books in the same vein, but none of them had a comparable impact. *The Jewel of Seven Stars* (1903) is a tale of Egyptian horrors involving the resurrection of a queen dead for thousands of years, and *The Lady of the Shroud* features a woman who poses as a vampire to thwart an international plot. Stoker died in 1912, just after completing *The Lair of the White Worm*. This novel, about a giant slug who lives beneath the earth and projects itself into the form of a mysterious woman, has more potential than perfection. The clumsy style shows all too clearly the effects of the severe illness from which Stoker was suffering. His last year recalled the debility of his childhood, when he was so weak that he did not leave his bed until the age of eight. *Dracula's Guest* (1914) was a posthumous collection of stories that included a fragment excised from *Dracula* as well as a pair of anthologist's favorites, "The Judge's House" and "The Squaw." The former is a good haunted-house story in which the ghost appears as a rat; the latter depicts a foolhardy American tourist who dies in an iron maiden which he has insisted on entering just for the thrill of it.

Dracula's history as a play commenced a few days after its publication, when it was read in a theater to protect the stage rights. The distinction of portraying the title character went to a Mr. Jones. A real adaptation was finally done in 1924 by actor Hamilton Deane, who played Van Helsing to Raymond Huntley's Dracula. Unanimously despised by the critics, the play was a huge success with the public.

A popularity surpassing even that of Stoker's famous character was enjoyed by Arthur

Conan Doyle's Sherlock Holmes, the fictional investigator who established the detective story as the favorite form for the consumption of pen-and-ink corpses. He handled many a gruesome case, including a few with supernatural overtones. Of course Holmes always found a logical explanation for apparently uncanny events, but many of the tales were effectively eerie. The most famous example is *The Hound of the Baskervilles*, in which the detective discovers a murderous canine ghost to be a well-trained animal covered with phosphorus. Similar cases include "The Adventure of the Devil's Foot," in which a rare poison creates the impression that its victims have died of fright; and "The Adventure of the Sussex Vampire," in which a woman caught sucking the blood of her child turns out to be drawing the poison from a wound administered by the real culprit.

One reaction to this sort of challenge was provided by the collected exploits of *Carnacki the Ghost-Finder* (1910) by William Hope Hodgson. A few of Carnacki's cases, like "The Horse of the Invisible," involve felonious fraud; but his investigations are usually concerned with genuine supernatural manifestations, often of the most grotesque type. "The Whistling Room," haunted by the spirit of a murdered jester, has a floor in which gigantic lips appear to produce hideous music. And "The Hog" is a filthy grunting force from another world which Carnacki keeps at bay with the use of an electric pentacle. This sort of detection had an interesting similarity to the life of Arthur Conan Doyle, who spent his last years seriously and hopefully investigating the possibility of communicating with the dead.

Hodgson, whose brief career was cut short by his death in the First World War, specialized not only in tales of psychic detection, but also in ghostly yarns about the sea. He had been a sailor for several years and later became an expert at conjuring up the mood of mystery and isolation of men adrift on the vast expanses of uncharted oceans. His most famous short stories of the sea are "The Derelict," in which an abandoned ship is covered with a strange mold that consumes any living creature coming into contact with the vessel; and "The Voice in the Night," in which two castaways feed on a fungus which eventually takes over their bodies, reducing them to shapeless gray masses, still unfortunately retaining their human intelligence. When potential rescuers approach, the sufferers are obliged to send them away, lest their affliction prove contagious. Other tales concern haunted ships and sea monsters.

Hodgson is most renowned for his four novels, *The Boats of the "Glen Carig," The House on the Borderland, The Ghost Pirates,* and *The Night Land,* all written between 1907 and 1912. Two of these consolidated the themes of his best sea stories, while *The House on the Borderland* and *The Night Land* moved in a new direction. Like *The King in Yellow,* these books sought to portray a different sort of horror, one that had considerable effect on later writers. They might technically be called science fiction, but Hodgson's intention was to express the mysteries of space and time, rather than to imagine the results of new discoveries or inventions. The idea of invaders from another dimension gets a persuasive and powerful treatment in *The House on the Borderland.* A manuscript found in a remote area tells the tale of a man whose isolated home is besieged by monsters. His defense of his house and his underground search for the creatures produce a mood of claustrophobic terror, while his vision of their source in an awesome infinity creates a breathless sense of wonder. This is probably his best novel, although many connoisseurs prefer *The Night Land,* a maddening combination of wild imagination, insufferable sentimentality, and tortured syntax. Presented as the work of a seventeenth-century man who dreams that he is living millions of years in the future, the book is written in a ridiculous and infuriating style that purports to indicate the narrator's era but in fact has no equivalent in the

Lee Brown Coye, a pulp magazine artist whose apparently simple work has a haunting long-term effect, drew this scene from William Hope Hodgson's story "The Hog" in 1946. *Courtesy of Lee Brown Coye.*

English language. In the world he describes, humanity is nearly extinct. The sun has gone out, the earth is alive with horrifying beings of every shape and size, and the few people left alive hide from an utterly inimical environment in a huge metal pyramid. Telepathically contacted by another colony of desperate people, the hero ventures out to bring them aid and encounters the most staggering array of outlandish adversaries ever committed to print. He finds love at the second pyramid, and the reader is apt to shudder anew at the maudlin excesses inspired in this encounter. Still, in its overall conception and in its best incidents, *The Night Land* is a compelling literary nightmare.

Horrors of a much more traditional sort were produced by the last great master of the Victorian ghost story, M. R. James. Without really breaking any new ground, the scholarly antiquarian brought to his work a sense of style and structure that has rarely been surpassed in macabre fiction. His academic work took most of his time, and he seems to have tossed off his dozens of cobwebby yarns to amuse himself and his friends. James was a devoted disciple of Le Fanu and shared his fondness for a slow beginning to set the scene and lull the reader. He wrote that "two ingredients most valuable in the concocting of a ghost story are, to me, the atmosphere and the nicely managed crescendo."

The first of his tales was written in 1894, and he continued to concoct them for more than thirty years. They were published in four volumes: *Ghost Stories of an Antiquary* (1904), *More Ghost Stories* (1911), *A Thin Ghost and Others* (1919), and *A Warning to the*

James McBryde was the artist for the first short story collection by M. R. James. "Oh, Whistle and I'll Come to You, My Lad" describes an unseen ghost that erupts from the victim's bedsheets.

Curious (1925). A few previously uncollected pieces were added to all the above to produce *Collected Ghost Stories* in 1931. The first two books are the best known and have supplied dozens of anthologies. They include such gems as "The Mezzotint," about a haunted picture that changes to portray the ghastly history of the house it depicts; "Oh, Whistle, and I'll Come to You, My Lad," concerning a musical instrument that calls up the spirits of the dead; and "Casting the Runes," in which a sorcerer sends a demon to punish a critic who gave his book on witchcraft a bad review. Most of the stories are enhanced by James's knowledge of English history; they are frequently set in old cathedrals or venerable country houses, or else they involve the discovery of curious relics. His ghosts, which appear only briefly, take some unusual forms. The one in "The Diary of Mr. Poynter" has a human shape but crawls on all fours and has a face entirely covered with hair; the one in "The Rose Garden" is just a face, "large, smooth and pink," with only one tooth. These unpleasant creatures have a way of getting uncomfortably close to their victims; as H. P. Lovecraft noted, they are often touched before they are seen. One that is heard before it is seen is the subject of "Rats," a seldom seen tale, one of the author's last, which is reprinted here from *Collected Ghost Stories*.

M. R. James, along with the rest of the men discussed in this survey of Victorian chillers, was an isolated toiler in his own literary graveyard. But the turn of the century saw a new development as a whole group of uncanny authors banded together to form a secret society. It was their solemn purpose to become masters of the lost art of magic.

MY FAVORITE MURDER

By Ambrose Bierce

Having murdered my mother under circumstances of singular atrocity, I was arrested and put upon my trial, which lasted seven years. In charging the jury, the judge of the Court of Acquittal remarked that it was one of the most ghastly crimes that he had ever been called upon to explain away.

At this, my attorney rose and said:

"May it please your Honor, crimes are ghastly or agreeable only by comparison. If you were familiar with the details of my client's previous murder of his uncle you would discern in his later offense (if offense it may be called) something in the nature of tender forbearance and filial consideration for the feelings of the victim. The appalling ferocity of the former assassination was indeed inconsistent with any hypothesis but that of guilt; and had it not been for the fact that the honorable judge before whom he was tried was the president of a life insurance company that took risks on hanging, and in which my client held a policy, it is hard to see how he could decently have been acquitted. If your Honor would like to hear about it for instruction and guidance of your Honor's mind, this unfortunate man, my client, will consent to give himself the pain of relating it under oath."

The district attorney said: "Your Honor, I object. Such a statement would be in the nature of evidence, and the testimony in this case is closed. The prisoner's statement should have been introduced three years ago, in the spring of 1881."

"In a statutory sense," said the judge, "you are right, and in the Court of Objections and Technicalities you would get a ruling in your favor. But not in a Court of Acquittal. The objection is overruled."

"I except," said the district attorney.

"You cannot do that," the judge said. "I must remind you that in order to take an exception you must first get this case transferred for a time to the Court of Exceptions on a formal motion duly supported by affidavits. A motion to that effect by your predecessor in office was denied by me during the first year of this trial. Mr. Clerk, swear the prisoner."

The customary oath having been administered, I made the following statement, which impressed the judge with so strong a sense of the comparative triviality of the offense for which I was on trial that he made no further search for mitigating circumstances, but simply instructed the jury to acquit, and I left the court, without a stain upon my reputation:

"I was born in 1856 in Kalamakee, Mich., of honest and reputable parents, one of whom Heaven has mercifully spared to comfort me in my later years. In 1867 the family came to California and settled near Nigger Head, where my father opened a road agency and prospered beyond the dreams of avarice. He was a reticent, saturnine man then, though his increasing years have now somewhat relaxed the austerity of his disposition, and I believe that nothing but his memory of the sad event for which I am now on trial prevents him from manifesting a genuine hilarity.

"Four years after we had set up the road agency an itinerant preacher came along, and having no other way to pay for the night's lodging that we gave him, favored us with an exhortation of such power that, praise God, we were all converted to religion. My father at once sent for his brother, the Hon. William Ridley of Stockton, and on his arrival turned over the agency to him, charging him nothing for the franchise nor plant—the latter consisting of a Winchester rifle, a sawed-off shotgun, and an assortment of masks made out of flour sacks. The family then moved to Ghost Rock and opened a dance house. It was called 'The Saints' Rest Hurdy-Gurdy,' and the proceedings each night began with prayer. It was there that my now sainted mother, by her grace in the dance, acquired the *sobriquet* of 'The Bucking Walrus.'

"In the fall of '75 I had occasion to visit Coyote, on the road to Mahala, and took the stage at Ghost Rock. There were four other passengers. About three miles beyond Nigger Head, persons whom I identified as my Uncle William and his two sons held up the stage. Finding nothing in the express box, they went through the passengers. I acted a most honorable part in the affair, placing myself in line with the others, holding up my hands and permitting myself to be deprived of forty dollars and a gold watch. From my behavior no one could have suspected that I knew the gentlemen who gave the entertainment. A few days later, when I went to Nigger Head and asked for the return of my money and watch my uncle and cousins swore they knew nothing of the matter, and they affected a belief that my father and I had done the job ourselves in dishonest violation of commercial good faith. Uncle William even threatened to retaliate by starting an opposition dance house at Ghost Rock. As 'The Saints' Rest' had become rather unpopular, I saw that this would assuredly ruin it and prove a paying enterprise, so I told my uncle that I was willing to overlook the past if he would take me into the scheme and keep the partnership a secret from my father. This fair offer he rejected, and I then perceived that it would be better and more satisfactory if he were dead.

"My plans to that end were soon perfected, and communicating them to my dear parents I had the gratification of receiving their approval. My father said he was proud of me, and my mother promised that although her religion forbade her to assist in taking human life I should have the advantage of her prayers for my success. As a preliminary measure looking to my security in case of detection I made an application for membership in that powerful order, the Knights of Murder, and in due course was received as a member of the Ghost Rock commandery. On the day that my probation ended I was for the first time permitted to inspect the records of the order and learn who belonged to it—all the rites of initiation having been conducted in masks. Fancy my delight when, in looking over the roll of membership, I found the third name to be that of my uncle, who indeed was junior vice-chancellor of the order! Here was an opportunity exceeding my wildest dreams—to murder I could add insubordination and treachery. It was what my good mother would have called 'a special Providence.'

"At about this time something occurred which caused my cup of joy, already full, to overflow on all sides, a circular cataract of bliss. Three men, strangers in that locality, were arrested for the stage robbery in which I had lost my money and watch. They were brought to trial and, despite my efforts to clear them and fasten the guilt upon three of the most respectable and worthy citizens of Ghost Rock, convicted on the clearest proof. The murder would now be as wanton and reasonless as I could wish.

"One morning I shouldered my Winchester rifle, and going over to my uncle's house, near Nigger Head, asked my Aunt Mary, his wife, if he were at home, adding that I had come to kill him. My aunt replied with her peculiar smile that so many gentlemen called on that errand and were afterward carried away without having performed it that I must excuse her for doubting my good faith in the matter. She said I did not look as if I would kill anybody, so, as a proof of good faith I leveled my rifle and wounded a Chinaman who happened to be passing the house. She said she knew whole families that could do a thing of that kind, but Bill Ridley was a horse of another color. She said, however, that I would find him over on the other side of the creek in the sheep lot; and she added that she hoped the best man would win.

"My Aunt Mary was one of the most fair-minded women that I have ever met.

"I found my uncle down on his knees engaged in skinning a sheep. Seeing that he had neither gun nor pistol handy I had not the heart to shoot him, so I approached him, greeted him pleasantly and struck him a powerful blow on the head with the butt of my rifle. I have a very good delivery and Uncle William lay down on his side, then rolled over on his back, spread out his fingers and shivered. Before he could recover the use of his limbs I seized the knife that he had been using and cut his hamstrings. You know, doubtless, that when you sever the *tendo Achillis* the patient has no further use of his leg; it is just the same as if he had no leg. Well, I parted them both, and when he revived he was at my service. As soon as he comprehended the situation, he said:

" 'Samuel, you have got the drop on me and can afford to be generous. I have only one thing to ask of you, and that is that you carry me to the house and finish me in the bosom of my family.'

"I told him I thought that a pretty reasonable request and I would do so if he would let me put him into a wheat sack; he would be easier to carry that way and if we were seen by the neighbors *en route* it would cause less remark. He agreed to that, and going to the barn I got a sack. This, however, did not fit him; it was too short and much wider than he; so I bent his legs, forced his knees up against his breast and got him into it that way, tying the sack above his head. He was a heavy man and I had all that I could do to get him on my back, but I staggered along for some distance until I came to a swing that some of the children had suspended to the branch of an oak. Here I laid him down and sat upon him to rest, and the sight of the rope gave me a happy inspiration. In twenty minutes my uncle, still in the sack, swung free to the sport of the wind.

"I had taken down the rope, tied one end tightly about the mouth of the bag, thrown the other across the limb and hauled him up about five feet from the ground. Fastening the other end of the rope also about the mouth of the sack, I had the satisfaction to see my uncle converted into a large, fine pendulum. I must add that he was not himself entirely aware of the nature of the change that he had undergone in his relation to the exterior world, though in justice to a good man's memory I ought to say that I do not think he would in any case have wasted much of my time in vain remonstrance.

"Uncle William had a ram that was famous in all that region as a fighter. It was in a state of chronic constitutional indignation. Some deep disappointment in early life had soured its disposition and it had declared war upon the whole world. To say that it would butt anything accessible is but faintly to express the nature and scope of its military activity: the universe was its antagonist; its methods that of a projectile. It fought like the angels and devils, in mid-air, cleaving the atmosphere like a bird, describing a parabolic curve and descending upon its victim at just the exact angle of incidence to make the most of its velocity and weight. Its momentum, calculated in foot-tons, was something incredible. It had been seen to destroy a four year old bull by a single impact upon that animal's gnarly forehead. No stone wall had ever been known to resist its downward swoop; there were no trees tough enough to stay it; it would splinter them into matchwood and defile their leafy honors in the dust. This irascible and implacable brute—this incarnate thunderbolt—this monster of the upper deep, I had seen reposing in the shade of an adjacent tree, dreaming dreams of conquest and glory. It was with a view to summoning it forth to the field of honor that I suspended its master in the manner described.

"Having completed my preparations, I imparted to the avuncular pendulum a gentle oscillation, and retiring to cover behind a contiguous rock, lifted up my voice in a long rasping cry whose diminishing final note was drowned in a noise like that of a swearing cat, which emanated from the sack. Instantly that formidable sheep was upon its feet and had taken in the military situation at a glance. In a few moments it had approached, stamping, to within fifty yards of the swinging foeman, who, now retreating and anon advancing, seemed to invite the fray. Suddenly I saw the beast's head drop earthward as if depressed by the weight of its enormous horns; then a dim, white, wavy streak of sheep prolonged itself from that spot in a generally horizontal direction to within about four yards of a point immediately beneath the enemy. There it struck sharply upward, and before it had faded from my gaze at the place whence it had set out I heard a horrid thump and a piercing scream, and my poor uncle shot forward, with a slack rope higher than the limb to which he was attached. Here the rope tautened with a jerk, arresting his flight, and back he swung in a breathless curve to the other end of his arc. The ram had fallen, a heap of indistinguishable legs, wool and horns, but pulling itself together and dodging as its antagonist swept downward it retired at random, alternately shaking its head and stamping its fore-feet. When it had backed about the same distance as that from which it had delivered the assault it paused again, bowed its head as if in prayer for victory and again shot forward, dimly visible as before—a prolonging white streak with monstrous undulations, ending with a sharp ascension. Its course this time was at a right angle to its former one, and its impatience so great that it struck the enemy before he had nearly reached the lowest point of his arc. In consequence he went flying round and round in a horizontal circle whose radius was about equal to half the length of the rope, which I forgot to say was nearly twenty feet long. His shrieks, *crescendo* in approach and *diminuendo* in recession, made the rapidity of his revolution more obvious to the ear than to the eye. He had evidently not yet been struck in a vital spot. His posture in the sack and the distance from the ground at which he hung compelled the ram to operate upon his lower extremities and the end of his back. Like a plant that has struck its root into some poisonous mineral, my poor uncle was dying slowly upward.

"After delivering its second blow the ram had not again retired. The fever of battle burned hot in its heart; its brain was intoxicated with the wine of strife. Like a pugilist who in his rage forgets his skill and fights ineffectively at half-arm's length, the angry beast endeavored to reach its fleeting foe by awkward vertical leaps as he passed overhead, sometimes, indeed, succeeding in striking him feebly, but more frequently overthrown by its own misguided eagerness. But as the impetus was exhausted and the man's circles narrowed in scope and diminished in speed, bringing him nearer to the ground, these tactics produced better results, eliciting a superior quality of screams, which I greatly enjoyed.

"Suddenly, as if the bugles had sung truce, the ram suspended hostilities and walked away, thoughtfully wrinkling and smoothing its great aquiline nose, and occasionally cropping a bunch of grass and slowly munching it. It seemed to have tired of war's alarms and resolved to beat the sword into a plowshare and cultivate the arts of peace. Steadily it held its course away from the field of fame until it had gained a distance of nearly a quarter of a mile. There it stopped and stood with its rear to the foe, chewing its cud and apparently half asleep. I observed, however, an occasional slight turn of its head, as if its apathy were more affected than real.

"Meantime Uncle William's shrieks had abated with his motion, and nothing was heard from him but long, low moans, and at long intervals my name, uttered in pleading tones exceedingly grateful to my ear. Evidently the man had not the faintest notion of what was being done to him, and was inexpressibly terrified. When Death comes cloaked in mystery he is terrible indeed. Little by little my uncle's oscillations diminished, and finally he hung motionless. I went to him and was about to give him the *coup de grâce,* when I heard and felt a succession of smart shocks which shook the ground like a series of light earthquakes, and turning in the direction of the ram, saw a long cloud of dust approaching me with inconceivable rapidity and alarming effect! At a distance of some thirty yards away it stopped short, and from the near end of it rose into the air what I at first thought a great white bird. Its ascent was so smooth and easy and regular that I could not realize its extraordinary celerity, and was lost in admiration of its grace. To this day the impression remains that it was a slow, deliberate movement, the ram—for it was that animal—being upborne by some power other than its own impetus, and supported through the successive stages of its flight with infinite tenderness and care. My eyes followed its progress through the air with unspeakable pleasure, all the greater by contrast with my former terror of its approach by land. Onward and upward the noble animal sailed, its head bent down almost between its knees, its fore-feet thrown back, its hinder legs trailing to rear like the legs of a soaring heron.

"At a height of forty or fifty feet, as fond recollection presents it to view, it attained its zenith and appeared to remain an instant stationary; then, tilting suddenly forward without altering the relative position of its parts, it shot downward on a steeper and steeper course with augmenting velocity, passed immediately above me with a noise like the rush of a cannon shot and struck my poor uncle almost squarely on the top of the head! So frightful was the impact that not only the man's neck was broken, but the rope too; and the body of the deceased, forced against the earth, was crushed to pulp beneath the awful front of that meteoric sheep! The concussion stopped all the clocks between Lone Hand and Dutch Dan's, and Professor Davidson, a distinguished authority in matters seismic, who happened to be in the vicinity, promptly explained that the vibrations were from north to southwest.

"Altogether, I cannot help thinking that in point of artistic atrocity my murder of Uncle William has seldom been excelled."

RATS

By M. R. James

"And if you was to walk through the bedrooms now, you'd see the ragged, mouldy bedclothes a-heaving and a-heaving like seas." "And a-heaving and a-heaving with what?" he says. "Why, with the rats under 'em."

But was it with the rats? I ask, because in another case it was not. I cannot put a date to the story, but I was young when I heard it, and the teller was old. It is an ill-proportioned tale, but that is my fault, not his.

It happened in Suffolk, near the coast. In a place where the road makes a sudden dip and then a sudden rise; as you go northward, at the top of that rise, stands a house on the left of the road. It is a tall red-brick house, narrow for its height; perhaps it was built about 1770. The top of the front has a low triangular pediment with a round window in the centre. Behind it are stables and offices, and such garden as it has is behind them. Scraggy Scotch firs are near it: an expanse of gorse-covered land stretches away from it. It commands a view of the distant sea from the upper windows of the front. A sign on a post stands before the door; or did so stand, for though it was an inn of repute once, I believe it is so no longer.

To this inn came my acquaintance, Mr. Thomson, when he was a young man, on a fine spring day, coming from the University of Cambridge, and desirous of solitude in tolerable quarters and time for reading. These he found, for the landlord and his wife had been in service and could make a visitor comfortable, and there was no one else staying in the inn. He had a large room on the first floor commanding the road and the view, and if it faced east, why, that could not be helped; the house was well built and warm.

He spent very tranquil and uneventful days: work all the morning, an afternoon perambulation of the country round, a little conversation with country company or the people of the inn in the evening over the then fashionable drink of brandy and water, a little more reading and writing, and bed; and he would have been content that this should continue for the full month he had at disposal, so well was his work progressing, and so fine was the April of that year—which I have reason to believe was that which Orlando Whistlecraft chronicles in his weather record as the "Charming Year."

One of his walks took him along the northern road, which stands high and traverses a wide common, called a heath. On the bright afternoon when he first chose this direction his eye caught a white object some hundreds of yards to the left of the road, and he felt it necessary to make sure what this might be. It was not long before he was standing by it, and found himself looking at a square block of white stone fashioned somewhat like the base of a pillar, with a square hole in the upper surface. Just such another you may see at this day on Thetford Heath. After taking stock of it he contemplated for a few minutes the view, which offered a church tower or two, some red roofs of cottages and windows winking in the sun, and the expanse of sea—also with an occasional wink and gleam upon it—and so pursued his way.

In the desultory evening talk in the bar, he asked why the white stone was there on the common.

"A old-fashioned thing, that is," said the landlord (Mr. Betts), "we was none of us alive when that was put there." "That's right," said another. "It stands pretty high," said Mr. Thomson, "I dare say a sea-mark was on it some time back." "Ah! yes," Mr. Betts agreed, "I 'ave 'eard they could see it from the boats; but whatever there was, it's fell to bits this long time." "Good job too," said a third, " 'twarn't a lucky mark, by what the old men used to say; not lucky for the fishin', I mean to say." "Why ever not?" said Thomson. "Well, I never see it myself," was the answer, "but they 'ad some funny ideas, what I mean, peculiar, them old chaps, and I shouldn't wonder but what they made away with it theirselves."

It was impossible to get anything clearer than this: the company, never very voluble, fell silent, and when next someone spoke it was of village affairs and crops. Mr. Betts was the speaker.

Not every day did Thomson consult his health by taking a country walk. One very fine afternoon found him busily writing at three o'clock. Then he stretched himself and rose, and walked out of his room into the passage. Facing him was another room, then the stair-head, then two more rooms, one looking out to the back, the other to the south. At the south end of the passage was a window, to which he went, considering with himself that it was rather a shame to waste such a fine afternoon. However, work was paramount just at the moment; he thought he would just take five minutes off and go back to it, and those five minutes he would employ—the Bettses could not possibly object—to looking at the other rooms in the passage, which he had never seen. Nobody at all, it seemed, was indoors; probably, as it was market day, they were all gone to the town, except perhaps a maid in the bar. Very still the house was, and the sun shone really hot; early flies buzzed in the window-panes. So he explored. The room facing his own was undistinguished except for an old print of Bury St. Edmunds; the two next him on his side of the passage were gay and clean, with one window apiece, whereas his had two. Remained the south-west room, opposite to the last which he had entered. This was locked; but Thomson was in a mood of quite indefensible curiosity, and feeling confident that there could be no damaging secrets in a place so easily got at, he proceeded to fetch the key of his own room, and when that did not answer, to collect the keys of the other three. One of them fitted, and he opened the door. The room had two windows looking south and west, so it was as bright and the sun as hot upon it as could be. Here there was no carpet, but bare boards; no pictures, no washing-stand, only a bed, in the farther corner: an iron bed, with mattress and bolster, covered with a bluish check counterpane. As featureless a room as you can well imagine, and yet there was something that made Thomson close the door very quickly and yet quietly behind him and lean against the window-sill in the passage, actually quivering all over. It was this, that under the counterpane someone lay, and not only lay, but stirred. That it was some *one* and not some *thing* was certain, because the shape of a head was unmistakable on the bolster; and yet it was all covered, and no one lies with covered head but a dead person; and this was not dead, not truly dead, for it heaved and shivered. If he had seen these things in dusk or by the light of a flickering candle, Thomson could have comforted himself and talked of fancy. On this bright day that was impossible. What was to be done? First, lock the door at all costs. Very gingerly he approached it and bending down listened, holding his breath; perhaps there might be a sound of heavy breathing, and a prosaic explanation. There was absolute silence. But as, with a rather tremulous hand, he put the key into its hole and turned it, it rattled, and on the instant a stumbling padding tread was heard coming towards the door. Thomson fled like a rabbit to his room and locked himself in: futile enough, he knew it was; would doors and locks be any obstacle to what he suspected? but it was all he could think of at the moment, and in fact nothing happened; only there was a time of acute suspense—followed by a misery of doubt as to what to do. The impulse, of course, was to slip away as soon as possible from a house which contained such an inmate. But only the day before he had said he should be staying for at least a week more, and how if he changed plans could he avoid the suspicion of having pried into places where he certainly had no business? Moreover, either the Bettses knew all about the inmate, and yet did not leave the house, or knew nothing, which equally meant that there was nothing to be afraid of, or knew just enough to make them shut up the room, but not enough to weigh on their spirits: in any of these cases it seemed that not much was to be feared, and certainly so far he had had no sort of ugly experience. On the whole the line of least resistance was to stay.

Well, he stayed out his week. Nothing took him past that door, and, often as he would pause in a quiet hour of day or night in the passage and listen, and listen, no sound whatever issued from that direction. You might have thought that Thomson would have made some attempt at ferreting out stories connected with the inn—hardly perhaps from Betts, but from the parson of the parish, or old people in the village; but no, the reticence which commonly falls on people who have had strange experiences, and believe in them, was upon him. Nevertheless, as the end of his stay drew near, his yearning after some kind of explanation grew more and more acute. On his solitary walks he persisted in planning out some way, the least obtrusive, of getting another daylight glimpse into that room, and eventually arrived at this scheme. He would leave by an afternoon train—about four o'clock. When his fly was waiting, and his luggage on it, he would make one last expedition upstairs to look round his own room and see if anything was left unpacked, and then, with that key, which he had contrived to oil (as if that made any difference!), the door should once more be opened, for a moment, and shut.

So it worked out. The bill was paid, the consequent small talk gone through while the fly was loaded: "pleasant part of the country—been very comfortable, thanks to you and Mrs. Betts—hope to come back some time," on one side: on the other, "very glad you've found satisfaction, sir, done our best—always glad to 'ave your good word—very much favoured we've been with the weather, to be sure." Then, "I'll just take a look upstairs in case I've left a book or something out—no, don't trouble, I'll be back in a minute." And as noiselessly as possible he stole to the door and opened it. The shattering of the illusion! He almost laughed aloud. Propped, or you might say sitting, on the edge of the bed was—nothing in the round world but a scarecrow! A scarecrow out of the garden, of course, dumped into the deserted room. . . . Yes; but here amusement ceased. Have scarecrows bare bony feet? Do their heads loll on to their shoulders? Have they iron collars and links of chain about their necks? Can they get up and move, if never so stiffly, across a floor, with wagging head and arms close at their sides? and shiver?

The slam of the door, the dash to the stair-head, the leap downstairs, were followed by a faint. Awaking, Thomson saw Betts standing over him with the brandy bottle and a very reproachful face. "You shouldn't a done so, sir, really you shouldn't. It ain't a kind way to act by persons as done the best they could for you." Thomson heard words of this kind, but what he said in reply he did not know. Mr. Betts, and perhaps even more Mrs. Betts, found it hard to accept his apologies and his assurances that he would say no word that could damage the good name of the house. However, they *were* accepted. Since the train could not now be caught, it was arranged that Thomson should be driven to the town to sleep there. Before he went the Bettses told him what little they knew. "They says he was landlord 'ere a long time back, and was in with the 'ighwaymen that 'ad their beat about the 'eath. That's how he come by his end: 'ung in chains, they say, up where you see that stone what the gallus stood in. Yes, the fishermen made away with that, I believe, because they see it out at sea and it kep' the fish off, according to their idea. Yes, we 'ad the account from the people that 'ad the 'ouse before we come. 'You keep that room shut up,' they says, 'but don't move the bed out, and you'll find there won't be no trouble.' And no more there 'as been; not once he haven't come out into the 'ouse, though what he may do now there ain't no sayin'. Anyway, you're the first I know on that's seen him since we've been 'ere: I never set eyes on him myself, nor don't want. And ever since we've made the servants' rooms in the stablin', we ain't 'ad no difficulty that way. Only I do 'ope, sir, as you'll keep a close tongue, considerin' 'ow an 'ouse do get talked about": with more to this effect.

The promise of silence was kept for many years. The occasion of my hearing the story at last was this: that when Mr. Thomson came to stay with my father it fell to me to show him to his room, and instead of letting me open the door for him, he stepped forward and threw it open himself, and then for some moments stood in the doorway holding up his candle and looking narrowly into the interior. Then he seemed to recollect himself and said: "I beg your pardon. Very absurd, but I can't help doing that, for a particular reason." What that reason was I heard some days afterwards, and you have heard now.

·5·

THE GOLDEN DAWN: A SECRET SOCIETY

The end of the nineteenth century brought with it a reaction against rationality similar to that of the Romantics but smaller in scope. There were sporadic outbreaks of interest in the uncanny, perhaps as a reaction to the scientific discoveries that distinguished the era. Numerous groups banded together for the study of psychic phenomena, some shamefully gullible and some strictly investigative; but none had such an impact on the world of fantastic fictions as the Order of the Golden Dawn. This secret society was unique, possibly because of the metaphysical lore it professed, but most certainly for the talented and influential writers that it inspired. Whether or not the Order of the Golden Dawn truly possessed a magical doctrine, there is something almost uncanny in the sheer number of its members who found fame as the authors of supernatural stories. And, considering that the purpose of the order was to achieve spiritual elevation, there is something a trifle disturbing in the fact that most of these men who wrote of the unknown dwelt on its terrors.

A veil of mystery still clings to the ghost of this extinguished organization. Not only were its teachings esoteric, but membership itself was rarely a public affair; even those who are positively known to have been members often chose to remain silent on the subject. Various volumes have appeared through the years purporting to expose the rituals of the order, but a definitive list of the men who practiced them seems unlikely to emerge. Among the more prominent occultists can certainly be included S. L. MacGregor Mathers, the group's founder; Aleister Crowley, perhaps the most notorious self-styled magician of modern times; and A. E. Waite, the designer of a rectified Tarot deck which has since become the standard. Among the authors enlightened by the Golden Dawn are the distinguished Irish poet William Butler Yeats, as well as such important tellers of terror tales as Arthur Machen and Algernon Blackwood. To these can be added, with varying degrees of certainty, the names of such writers as Sax Rohmer, Lord Dunsany, G. K. Chesterton, H. Rider Haggard, Talbot Mundy, and even, according to one source, Bram Stoker. A list like this suggests that nearly every British author of the uncanny in this generation was initiated into the Order of the Golden Dawn. And the proceedings acquire an appropriately grim tone when it is noted that one of the charter members was the coroner for the City of London.

It is somewhat surprising that among all these literary figures, the one least associated with the bizarre should have been the least reticent about his occult experiences. This was William Butler Yeats, the respectable Nobel Prize winner, who was introduced into the society by its leader, Mathers, in 1887. Yeats described a gaunt, autocratic individual who had the ability to induce visions in his followers. Mathers handed a small symbol to the poet, and "there rose before me mental images that I could not control: a desert and black Titan raising himself up by his two hands from the middle of a heap of ancient ruins." This strange picture, which Mathers described as a fire elemental, seems to have inspired a later poem, "The Second Coming," in which Yeats depicts a stone colossus rising out of the Holy Land to herald a millennium of horror. Immersed since boyhood in Irish myth, Yeats found it easy to master the symbolism of the Golden Dawn's rituals, which apparently played no small part in the formulation of the mystical philosophy he described in *A Vision* (1925).

The birth of the order seems to have been inspired by the discovery of certain ancient books and manuscripts on the subject of magic, which in turn brought Mathers into contact with magical societies already established in Europe. All of this might have been sufficiently mysterious, but Mathers was not above suggesting that he had been personally instructed by a spiritual figure from the distant past. Other members became increasingly annoyed by his aloof and arrogant manner, especially the one who had

"Resistance—The Black Idol," by the Czech artist Frantisek Kupka, might almost be an illustration for the William Butler Yeats poem "The Second Coming," which seems to have been inspired by a vision received from the Order of the Golden Dawn.

Two cards from the major arcana of Waite's Tarot. The design for Death is original (tradition shows a naked skeleton walking with a scythe); the Devil is close to the decks of previous centuries. The cards represent, respectively, Scorpio and Capricorn.

brought him the first of those magical manuscripts. Eventually arguments about authority were to tear the Order of the Golden Dawn apart, amid hurled curses that were intended to be deadly. But if Mathers could be a grim and forbidding character, he also had a warmer side, manifested in such disparate activities as housing and instructing his followers without charge or releasing mice from traps to keep them as pets. He also had some eccentricities (besides the obvious one of wishing to be a wizard): he became unaccountably enamored of Scotland, which led him to adopt the name MacGregor and to wear kilts. He also fancied himself a military strategist and looked forward with some enthusiasm to the world war he predicted. Yet, despite his affectations, he was not entirely devoid of humor, especially when dismissing neurotic seekers of free advice. To a woman who complained of rotting corpses who visited her at night and attempted to climb into her bed, he merely commented, "Very bad taste on both sides."

Mathers had the personality to keep the group going for as long as it lasted, but the most permanent contribution to the spread of occult studies was made by Arthur Edward Waite. He was only one of several who published surveys of the unknown territory, but the deck of Tarot cards he designed has, with the expiration of copyright, gone into universal circulation. It has, at least for popular consumption, superseded the decks of previous centuries and has influenced most of the cards and commentaries that have appeared subsequently. Indeed, several purportedly authoritative works on the occult have made the error of assuming an ancient history for variations that appear only in Waite's comparatively modern work. The artist who executed his plans was Pamela Coleman Smith; several other experts have followed this arrangement—that the cards should be designed by a man and drawn by a woman. The Tarot, which was vital to the teachings of the Golden Dawn, is most widely known as a pack of cards for telling fortunes, but occultists claim that this is little more than a legend designed to keep the cards in circulation while disguising their true purpose. The Tarot is in fact a picture book of seventy-eight pages, drawn to depict the secrets of creation in symbolic form. The four suits represent the four elements of alchemy: wands (clubs) are fire, swords (spades) are air, cups (hearts) are water, and coins (diamonds) are earth. The value of the cards can be determined, at least in part, by juxtaposing their alchemical and numerological significances. More important than these cards, called the minor arcana, from which the modern poker deck evolved, are the major arcana, a series of twenty-two "jokers" which are richer in meaning, bearing such resonant titles as Death, the Devil, the Magician,

Waite's Seven of Cups and Three of Swords. His most important innovation was the creation of pictures for the minor arcana, which formerly consisted of only a number of pips, like modern playing cards.

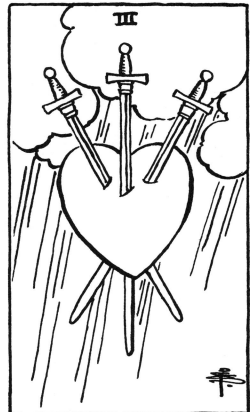

the High Priestess, and the Hanged Man. Each of these represents a number of things: a planet or sign of the zodiac, a color, a direction, a bodily function, a musical note, a state of mind, and a letter of the Hebrew alphabet. These correspondences seem to suggest hidden relationships, and contemplation of the Tarot is said to set the mind in tune with higher forces. Occult lore, now apparently confirmed by science, teaches that all matter is composed of the same stuff, which is, in essence, energy. Thought is said to be another manifestation of the same energy, making it theoretically possible to alter the material world by concentration and willpower. There is little doubt that some people have been able to do surprising things by working along these lines, although the technique is less likely to produce a sudden miracle than a gradual change in conditions. Those who are sufficiently advanced to work faster are usually assumed to be too spiritual to supply themselves spontaneously with palaces or piles of pearls. At any rate, study of the cards and their symbolism purportedly prepares the mind for such interesting activities. There is something irresistibly fascinating in their mere appearance and something a bit uncanny in their attributions: how did their creators, centuries ago, know exactly how many cards would be needed to account for all the planets in our solar system, three of which had yet to be discovered? The most impressive contemporary commentary on this intriguing topic is by Paul Foster Case, who claims, strangely enough, to have received his information via the Order of the Golden Dawn.

Not to be outdone by Waite, another member of the secret society created his own Tarot, although the designs are so eccentric that they have never been widely accepted. This was Aleister Crowley, the most famous and flamboyant magician of the group and the one who seems most to blame for its disintegration. He was first a sort of lieutenant to Mathers, who hoped that the energetic newcomer would help him to assert his control over rebellious members of the order. Rarely has one man so grossly underestimated another. Crowley certainly succeeded in alienating the rival factions, but it was only the first step in his plans to achieve control himself. He declared that a vision he had experienced in Egypt included instructions that he should become leader of the Golden Dawn. Mathers was furious. Each accused the other of attempted murder by magic and began casting sinister spells in retaliation. This long-distance duel continued for years, and when Mathers finally died in 1918, numerous persons (Yeats at least temporarily among them) were convinced that Crowley's curses had finally proved fatal. Previously, Crowley had started his own organization, the Silver Star, with rituals based on those of the Golden Dawn. Similar splinter groups, each claiming to possess the "most truthful" truth of all, caused the collapse of the original order, and matters hardly improved when Crowley spitefully published its secret rituals in his magazine, *The Equinox.*

Crowley in fact was a great one for publishing things. Yet few of his works can be classified as fantasy fiction, unless it is assumed that all his volumes of instruction in magic are merely the result of an overactive imagination. In a sense, this may be an accurate assessment, since he acknowledges in his do-it-yourself books that the rituals he describes are primarily aids to concentration and that the real work is done by the magician's mental processes. At any rate, most of his own efforts, like those of his former colleagues, seem to have been directed not toward performing miracles but rather in attempting to communicate with spirits. Consequently, results tended to be subjective and difficult to assess. What was obvious about Crowley is that he was a wild man. He shaved his head, sharpened his teeth, and relished his reputation as the wickedest man in the world. "Do what thou wilt shall be the whole of the law" became his motto, and he traveled from country to country indulging in orgies featuring bizarre sex and numerous drugs. Rumors that he was a killer and cannibal were never supported by hard evidence, but he could hardly be described as a good influence. Several of his followers lost their minds or committed suicide. He wrote pornographic poetry as well as instruction books, but when it came to describing in fiction what he called "Magick," he was oddly restrained. His *Diary of a Drug Fiend* shows a mystical figure not unlike himself benevolently giving addicts the strength to cure themselves, although it was his own policy to increase his intake constantly, thus demonstrating his superiority to any outside influence. His one occult novel, *Moonchild* (1917), is disappointingly tame; his colorful reputation is better served by W. Somerset Maugham's uneven novel *The Magician*, which offers a fictionalized Crowley bent on the creation of artificial life through witchcraft.

In an atmosphere created by men like Mathers, Crowley, and Waite, it is hardly surprising that the writers around them made the supernatural their subject. Perhaps the most important, and certainly the most controversial, of these authors was Arthur Machen. He has been described by various critics as the best and the worst author in the genre. His rich, resonant style is something of an acquired taste, and his themes are as dramatic to some as they are disgusting to others. Born in Wales in 1863, Machen lived to be eighty-four; but most of his best writing was done before the turn of the century. He came to London as a young man, changed his name from Arthur Jones, and settled down to a life of loneliness and poverty. The Golden Dawn apparently supplied him with companionship as well as source material, and he also drew on Welsh legends about the mysterious powers of primeval nature. Never able to make a decent living with his pen, he became a traveling actor in 1901, abandoning literature for years. His brief moment of glory as a writer came in 1914, through a maddening set of circumstances not devoid of supernatural overtones. On September 29 of that year, a newspaper printed a brief tale by Machen called "The Bowmen." It was a story of the First World War and of how British troops had been aided in the battle of Mons by the ghostly arrows of their ancestors. The story created a sensation, not so much because of its merits as because it was believed to be true! Reports were circulated by participants in the battle that St. George and an army of angels had indeed fought for England, and Machen's little fantasy became fact for thousands. It was a great morale builder, and nobody paid much attention to the author's plaintive insistence that he had imagined the whole thing. It is possible to construct a theory demonstrating that both Machen and the men at Mons were telling the truth by assuming that the miraculous tale had been transmitted to the writer by some sort of telepathy. In any case, it was a shattering experience for Machen, who put the story in a book that sold better than anything he had done before, and he continued to refer to the incident in his later works as a bewildering example of human gullibility.

Many of Machen's best terror tales appeared within the space of a year. Two 1894 stories, "The Great God Pan" and "The Inmost Light," represent his debut in the field; they were followed in 1895 by the dazzling episodic novel *The Three Impostors*, which was actually written several years earlier. This novel, which contains some of his most vivid horrors, takes the form of a detective story in which two gentlemen of leisure entertain themselves by attempting to unravel a mystery concerning an ancient coin and a stranger who appears to be in mortal danger. They encounter three impostors, who tell them astounding stories about why they, too, are seeking the desperate young man wearing spectacles. But these three are finally revealed as members of a sinister secret society, although not in time to prevent them from destroying their prey. The bulk of the book is devoted to the tales with which the amateur detectives are beguiled; the best of them, "Novel of the White Powder," is reprinted at the end of this chapter.

This chronicle of demonic disintegration includes suggestions of Machen's major theme, the ancient evil still alive in the backwaters of Britain. Here it is presented through the motif of a preternatural potion, indicating the influence of Le Fanu and Stevenson. Another of the fabulous yarns from *The Three Impostors*, "The Novel of the Black Seal," features the same theme of reversion as an anthropologist discovers that myths about fairies and goblins hide a hideous truth about primitive and malignant beings lurking in the English countryside. The supernatural that Machen portrays is subhuman rather than superhuman, not exotically gifted but crude, stunted, and bestial. Animals themselves are the source of *The Terror* (1917); they revolt against the human race and its overwhelming war. Stories like "The Great God Pan" and "The White People" suggest the revolting results of crossbreeding humans and these loathsome throwbacks; the implications seem to have distressed Machen's detractors. He has been criticized by some for relying too much on gruesome physical details and conversely because he relies too much on the idea of unspeakable, indescribable horrors. Perhaps some indication of his value as a writer can be gained from the realization that he was supported in his old age with funds raised by such distinguished men of letters as T. S. Eliot and George Bernard Shaw.

An interesting contrast to Machen's career is provided by Algernon Blackwood, his chief rival as a creator of supernatural short stories among the members of the Golden Dawn. Blackwood matched Machen's longevity, surviving from 1869 until 1951; but instead of giving up literature at an early age, he was a late bloomer whose first fiction was published when he was thirty-six. He achieved his greatest recognition through readings on British Broadcasting Company programs, which he did long past the age when most men retire. Many of his terror tales, like Machen's, are set in the wilds of a primitive nature; but Blackwood was less concerned with the brutishness at the edge of civilization, concentrating instead on the idea of awe-inspiring spiritual entities that rule the lands beyond man's domain. His best stories have a mystical flavor, deriving their most powerful effects from the suggestion that spirits are seductive, capable of absorbing human souls into an unearthly ecstasy.

"These stories, I think," wrote Blackwood, "were the accumulated repressed results of dreams, yearnings, hopes, and fears due to early Evangelical upbringing, ecstasies tasted in wild nature, draughts of bitter kind in New York's underworld life, and a wild certainty, if still half a dream, that human consciousness holds illimitable possibilities now only latent." He was raised in a zealously religious household and grew up with a fear of damnation which was finally allayed by his occult studies. At twenty he emigrated to Canada, where he failed as a farmer. He then traveled to the United States, where he was, among other things, a gold prospector, and he finally ended up in New York where he endured periods of terrible poverty occasionally relieved by employment as a newspaper reporter. He returned to England after ten years and became known as an author after an enthusiastic friend took some of his tales to a publisher. His most famous stories appeared within a few years of his debut, but he continued to write for decades.

Blackwood's first book, *The Empty House* (1906), is a collection of comparatively ordinary ghost stories; but his second, *The Listener* (1907), includes "The Willows," a long story generally regarded as his masterpiece. It depicts the adventures of two vacationers boating on the Danube who are trapped on an island and menaced by strange, shadowy figures. It is a compelling example of Blackwood's ability to create atmosphere and to describe subjective experiences in which the supernatural is sensed rather than seen. Based on his own impressions during a similar trip, "The Willows" ends with the travelers escaping after the spirits around them claim another victim, whose corpse they discover floating in the river. When Blackwood took the same trip again after writing this story, he and his companion found a body in the water at the same point described in the story. As Blackwood commented wryly, "A coincidence, of course!"

In fact, Blackwood claimed that most of his tales had their origin in his own strange experiences and that it was virtually impossible for him to write a story unless his mystical faculties were stimulated. Among the stories in *John Silence, Physician Extraordinary* (1908) is "Secret Worship," describing a man who returns to the boarding school in Germany that he attended as a boy, only to learn that it has fallen into the hands of devil worshipers. Blackwood asserted that this is what had happened to his own school in the Black Forest. "Ancient Sorceries," in the same volume, describes a French town where Blackwood had had a vision that all the inhabitants could transform themselves into cats. The hero of these stories, John Silence, is the author's most famous character and perhaps the best example of the occult detective, although he is less likely to participate in adventures than to observe them. Silence's experiences include one with a werewolf in Canada, but it does not compare with "The Wendigo" (1910), about a legendary demon of the Canadian backwoods with which the author claimed a nodding acquaintance. What is important in his work, however, is less the variety of plots than the absolute conviction with which Blackwood infuses them. He is without peer in expressing the mental processes of men in the presence of the uncanny and in making his apparitions seem to be experiences rather than events. He is the rare writer in the field who can be subtle without losing impact.

At the opposite end of the spectrum is Blackwood's flamboyant colleague Arthur Sarsfield Ward, who wrote under the name Sax Rohmer. His gift for outlandish melodrama brought him greater financial success than anyone else in the Order of the Golden Dawn, so much so that in later years he signed himself $ax Rohmer. "I couldn't keep track of the money," he declared. "I just gave up and spent it." Most of his fortune was due to the creation of Dr. Fu Manchu, a fiendish Oriental villain who is estimated to have earned Rohmer more than two million dollars, although books about him constitute only a small part of the author's works, a mere dozen volumes. Fu Manchu was the subject of Rohmer's first book, in 1913, and his last, published just before he died in 1959 at the age of seventy-six. The original volume, *The Mystery of Dr. Fu-Manchu* (Rohmer soon eliminated the hyphen), appeared in America as *The Insidious Dr. Fu-Manchu.* Like the next two books, it was a collection of short stories that had originally appeared in magazines. The villain dies at the end of each; the third death was expected to prove fatal; but Fu Manchu was revived after thirteen years to appear in a series of full-fledged novels that are artistically superior to the original tales, although they lack period charm. In fact the sinister Chinese mastermind lasts so long that he eventually runs into trouble with his homeland's new Communist government, becoming a quasi-hero in the process. He is more effective when his motives are unmixedly malicious. Tall, gaunt, and bald, with green eyes like a cat's, Dr. Fu Manchu is the world's champion mad scientist, employing wild inventions combined with a touch of old-style sorcery. Zombies, giant spiders, plagues, untraceable poisons, and an elixir of youth are the devices against which struggled the doctor's dauntless opponent, Nayland Smith.

In his last decade Rohmer attempted to rival this outrageous but enthralling series with one about a powerful villainess, Sumuru, bent, like Fu Manchu, on conquering the

world, but employing an army of women. Sumuru does not really compare with her male predecessor, but she is an improvement on the character introduced and abandoned in Rohmer's second novel, *The Sins of Severac Bablon* (1914). Bablon was in effect a Jewish Fu Manchu, a descendant of the ancient kings of Israel described by Rohmer as a "Jewish Robin Hood." Too dignified to take over the planet, Bablon is content to chastise or reform wealthy Jews who sully the name of his people.

Rohmer's third book and his sole venture into nonfiction was *The Romance of Sorcery* (1914), a history of magic and magicians that seems to have been heavily influenced by his Golden Dawn indoctrination, although he does not refer directly to personal experience. His third novel, and probably his best, appeared the same year as a magazine serial and four years later in book form. This was *Brood of the Witch Queen*, a supernatural thriller devoid of the author's usual pseudoscientific explanations, concerning a young man who is a revitalized relic of ancient Egypt at large in modern England. Rohmer's occult lore was never as well employed as in this tale of a malevolent magician's use of elemental spirits, and he never equaled the claustrophobic chills of the scenes in the bowels of a pyramid. His other books with predominantly uncanny themes include *The Dream Detective* (1920), the adventures of psychic detective Moris Klaw; *The Green Eyes of Bast* (1920), about a lycanthropic cat-woman; *Grey Face* (1924), about a modern alchemist who has discovered the secret of making gold and prolonging life; and *The Bat Flies Low* (1935), which is particularly interesting because of the way the author uses occult lore to anticipate the theories of nuclear physics. The book describes a secret process for producing power, guarded since time immemorial by an Egyptian cult. An American utility company steals the secret, but the attempt to try it out produces an explosion that rocks the world.

Rohmer could hardly pass for a stylist; most of his works are fast-paced action tales, not really very well written. Thus he stands in contrast to Edward John Moreton Drax Plunkett, eighteenth Baron Dunsany, known to his readers as Lord Dunsany. He remarked near the end of his career with some truth and more egotism, "I can't think of any great prose writers who have come up to the standards I have set for prose." He was equally adept at lyrical evocations of mythical domains or at caustically witty commentaries on modern culture, and his writing is impressive, if not quite as good as he thought. His themes are usually supernatural, and a note of terror is frequently sounded; but his work is characterized by the contrasting qualities of mystical beauty and ironic humor. The Irish baron first achieved fame as a dramatist; his first play was produced in 1909 at Dublin's Abbey Theatre, where the great poetic plays of Yeats were presented. Dunsany made his debut with *The Glittering Gate*, a typical piece of whimsy about burglars who attempt the job of breaking and entering into Heaven. Thieves were among his favorite characters, appearing again in his most frightening and effective play, *A Night at an Inn*. This employed the device of an idol's stolen eye; but in this case it is not his agents who recover the gem, but the great stone god himself.

Dunsany's first book was *The Gods of Pegana* (1905), which began his creation of an original mythology. This series of stories or sketches describes the universe as originating with Mana-Yood-Sushai, who created lesser gods and then retired. In stately, almost biblical language, Dunsany depicts an artificial religion that is the background for his

Boris Karloff as Sax Rohmer's insidious Oriental, and Myrna Loy as his daughter, from the 1932 film *The Mask of Fu Manchu. Courtesy of MGM.*

later tales of heroes and rogues in *The Sword of Welleran* (1908) and *The Book of Wonder* (1912). His inventiveness proved very influential in later decades, as a number of writers, among them H. P. Lovecraft and Clark Ashton Smith, adopted the idea of inventing their own supernatural entities instead of dealing with those that had traditionally existed. Dunsany's private life contrasted starkly to his literary work; he was a bluff, hearty man, a professional soldier who fought in two wars and devoted most of his later years to hunting. Almost the epitome of the old-style British aristocrat, he claimed that his writing was done rapidly without revision during his spare time. Later stories, like those in *Tales of Wonder* (1916), brought the fantastic into the modern world, with increasing doses of comedy. This tendency culminated in the appearance of his best-known character, who narrated five books beginning with *Travel Tales of Mr. Joseph Jorkens* in 1931. Jorkens, the alcoholic member of a staid English club, specializes in spinning outrageous tall tales in exchange for free drinks. Dunsany used his own extensive travels to provide backgrounds for these frequently hilarious yarns of the occult. Of all Dunsany's stories, the most widely known is the atypical and unnerving "Two Bottles of Relish," in which investigators gradually realize, without ever actually saying so, that they cannot find the corpse they are seeking because the murderer, normally a vegetarian, has eaten it. Dunsany lived to the age of seventy-nine, suggesting, as with Blackwood, Machen, and Rohmer, that one of the Golden Dawn's secrets may have had something to do with longevity.

Dunsany's glib pen was rivaled by that of G. K. Chesterton, a prolific master of paradox who devoted most of his time to essays but is now remembered almost exclusively for his fiction. In 1911 he published the first of five books of detective stories, *The Innocence of Father Brown.* Considered by connoisseurs to be nearly the equal of Poe's Dupin and Doyle's Sherlock Holmes, Chesterton's detective is a small, rotund priest who solves mysteries by intuition and induction. Chesterton specialized in the description of terrifying, apparently supernatural crimes which are finally revealed to have rational explanations. Among Father Brown's classic cases are "The Invisible Man," in which a murderer passes unseen before witnesses by the simple but ingenious expedient of posing as a mailman; and "The Hammer of God," in which a deathblow of apparently superhuman strength is delivered by a killer who drops the weapon from a church tower. Chesterton himself was the model for Dr. Gideon Fell, the obese, blustering, mustachioed detective created by John Dickson Carr, the modern master of the macabre mystery. Chesterton's ventures into fantasy were less frequent than his detective tales, but on one occasion at least he created a minor classic: *The Man Who Was Thursday* (1908). This novel, subtitled *A Nightmare*, is a brilliant example of Chesterton's ability to shift ground beneath the reader's feet, each apparent conception of the plot astoundingly giving way to another without any loss of coherence or excitement. The story concerns an idealist who infiltrates an anarchist organization only to discover that everyone else there is also a spy, except the jovial leader Sunday, who is revealed as a practical joker with all the powers of time and space at his command. Chesterton, like Arthur Machen, converted to Roman Catholicism, apparently inspired less by the doctrine of the church than by a love of mysticism and ritual which may have been echoed by the Order of the Golden Dawn.

The bookish, urbane Chesterton produced literature in keeping with his character; a type with wider appeal came from the pens of two more adventurous authors, Sir Henry Rider Haggard and Talbot Mundy. Haggard spent much of his early life in Africa as secretary to the governor of Natal. He later became interested in agriculture and at one

"Mung and the Beast of Mung," sinister supernatural figures from Lord Dunsany's *Gods of Pegana*, illustrated by S. H. Sime.

Another fearsome figure from Dunsany's synthetic mythology, enigmatically entitled "It." The artist, Sime, worked so closely with the author that his pictures often became the inspiration for the stories.

time was an ostrich farmer in Pretoria. Despite what might appear to be the strange nature of that venture, he was an expert in his field and earned his knighthood through research and writing on farming techniques. Yet greater fame and a larger income came from his romantic novels of Africa. His first success was *King Solomon's Mines* (1886), the enthralling tale of a jungle treasure hunt; but both Haggard and his audience seem to have had a special fondness for his novel of a lost African civilization, *She* (1887), which spawned several sequels over the next four decades. *She* is the story of explorers who discover the city ruled by Ayesha, an immortal queen called She-Who-Must-Be-Obeyed. Ayesha, domineering and beautiful, recognizes one of the men as the incarnation of her lover, Kallikrates, dead for thousands of years. She offers to share her throne with him and reveals the secret of her longevity, a magical flame whose touch preserves life. When her lover is reluctant to enter the fire, Ayesha impatiently precedes him, but a second exposure to the flame proves to be her undoing, and she dies, a hideously withered hag. The deathless love of a dynamic lady proved to be a compelling concept for countless Victorian readers, and numerous novels appeared subsequently that were variations on the same theme; some of the best were written by the twentieth-century American A. Merritt. Haggard himself made a comeback in 1905 with *Ayesha, or The Return of She,* which shows Leo Vincey, the hero of the first novel, meeting the reincarnation of Ayesha in the form of an Asian priestess. Neither survives this encounter, although readers are assured that they will meet in another world, if not another novel. Instead, Haggard went further into the past for *She and Allan* (1921), recounting previous adventures of Ayesha with the hero of other Haggard novels. *Wisdom's Daughter* (1923) must have disappointed all but the most devoted admirers of Ayesha, because it was merely an elaborate retelling of her origin, already described in the other books. Still, there is something intriguing about Haggard's idea, at least in the original version, and *She* became something of a minor classic, later inspiring several motion pictures.

A writer who handled the theme of occult adventure in exotic settings with considerably more skill was Talbot Mundy. Like Haggard, he was for a time in the British Empire's colonial service; although he spent most of his time in India, he also traveled in Tibet, Africa, and Australia. Particularly enthralled by the magic and mystery of these lands, Mundy made an extensive study of the subject and declared that while he found some fraud, he also found enough evidence to confirm his belief in the supernatural. He emigrated to the United States in 1911 and almost immediately embarked on a career as an author, most of his work appearing in popular magazines before book publication. Often Mundy's occult inclinations provided little more than the spice for an action saga, as in the case of his early success, *King of the Khyber Rifles* (1916). This is primarily concerned with efforts to frustrate an Indian rebellion during the First World War; but the hero, Athelstan King, is aided by the beautiful Yasmini, whose powers include the ability to see the past and the future in a crystal. She tries unsuccessfully to lure King into a liaison of passion and political power, foreshadowing Mundy's typical use of the supernatural not as a threat, but as a temptation to abandon the stern demands of duty. Another of Mundy's British Secret Service heroes is James Grim, known as Jimgrim, who Mundy claimed was based on an intelligence officer he had met in Palestine, "who very kindly introduced me to the lewder fellows of the baser sort with whom it was his business to deal." Jimgrim and his shady entourage were teamed with King to investigate *The Nine Unknown* (1922), a group possessing untold knowledge who secretly control the destiny of the human race. The adventurers never uncover the Nine, but they do manage to defeat nine impostors who are using the reputation of their betters for nefarious purposes, and they also get a glimpse of the

The immortal queen Ayesha bathing in her magical fire in a scene from Haggard's *She*, illustrated by Maurice Greiffenhagen.

Nine's process for converting gold into an elixir of life which flows into a sacred river. In *The Devil's Guard* (1926), Jimgrim and his men venture into the Tibetan Himalayas where they become involved with a band of wicked wizards, one of whom is a former friend who wishes to corrupt the dauntless band. In *Jimgrim* (1931), the hero again ventures into the mystic mountains to defeat a magician who has gained the knowledge of lost Atlantis. Jimgrim resorts to the use of a magical drug to battle this almost omnipotent opponent, yielding at last to the lure of the uncanny and sacrificing his life to save the world from destruction. Mundy's other novels of the unknown India include *Om* (1923) and *Full Moon* (1935); but he is perhaps best remembered for the series of sagas that began in 1934 with *Tros of Samothrace*, huge novels about a warrior in the days of Caesar and Cleopatra which are almost completely devoid of supernatural incidents.

The conviction that the writers from the Order of the Golden Dawn brought to their work, combined with their long careers, enabled them virtually to dominate the literature of the supernatural for decades. Of course, they were not alone. Even in the golden days of the Golden Dawn, around the turn of the century, other artists were banding together, albeit in less formalized organizations, whose purposes included the description of the uncanny and the evil. Decades before, the poet and painter Dante Gabriel Rossetti and his associates had formed the Pre-Raphaelite Brotherhood, dedicated to principles of mysticism, symbolism, and medievalism in the arts. A macabre air hovers around the work of these men, exemplified by incidents in Rossetti's life that might have been imagined by Poe. Rossetti was so passionately attached to his wife and model that when she died, he had the manuscripts of his best poems buried in her coffin. Seven years later she was exhumed so that he could recover his work and have it published. Afterward, he became convinced that she was haunting him, embodied in the form of birds. Rossetti's sister Christina produced a poem, "Goblin Market" (1862), that anticipated and may have influenced Arthur Machen's view of the little folk as sinister tempters. Perhaps the greatest of the group was William Morris, a Renaissance man who achieved remarkable results in various fields of creative endeavor. He wrote numerous fantasies in poetry and prose, but the horrific element is largely lacking.

The Pre-Raphaelites did not survive into the twentieth century, but their influence continued, in a somewhat decadent form, through a younger group centered around the flamboyant figure of Oscar Wilde. The chief outlet for their work was the controversial periodical *The Yellow Book*, which seemed dedicated to outraging Victorian sensibilities. Wilde claimed that art should not be bound by morality, and he and his colleagues delighted in exploring the possibilities of evil, at least in their works. Wilde produced a macabre masterpiece in *The Picture of Dorian Gray* (1891), which was considered a shocking book by conservative critics not because it was frightening, but because it contained suggestions of wickedness and sin. The novel concerns a young man whose portrait absorbs all the effects of his debauched existence while he remains young and fresh in appearance, for no other reason than that he wished aloud that it might be so. After years of this unnatural career, he attacks the portrait with a knife in a fit of fury, with his own transformation and destruction as the result. Although usually praised for its witty dialogue and titillating hints of depravity, *Dorian Gray* is also a powerful terror tale, recognizable, at least in summary, to a wider public than the author's celebrated comedies. The illustrator of some of Wilde's work was Aubrey Beardsley, the exquisite black-and-white delineator whose principal subject seemed to be corruption in all its forms. Beardsley also did some drawings for Poe's stories and designed several remarkably restrained title pages for books by Arthur Machen.

A drawing by Aubrey Beardsley for a tale of terror which is also generally regarded as the world's first detective story, Poe's "Murders in the Rue Morgue."

The Order of the Golden Dawn, influenced in part by these illustrious predecessors, exemplified the English tradition of superior stories of the supernatural. While it might be said to have represented the finest flowering of the genre within a narrow span of space and time, it was by no means the end of English expression in the field. A number of skillful writers continued to make important contributions, some of them achieving a modest sort of immortality with but a single short tale. Such was the case with W. W. Jacobs, who wrote "The Monkey's Paw" (1902) in which three wishes, used to revive a dead son, turn from a blessing into a curse. This later became a popular play. Oliver Onions and Robert Hichens are well remembered for "The Beckoning Fair One" (1911) and "How Love Came to Professor Guildea" (1905), two chilling accounts of lovelorn female spirits who drive their victims mad. W. F. Harvey contributed at least two minor masterpieces: "August Heat" (1910) describes two men whose premonitions of each other's deaths drive them irresistibly toward murder, and "The Beast with Five Fingers," published in 1925, is the definitive treatment of the crawling-hand theme. The distinguished poet Walter de la Mare is responsible for several atmospheric pieces like "Seaton's Aunt," "A Recluse," and "Out of the Deep" which are so subtly done that the presence of the uncanny must be intuited from insufficient evidence.

The eccentric style of M. P. Shiel has produced several chilling short stories; his most famous work is a novel about the last survivor of the human race, *The Purple Cloud* (1901). Such serious novelists as L. P. Hartley and John Metcalfe have contributed to a more lurid literature; Hartley's "The Travelling Grave" is among the most grotesque tales in English, and Metcalfe's collection *The Smoking Leg* contains a wide variety of uncanny effects. Working in the tradition of Le Fanu and M. R. James, H. R. Wakefield has produced several volumes of fine ghost stories, including *They Return at Evening, The Clock Strikes Twelve,* and the beautifully titled *Imagine a Man in a Box.*

Among those who have devoted a larger portion of their careers to the field, no two authors more vividly exemplify its potential range than John Collier and Dennis Wheatley. Collier is a superb stylist and imaginative innovator whose short stories are polished gems of black comedy, more disturbing than many comparatively impassioned works because of their cruelly aloof and ironic tone. No summary can do justice to his tales; but among his classic conceptions are "The Chaser," in which infallible love potions are sold cheaply by a shrewd sorcerer who realizes that he is merely establishing a clientele for his very expensive but undetectable poisons; "Evening Primrose," in which a young man seeks refuge from society by moving into a luxurious department store, only to find that he is but one of many such misfits whose lives are more dreadful than the ones they abandoned; and "Green Thoughts," in which a man-eating plant gives evidence against a killer when its blossoms duplicate the heads of his victims. Most of his best stories have been collected in the book *Fancies and Goodnights* (1951).

Dennis Wheatley, whose books have sold many millions of copies all over the world, can hardly compare with Collier as a master of the language, but his sprawling novels of action and intrigue are compelling reading. Among thrillers of nearly every type, his tales of black magic are the most impressive. Beginning with *The Devil Rides Out* (1935), Wheatley has written a series of novels in which the suave Duke de Richleau combats energetic bands of Satanists. While his novels are more exciting than atmospheric, Wheatley displays a thorough knowledge of his subject, and many of his books contain a note cautioning readers against dabbling in magic. *Strange Conflict* (1941) contains his most unusual plot, as de Richleau fights the Second World War on the astral plane to defeat those enemies who are using the supernatural for purposes of espionage. The same theme appears in *They Used Dark Forces* (1964); it represents more than a writer's pipe dream, for Hitler is known to have employed magicians, fraudulent or not, and British Intelligence, with which Wheatley was connected, used its own astrologers to anticipate Axis plans in order to counter them.

Frightening fiction has continued unabated to the present day, and it is in many respects the most satisfactory medium for the creation of macabre moods. Yet even as the Golden Dawn was instructing its initiates in the secrets that produced so many sinister stories, a new miracle was in the offing that cast a blinding shadow over the printed page. It was the motion picture, which, even without the magic of words, would bring more monsters to more millions than ever before.

NOVEL OF THE WHITE POWDER

By Arthur Machen

My name is Leicester; my father, Major-General Wyn Leicester, a distinguished officer of artillery, succumbed five years ago to a complicated liver complaint acquired in the deadly climate of India. A year later my only brother, Francis, came home after an exceptionally brilliant career at the University, and settled down with the resolution of a hermit to master what has been well called the great legend of the law. He was a man who seemed to live in utter indifference to everything that is called pleasure; and though he was handsomer than most men, and could talk as merrily and wittily as if he were a mere vagabond, he avoided society, and shut himself up in a large room at the top of the house to make himself a lawyer. Ten hours a day of hard reading was at first his allotted portion; from the first light in the east to the late afternoon he remained shut up with his books, taking a hasty half-hour's lunch with me as if he grudged the wasting of the moments, and going out for a short walk when it began to grow dusk. I thought that such relentless application must be injurious, and tried to cajole him from the crabbed textbooks, but his ardour seemed to grow rather than diminish, and his daily tale of hours increased. I spoke to him seriously, suggesting some occasional relaxation, if it were but an idle afternoon with a harmless novel; but he laughed, and said that he read about feudal tenures when he felt in need of amusement, and scoffed at the notions of theatres, or a month's fresh air. I confessed that he looked well, and seemed not to suffer from his labours, but I knew that such unnatural toil would take revenge at last, and I was not mistaken. A look of anxiety began to lurk about his eyes, and he seemed languid, and at last he avowed that he was no longer in perfect health; he was troubled, he said, with a sensation of dizziness, and awoke now and then of nights from fearful dreams, terrified and cold with icy sweats. "I am taking care of myself," he said, "so you must not trouble; I passed the whole of yesterday afternoon in idleness, leaning back in that comfortable chair you gave me, and scribbling nonsense on a sheet of paper. No, no; I will not overdo my work; I shall be well enough in a week or two depend upon it."

Yet in spite of his assurances I could see that he grew no better, but rather worse; he would enter the drawing-room with a face all miserably wrinkled and despondent, and endeavour to look gaily when my eyes fell on him, and I thought such symptoms of evil omen, and was frightened sometimes at the nervous irritation of his movements, and at glances which I could not decipher. Much against his will, I prevailed on him to have medical advice, and with an ill grace he called in our old doctor.

Dr. Haberden cheered me after examination of his patient.

"There is nothing really much amiss," he said to me. "No doubt he reads too hard and eats hastily, and then goes back again to his books in too great a hurry, and the natural sequence is some digestive trouble and a little mischief in the nervous system. But I think—I do indeed, Miss Leicester—that we shall be able to set this all right. I have written him a prescription which ought to do great things. So you have no cause for anxiety."

My brother insisted on having the prescription made up by a chemist in the neighbourhood. It was an odd, old-fashioned shop, devoid of the studied coquetry and calculated glitter that make so gay a show on the counters and shelves of the modern apothecary; but Francis liked the old chemist, and believed in the scrupulous purity of his drugs. The medicine was sent in due course, and I saw that my brother took it regularly after lunch and dinner. It was an innocent-looking white powder, of which a little was dissolved in a glass of cold water; I stirred it in, and it seemed to disappear, leaving the water clear and colorless. At first Francis seemed to benefit greatly; the weariness vanished from his face, and he became more cheerful than he had ever been since the time when he left school; he talked gaily of reforming himself, and avowed to me that he had wasted his time.

"I have given too many hours to law," he said, laughing; "I think you have saved me in the nick of time. Come, I shall be Lord Chancellor yet, but I must not forget life. You and I will have a holiday together before long; we will go to Paris and enjoy ourselves, and keep away from the Bibliothèque Nationale."

I confessed myself delighted with the prospect.

"When shall we go?" I said. "I can start the day after to-morrow if you like."

"Ah! that is perhaps a little too soon; after all, I do not know London yet, and I suppose a man ought to give the pleasures of his own country the first choice. But we will go off together in a week or two, so try and furbish up your French. I only know law French myself, and I am afraid that wouldn't do."

We were just finishing dinner, and he quaffed off his medicine with a parade of carousal as if it had been wine from some choicest bin.

"Has it any particular taste?" I said.

"No; I should not know I was not drinking water," and he got up from his chair and began to pace up and down the room as if he were undecided as to what he should do next.

"Shall we have coffee in the drawing-room?" I said; "or would you like to smoke?"

"No, I think I will take a turn; it seems a pleasant evening. Look at the afterglow; why, it is as if a great city were burning in flames, and down there between the dark houses it is raining blood fast. Yes, I will go out; I may be in soon, but I shall take my key; so good-night, dear, if I don't see you again."

The door slammed behind him, and I saw him walk lightly down the street, swinging his malacca cane, and I felt grateful to Dr. Haberden for such an improvement.

I believe my brother came home very late that night, but he was in a merry mood the next morning.

"I walked on without thinking where I was going," he said, "enjoying the freshness of the air, and livened by the crowds as I reached more frequented quarters. And then I met an old college friend, Orford, in the press of the pavement, and then—well, we enjoyed ourselves. I have felt what it is to be young and a man; I find I have blood in my veins, as other men have. I made an appointment with Orford for to-night; there will be a little party of us at the restaurant. Yes; I shall enjoy myself for a week or two, and hear the chimes at midnight, and then we will go for our little trip together."

Such was the transmutation of my brother's character that in a few days he became a lover of pleasure, a careless and merry idler of western pavements, a hunter out of snug restaurants, and a fine critic of fantastic dancing; he grew fat before my eyes, and said no more of Paris, for he had clearly found his paradise in London. I rejoiced, and yet wondered a little; for there was, I thought, something in his gaiety that indefinitely displeased me, though I could not have defined my feeling. But by degrees there came a change; he returned still in the cold hours of the morning, but I heard no more about his pleasures, and one morning as we sat at breakfast together I looked suddenly into his eyes and saw a stranger before me.

"Oh, Francis!" I cried. "Oh, Francis, Francis, what have you done?" and rending sobs cut the words short. I went weeping out of the room; for though I knew nothing, yet I knew all, and by some odd play of thought I remembered the evening when he first went abroad, and the picture of the sunset sky glowed before me; the clouds like a city in burning flames, and the rain of blood. Yet I did battle with such thoughts, resolving that perhaps, after all, no great harm had been done, and in the evening at dinner I resolved to press him to fix a day for our holiday in Paris. We had talked easily enough, and my brother had just taken his medicine, which he continued all the while. I was about to begin my topic when the words forming in my mind vanished, and I wondered for a second what icy and intolerable weight oppressed my heart and suffocated me as with the unutterable horror of the coffin-lid nailed down on the living.

We had dined without candles; the room had slowly grown from twilight to gloom, and the walls and corners were indistinct in the shadow. But from where I sat I looked out into the street; and as I thought of what I would say to Francis, the sky began to flush and shine, as it had done on a well-remembered evening, and in the gap between two dark masses that were houses an awful pageantry of flame appeared—lurid whorls of writhed cloud, and utter depths burning, grey masses like the fume blown from a smoking city, and an evil glory blazing far above shot with tongues of more ardent fire, and below as if there were a deep pool of blood. I looked down to where my brother sat facing me, and the words were shaped on my lips, when I saw his hand resting on the table. Between the thumb and forefinger of the closed hand there was a mark, a small patch about the size of a sixpence, and somewhat of the colour of a bad bruise. Yet, by some sense I cannot define, I knew that what I saw was no bruise at all; oh! if human flesh could burn with flame, and if flame could be black as pitch, such was that before me. Without thought or fashioning of words grey horror shaped within me at the sight, and in an inner cell it was known to be a brand. For the moment the stained sky became dark as midnight, and when the light returned to me I was alone in the silent room, and soon after I heard my brother go out.

Late as it was, I put on my hat and went to Dr. Haberden, and in his great consulting room, ill lighted by a candle which the doctor brought in with him, with stammering lips, and a voice that would break in spite of my resolve, I told him all, from the day on which my brother began to take the medicine down to the dreadful thing I had seen scarcely half an hour before.

When I had done, the doctor looked at me for a minute with an expression of great pity on his face.

"My dear Miss Leicester," he said, "you have evidently been anxious about your brother; you have been worrying over him, I am sure. Come, now, is it not so?"

"I have certainly been anxious," I said. "For the last week or two I have not felt at ease."

"Quite so; you know, of course, what a queer thing the brain is?"

"I understand what you mean; but I was not deceived. I saw what I have told you with my own eyes."

"Yes, yes of course. But your eyes had been staring at that very curious sunset we had tonight. That is the only explanation. You will see it in the proper light to-morrow, I am sure. But, remember, I am always ready to give any help that is in my power; do not scruple to come to me, or to send for me if you are in any distress."

I went away but little comforted, all confusion and terror and sorrow, not knowing where to turn. When my brother and I met the next day, I looked quickly at him, and noticed, with a sickening at heart, that the right hand, the hand on which I had clearly seen the patch as of a black fire, was wrapped up with a handkerchief.

"What is the matter with your hand, Francis?" I said in a steady voice.

"Nothing of consequence. I cut a finger last night, and it bled rather awkwardly. So I did it up roughly to the best of my ability."

"I will do it neatly for you, if you like."

"No, thank you, dear; this will answer very well. Suppose we have breakfast; I am quite hungry."

We sat down and I watched him. He scarcely ate or drank at all, but tossed his meat to the dog when he thought my eyes were turned away; there was a look in his eyes that I had never yet seen, and the thought flashed across my mind that it was a look that was scarcely human. I was firmly convinced that awful and incredible as was the thing I had seen the night before, yet it was no illusion, no glamour of bewildered sense, and in the course of the evening I went again to the doctor's house.

He shook his head with an air puzzled and incredulous, and seemed to reflect for a few minutes.

"And you say he still keeps up the medicine? But why? As I understand, all the symptoms he complained of have disappeared long ago; why should he go on taking the stuff when he is quite well? And by the by, where did he get it made up? At Sayce's? I never send any one there; the old man is getting careless. Suppose you come with me to the chemist's; I should like to have some talk with him."

We walked together to the shop; old Sayce knew Dr. Haberden, and was quite ready to give any information.

"You have been sending that in to Mr. Leicester for some weeks, I think, on my prescription," said the doctor, giving the old man a pencilled scrap of paper.

The chemist put on his great spectacles with trembling uncertainty, and held up the paper with a shaking hand.

"Oh, yes," he said, "I have very little of it left; it is rather an uncommon drug, and I have had it in stock some time. I must get in some more, if Mr. Leicester goes on with it."

"Kindly let me have a look at the stuff," said Haberden, and the chemist gave him a glass bottle. He took out the stopper and smelt the contents, and looked strangely at the old man.

"Where did you get this?" he said, "and what is it? For one thing, Mr. Sayce, it is not what I prescribed. Yes, yes, I see the label is right enough, but I tell you this is not the drug."

"I have had it a long time," said the old man in feeble terror; "I got it from Burbage's in the usual way. It is not prescribed often, and I have had it on the shelf for some years. You see there is very little left."

"You had better give it to me," said Haberden. "I am afraid something wrong has happened."

We went out of the shop in silence, the doctor carrying the bottle neatly wrapped in paper under his arm.

"Dr. Haberden," I said, when we had walked a little way—"Dr. Haberden."

"Yes," he said, looking at me gloomily enough.

"I should like you to tell me what my brother has been taking twice a day for the last month or so."

"Frankly, Miss Leicester, I don't know. We will speak of this when we get to my house."

We walked on quickly without another word till we reached Dr. Haberden's. He asked me to sit down, and began pacing up and down the room, his face clouded over, as I could see, with no common fears.

"Well," he said at length, "this is all very strange; it is only natural that you should feel alarmed, and I must confess that my mind is far from easy. We will put aside, if you please, what you told me last night and this morning, but the fact remains that for the last few weeks Mr. Leicester has been impregnating his system with a drug which is completely unknown to me. I tell you, it is not what I ordered; and what the stuff in the bottle really is remains to be seen."

He undid the wrapper, and cautiously tilted a few grains of the white powder on to a piece of paper, and peered curiously at it.

"Yes," he said, "it is like the sulphate of quinine, as you say; it is flaky. But smell it."

He held the bottle to me, and I bent over it. It was a strange, sickly smell, vaporous and overpowering, like some strong anaesthetic.

"I shall have it analysed," said Haberden; "I have a friend who has devoted his whole life to chemistry as a science. Then we shall have something to go upon. No, no; say no more about that other matter; I cannot listen to that; and take my advice and think no more about it yourself."

That evening my brother did not go out as usual after dinner.

"I have had my fling," he said with a queer laugh, "and I must go back to my old ways. A little law will be quite a relaxation after so sharp a dose of pleasure," and he grinned to himself, and soon after went up to his room. His hand was still all bandaged.

Dr. Haberden called a few days later.

"I have no special news to give you," he said. "Chambers is out of town, so I know no more about that stuff than you do. But I should like to see Mr. Leicester, if he is in."

"He is in his room," I said; "I will tell him you are here."

"No, no, I will go up to him; we will have a little quiet talk together. I dare say that we have made a good deal of fuss about a very little; for, after all, whatever the powder may be, it seems to have done him good."

The doctor went upstairs, and standing in the hall I heard his knock, and the opening and shutting of the door; and then I waited in the silent house for an hour, and the stillness grew more and more intense as the hands of the clock crept round. Then there sounded from above the noise of a door shut sharply, and the doctor was coming down the stairs. His footsteps crossed the hall, and there was a pause at the door; I drew a long, sick breath with difficulty, and saw my face white in a little mirror, and he came in and stood at the door. There was an unutterable horror shining in his eyes; he steadied himself by holding the back of a chair with one hand, his lower lip trembled like a horse's, and he gulped and stammered unintelligible sounds before he spoke.

"I have seen that man," he began in a dry whisper. "I have been sitting in his presence for the last hour. My God! And I am alive and in my senses! I, who have dealt with death all my life, and have dabbled with the melting ruins of the earthly tabernacle. But not this, oh! not this," and he covered his face with his hands as if to shut out the sight of something before him.

"Do not send for me again, Miss Leicester," he said with more composure. "I can do nothing in this house. Good-bye."

As I watched him totter down the steps, and along the pavement towards his house, it seemed to me that he had aged by ten years since the morning.

My brother remained in his room. He called out to me in a voice I hardly recognized that he was very busy, and would like his meals brought to his door and left there, and I gave the order to the servants. From that day it seemed as if the arbitrary conception we call time had been annihilated for me; I lived in an ever-present sense of horror, going through the routine of the house mechanically, and only speaking a few necessary words to the servants. Now and then I went out and paced the streets for an hour or two and came home again; but whether I were without or within, my spirit delayed before the closed door of the upper room, and, shuddering, waited for it to open. I have said that I scarcely reckoned time; but I suppose it must have been a fortnight after Dr. Haberden's visit that I came home from my stroll a little refreshed and lightened. The air was sweet and pleasant, and the hazy form of green leaves, floating cloud-like in the square, and the smell of blossoms, had charmed my senses, and I felt happier and walked more briskly. As I delayed a moment at the verge of the pavement, waiting for a van to pass by before crossing over to the house, I happened to look up at the windows, and instantly there was the rush and swirl of deep cold waters in my ears, my heart leapt up and fell down, down as into a deep hollow, and I was amazed with a dread and terror without form or shape. I stretched out a hand blindly through the folds of thick darkness, from the black and shadowy valley, and held myself from falling, while the stones beneath my feet rocked and swayed and tilted, and the sense of solid things seemed to sink away from under me. I had glanced up at the window of my brother's study, and at that moment the blind was drawn aside, and something that had life stared out into the world. Nay, I cannot say I saw a face or any human likeness; a living thing, two eyes of burning flame glared at me, and they were in the midst of something as formless as my fear, the symbol and presence of all evil and all hideous corruption. I stood shuddering and quaking as with the grip of ague, sick with unspeakable agonies of fear and loathing, and for five minutes I could not summon force or motion to my limbs. When I was within the door, I ran up the stairs to my brother's room and knocked.

"Francis, Francis," I cried, "for Heaven's sake, answer me. What is the horrible thing in your room? Cast it out, Francis; cast it from you."

I heard a noise as of feet shuffling slowly and awkwardly, and a choking, gurgling sound, as if some one was struggling to find utterance, and then the noise of a voice, broken and stifled, and words that I could scarcely understand.

"There is nothing here," the voice said. "Pray do not disturb me. I am not very well to-day."

I turned away, horrified, and yet helpless. I could do nothing, and I wondered why Francis had lied to me, for I had seen the appearance beyond the glass too plainly to be deceived, though it was but the sight of a moment. And I sat still, conscious that there had been something else, something I had seen in the first flash of terror, before those burning eyes had looked at me. Suddenly I remembered; as I lifted my face the blind was being drawn back, and I had had an instant's glance of the thing that was moving it, and in my recollection I knew that a hideous image was engraved forever on my brain. It was not a hand; there were no fingers that held the blind, but a black stump pushed it aside, the mouldering outline and the clumsy movement as of a beast's paw had glowed into my senses before the darkling waves of terror had overwhelmed me as I went down quick into the pit. My mind was aghast at the thought of this, and of the awful presence that dwelt with my brother in his room; I went to his door and cried to him again, but no answer came. That night one of the servants came up to me and told me in a whisper that for three days food had been regularly placed at the door and left untouched; the maid had knocked but had received no answer; she had heard the noise of shuffling feet that I had noticed. Day after day went by, and still my brother's meals were brought to his door and left untouched; and though I knocked and called again and again, I could get no answer. The servants began to talk to me; it appeared they were as alarmed as I; the cook said that when my brother first shut himself up in his room she used to hear him come out at night and go about the house; and once, she said, the hall door had opened and closed again, but for several nights she had heard no sound. The climax came at last; it was in the dusk of the evening, and I was sitting in the darkening dreary room when a terrible shriek jarred and rang harshly out of the silence, and I heard a frightened scurry of feet dashing down the stairs. I waited, and the servant-maid staggered into the room and faced me, white and trembling.

"Oh, Miss Helen!" she whispered; "oh! for the Lord's sake, Miss Helen, what has happened? Look at my hand, miss; look at that hand!"

I drew her to the window, and saw there was a black wet stain upon her hand.

"I do not understand you," I said. "Will you explain to me?"

"I was doing your room just now," she began. "I was turning down the bed-clothes, and all of a sudden there was something fell upon my hand, wet, and I looked up, and the ceiling was black and dripping on me."

I looked hard at her and bit my lip.

"Come with me," I said. "Bring your candle with you."

The room I slept in was beneath my brother's, and as I went in I felt I was trembling. I looked up at the ceiling, and saw a patch, all black and wet, and a dew of black drops upon it, and a pool of horrible liquor soaking into the white bed-clothes.

I ran upstairs and knocked loudly.

"Oh, Francis, Francis, my dear brother," I cried, "what has happened to you?"

And I listened. There was a sound of choking, and a noise like water bubbling and regurgitating, but nothing else, and I called louder, but no answer came.

In spite of what Dr. Haberden had said, I went to him; with tears streaming down my cheeks I told him all that had happened, and he listened to me with a face set hard and grim.

"For your father's sake," he said at last, "I will go with you, though I can do nothing."

We went out together; the streets were dark and silent, and heavy with heat and a drought of many weeks. I saw the doctor's face white under the gas-lamps, and when we reached the house his hand was shaking.

We did not hesitate, but went upstairs directly. I held the lamp, and he called out in a loud, determined voice—

"Mr. Leicester, do you hear me? I insist on seeing you. Answer me at once."

There was no answer, but we both heard that choking noise I have mentioned.

"Mr. Leicester, I am waiting for you. Open the door this instant, or I shall break it down." And he called a third time in a voice that rang and echoed from the walls—

"Mr. Leicester! For the last time I order you to open the door."

"Ah!" he said, after a pause of heavy silence, "we are wasting time here. Will you be so kind as to get me a poker, or something of the kind?"

I ran into a little room at the back where odd articles were kept, and found a heavy adze-like tool that I thought might serve the doctor's purpose.

"Very good," he said, "that will do, I dare say. I give you notice, Mr. Leicester," he cried loudly at the keyhole, "that I am now about to break into your room."

Then I heard the wrench of the adze, and the woodwork split and cracked under it; with a loud crash the door suddenly burst open, and for a moment we started back aghast at a fearful screaming cry, no human voice, but as the roar of a monster, that burst forth inarticulate and struck at us out of the darkness.

"Hold the lamp," said the doctor, and we went in and glanced quickly round the room.

"There it is," said Dr. Haberden, drawing a quick breath; "look, in that corner."

I looked, and a pang of horror seized my heart as with a white-hot iron. There upon the floor was a dark and putrid mass, seething with corruption and hideous rottenness, neither liquid nor solid, but melting and changing before our eyes, and bubbling with unctuous oily bubbles like boiling pitch. And out of the midst of it shone two burning points like eyes, and I saw a writhing and stirring as of limbs, and something moved and lifted up what might have been an arm. The doctor took a step forward, raised the iron bar and struck at the burning points; he drove in the weapon, and struck again and again in the fury of loathing.

A week or two later, when I had recovered to some extent from the terrible shock, Dr. Haberden came to see me.

"I have sold my practice," he began, "and to-morrow I am sailing on a long voyage. I do not know whether I shall ever return to England; in all probability I shall buy a little land in California, and settle there for the remainder of my life. I have brought you this packet, which you may open and read when you feel able to do so. It contains the report of Dr. Chambers on what I submitted to him. Good-bye, Miss Leicester, good-bye."

When he was gone I opened the envelope; I could not wait, and proceeded to read the papers within. Here is the manuscript, and if you will allow me, I will read you the astounding story it contains.

"My dear Haberden," the letter began, "I have delayed inexcusably in answering your questions as to the white substance you sent me. To tell you the truth, I have hesitated for some time as to what course I should adopt, for there is a bigotry and orthodox standard in physical science as in theology, and I knew that if I told you the truth I should offend rooted prejudices which I once held dear myself. However, I have determined to be plain with you, and first I must enter into a short personal explanation.

"You have known me, Haberden, for many years as a scientific man; you and I have often talked of our profession together, and discussed the hopeless gulf that opens before the feet of those who think to attain to truth by any means whatsoever except the beaten way of experiment and observation in the sphere of material things. I remember the scorn with which you have spoken to me of men of science who have dabbled a little in the unseen, and have timidly hinted that perhaps the senses are not, after all, the eternal, impenetrable bounds of all knowledge, the everlasting walls beyond which no human being has ever passed. We have laughed together heartily, and I think justly, at the 'occult' follies of the day, disguised under various names—the mesmerisms, spiritualisms, materializations, theosophies, all the rabble rout of imposture, with their machinery of poor tricks and feeble conjuring, the true back-parlour of shabby London streets. Yet, in spite of what I have said, I must confess to you that I am no materialist, taking the word of course in its usual signification. It is now many years since I have convinced myself—convinced myself, a sceptic, remember—that the old ironbound theory is utterly and entirely false. Perhaps this confession will not wound you so sharply as it would have done twenty years ago; for I think you cannot have failed to notice that for some time hypotheses have been advanced by men of pure science which are nothing less than transcendental, and I suspect that most modern chemists and biologists of repute would not hesitate to subscribe the *dictum* of the old Schoolman, *Omnia exeunt in mysterium*, which means, I take it, that every branch of human knowledge if traced up to its source and final principles vanishes into mystery. I need not trouble you now with a detailed account of the painful steps which led me to my conclusions; a few simple experiments suggested a doubt as to my then standpoint, and a train of thought that rose from circumstances comparatively trifling brought me far; my old conception of the universe has been swept away, and I stand in a world that seems as strange and awful to me as the endless waves of the ocean seen for the first time, shining, from a peak in Darien. Now I know that the walls of sense that seemed so impenetrable, that seemed to loom up above the heavens and to be founded below the depths, and to shut us in for evermore, are no such everlasting impassable barriers as we fancied, but thinnest and most airy veils that melt away before the seeker, and dissolve as the early mist of the morning about the brooks. I know that you never adopted the extreme materialistic position; you did not go about trying to prove a universal negative, for your logical sense withheld you from that crowning absurdity; but I am sure that you will find all that I am saying strange and repellent to your habits of thought. Yet, Haberden, what I tell you is the truth, nay, to adopt our common language, the sole and scientific truth, verified by experience; and the universe is verily more splendid and more awful than we used to dream. The whole universe, my friend, is a tremendous sacrament; a mystic, ineffable force and energy, veiled by an outward form of matter; and man, and the sun and the other stars, and the flower of the grass, and the crystal in the test-tube, are each and every one as spiritual, as material, and subject to an inner working.

"You will perhaps wonder, Haberden, whence all this tends; but I think a little thought will make it clear. You will understand that from such a standpoint the whole view of things is changed, and what we thought incredible and absurd may be possible enough. In short, we must look at legend and belief with other eyes, and be prepared to accept tales that had become mere fables. Indeed this is no such great demand. After all, modern science will concede as much, in a hypocritical manner; you must not, it is true, believe in witchcraft, but you may credit hypnotism; ghosts are out of date, but there is a good deal to be said for the theory of telepathy. Give superstition a Greek name, and believe in it, should almost be a proverb.

"So much for my personal explanation. You sent me, Haberden, a phial, stoppered and sealed, containing a small quantity of flaky white powder, obtained from a chemist who has been dispensing it to one of your patients. I am not surprised to hear that this powder refused to yield any results to your analysis. It is a substance which was known to a few many hundred years ago, but which I never expected to have submitted to me from the shop of a modern apothecary. There seems no reason to doubt the truth of the man's tale; he no doubt got, as he says, the rather uncommon salt you prescribed from the wholesale chemist's; and it has probably remained on his shelf for twenty years, or perhaps longer. Here what we call chance and coincidence begin to work; during all these years the salt in the bottle was exposed to certain recurring variations of temperature, variations probably ranging from 40° to 80°. And, as it happens, such changes, recurring year after year at irregular intervals, and with varying degrees of intensity and duration, have constituted a process, and a process, so complicated and so delicate, that I question whether modern scientific apparatus directed with the utmost precision could produce the same result. The white powder you sent me is something very different from the drug you prescribed; it is the powder from which the wine of the Sabbath, the *Vinum Sabbati*, was prepared. No doubt you have read of the Witches' Sabbath, and have laughed at the tales which terrified our ancestors; the black cats, and the broomsticks, and dooms pronounced against some old woman's cow. Since I have known the truth I have often reflected that it is on the whole a happy thing that such burlesque as this is believed, for it serves to conceal much that it is better should not be known generally. However, if you care to read the appendix to Payne Knight's monograph, you will find that the true Sabbath was something very different, though the writer has very nicely refrained from printing all he knew. The secrets of the true Sabbath were the secrets of remote times surviving into the Middle Ages, secrets of an evil science which existed long before Aryan man entered Europe. Men and women, seduced from their homes on specious pretences, were met by beings well qualified to assume, as they did assume, the part of devils, and taken by their guides to some desolate and lonely place, known to the initiate by long tradition, and unknown to all else. Perhaps it was a cave in some bare and wind-swept hill, perhaps some inmost recess of a great forest, and there the Sabbath was held. There, in the blackest hour of night, the *Vinum Sabbati* was prepared, and this evil graal was poured forth and offered to the neophytes, and they partook of an infernal sacrament; *sumentes calicem principis inferorum*, as an old author well expresses it. And suddenly, each one that had drunk found himself attended by a companion, a share of glamour and unearthly allurement, beckoning him apart, to share in joys more exquisite, more piercing than the thrill of any dream, to the consummation of the marriage of the Sabbath. It is hard to write of such things as these, and chiefly because that shape that allured with loveliness was no hallucination, but, awful as it is to express, the man himself. By the power of that Sabbath wine, a few grains of white powder thrown into a glass of water, the house of life was riven asunder and the human trinity dissolved, and the worm which never dies, that which lies sleeping within us all, was made tangible and an external thing, and clothed with a garment of flesh. And then, in the hour of midnight, the primal fall was repeated and re-presented, and the awful thing veiled in the mythos of the Tree in the Garden was done anew. Such was the *nuptiæ Sabbati*.

"I prefer to say no more; you, Haberden, know as well as I do that the most trivial laws of life are not to be broken with impunity; and for so terrible an act as this, in which the very inmost place of the temple was broken open and defiled, a terrible vengeance followed. What began with corruption ended also with corruption."

Underneath is the following in Dr. Haberden's writing:—

"The whole of the above is unfortunately strictly and entirely true. Your brother confessed all to me on that morning when I saw him in his room. My attention was first attracted to the bandaged hand, and I forced him to show it to me. What I saw made me, a medical man of many years' standing, grow sick with loathing, and the story I was forced to listen to was infinitely more frightful than I could have believed possible. It has tempted me to doubt the Eternal Goodness which can permit nature to offer such hideous possibilities; and if you had not with your own eyes seen the end, I should have said to you—disbelieve it all. I have not, I think, many more weeks to live, but you are young, and may forget all this.

"JOSEPH HABERDEN, M.D."

In the course of two or three months I heard that Dr. Haberden had died at sea shortly after the ship left England.

·6·

THE SILVER KEY: MASS MARKETS

The birth of the twentieth century gave fantasies of fear a new look. Within the space of a generation, science showered mankind with such surprising devices as electric lights, telegraphs, telephones, horseless carriages, airplanes, and cornflakes. Among the results were opportunities for expression in media innovations like motion pictures, phonograph records, and even comic strips. Old monsters are never far behind new mediums, and the brain behind half of this wild pioneering, Thomas Alva Edison, was also responsible for the first *Frankenstein* film, now lost, in 1910.

Actually, movies with macabre motives had begun to appear years earlier. The French director Georges Méliès had begun making bizarre motion pictures in the last decade of the nineteenth century. He was the first great innovator in the field of camera trickery, and he delighted especially in stopping the film to change somebody or something into something else. He used double exposures to create gigantic figures and pioneered the use of specially constructed sets for his fantastic featurettes. Although he frequently used supernatural or science fiction subjects, the tone of his work was essentially light and playful. He made little attempt to induce a mood of menace but rather communicated the fabulous fun of playing with a new toy. His *Trip to the Moon* is still especially enjoyable, but his principal contribution was proving that motion pictures were capable of visualizing the incredible in a way that had never been possible before.

Many silent films have been lost to posterity, some so completely that no one is aware that they ever existed. For the first few years they tended to steer clear of anything too shocking—audiences were horrified to see guns fired out of the screen at them, or trains rushing toward the camera. Nothing much stronger seems to have been required or even tolerated. Gradually a few films began to touch on the grim or the grotesque, but it is difficult to determine which, if any, should be regarded as the first "horror movie." The title might as well go to one of countless versions of *Dr. Jekyll and Mr. Hyde.* The first American production, made in 1908, was a photographic record of a stage play. Two years later the Edison *Frankenstein* appeared, with Charles Ogle as a monster who looks a bit foolish in the few remaining stills. The story was shortened almost beyond recognition and provided with a happy ending in which the monster is improbably destroyed by the love between Frankenstein and his bride. Whoever wrote the script had unwittingly set the pattern for almost every future film in the genre. In contravention of the literary

As the Phantom of the Opera (1925), Lon Chaney created a fearsome face which may well be the finest monster makeup, in spite of subsequent technical advances. He had no competition from later actors, who were prohibited by union rules from donning their own disguises. *Courtesy of Universal Pictures.*

Charles Ogle portrayed the monster in Thomas Edison's 1910 film production *Frankenstein*.

tradition, screenplays seemed to require the presence of a courting couple who survive to live happily ever after. If the original story failed to provide this sort of optimistic love interest, it would be added, regardless of its effect on the theme.

This early reluctance to present unadulterated horror on the screen led many nightmarish movies to reassure their viewers by presenting them as a dream of the leading character. Such was the case in *Life without Soul* (1915), a second version of the Frankenstein story which featured Percy Darrell Standing as a monster without makeup. Neither of these films seems to have met with much success; movie audiences apparently acquired their taste for the macabre rather slowly. Even D. W. Griffith, the greatest director of his day, produced something less than a sensation with his *The Avenging*

Conscience (1914), an appropriately titled Poe adaptation loosely based on "The Tell-Tale Heart" in which the hero escapes punishment for murder by the standard route: he wakes up.

The majority of the masterpieces in the silent cinema of the sinister were made in Germany, where the public seemed more willing to play the game. German films produced the first actors to specialize in repulsive roles, among them Paul Wegener and Conrad Veidt. In 1913 Wegener starred in *The Student of Prague*, who is haunted by his double after selling his soul to the devil. He codirected and played the title role in *The Golem* (1915), an adaptation of a Jewish legend, hundreds of years old. The Golem is a statue brought to life by a rabbi to protect his people from religious persecution. The film portrays it as being discovered and revived in modern times. Predictably, the monster

Paul Wegener directed and starred in *The Golem* (1920), the best of his three films about the legendary living statue.

Conrad Veidt and Lil Dagover in the influential German film *The Cabinet of Dr. Caligari*. The expressionistic sets were designed by Hermann Warm, Walter Reimann, and Walter Röhrig.

runs amok, but is destroyed when the heroine removes the magical symbol that has animated its clay body. A sequel two years later, *The Golem and the Dancing Girl*, was a comedy in which Wegener played himself, impersonating his famous character for a practical joke. He returned to the role in a 1920 film, again called *The Golem*, which is probably the best of the lot, based as it was on the original story with its medieval setting and strong motivation. The fact that the character lasted through three movies anticipated the great successes of the talking picture's monsters, who were hardly worth their salt unless they could spawn a sequel or two.

Conrad Veidt surpassed Wegener by landing the role of the sinister somnambulist Cesare in *The Cabinet of Dr. Caligari* (1919), still usually cited in lists of the most important films ever made. Directed by Robert Wiene, from a screenplay by Carl Mayer and Hans Janowitz, this expressionist film went a long way toward proving that movies in general, and horror movies in particular, could be substantial works of art. The plot concerns a wandering showman, Dr. Caligari (Werner Krauss), who keeps the black-clad Cesare in a coffin, waking him periodically so that he may tell fortunes for crowds. At night he sends the creature out to commit murders, apparently only so that the dire predictions of the day will come true. Cesare kidnaps the heroine, but he collapses after a grueling chase, and Caligari is revealed to be the proprietor of a local madhouse. The story is less important than its treatment; the film made startling use of grotesque sets that were like nothing ever seen on the screen before. There was no attempt at realism. Rather, the twisted, contorted backgrounds through which the actors moved were extensions of the mood of madness and murder. Ingeniously arranged false perspectives made the somnambulist's flight a dizzy demonstration of geometry gone wild. Veidt looks very much like a walking corpse, and the scene in which he slowly comes to life, his nostrils twitching as if they had never smelled fresh air before, is a small gem of pantomime. His later work in macabre movies included a dual role in the Jekyll-Hyde imitation *The Head of Janus* (1920) and the lead in Wiene's *Hands of Orlac* (1925), about a man who has his amputated hands replaced by surgery and becomes convinced that he has lost control over them when he discovers that they are those of a murderer. As if to emphasize the similarity in their careers, Veidt next took Paul Wegener's role in a 1926 remake of *The Student of Prague*.

Germans also produced the first Dracula film, *Nosferatu* (1922). Like *The Head of Janus*, this movie changed some names and details of the literary work from which it was lifted; but the deception was unsuccessful. Bram Stoker's widow sued the production company, which promptly went bankrupt, and the movie was withdrawn from circulation, although a few copies escaped the court order that they be destroyed. F. W. Murnau directed the adaptations of both Stevenson's and Stoker's classics. *Nosferatu* is a grotesque film, about half terrifying and half just terrible. The vampire Orlock, played under a pseudonym by one Max Schreck (his last name means "terror"), has such an outrageous appearance that he could never pass for normal as Dracula did. A bald, snaggle-toothed fiend with pointed ears and huge claws, he is accompanied by a retinue of rats. There is nothing suave about him, but some of his appearances are startling. When he crosses the sea in search of new victims, his coffin is opened by a curious sailor, and Schreck pops up like a jack-in-the-box. Murnau has some feeling for the workaday world of the vampire, as in one quaint shot of Orlock entering a new town, scurrying through the twilit streets, bent double by the weight of the coffin he carries on his back. The adapter, Henrik Galeen, seems to have invented the idea that a vampire could be destroyed by sunlight. This concept was to be repeated in many later films, although Stoker's Dracula could walk abroad at noon without ill effect.

Max Schreck was the first film Dracula, in F. W. Murnau's *Nosferatu* (1922), a German adaptation that gave the vampire an incredibly bizarre look.

Fritz Lang, whose career spanned several decades and two continents, directed several important fantasy films during the great era of Germany's silent screen. None of them seems intended primarily to frighten the audience, but many of them have their awe-inspiring moments. *Dr. Mabuse* (1922) depicts a master criminal who plots to dominate the world through hypnotism, and *Siegfried* (1924) features a fight with a dragon. Lang's most elaborately produced and vividly realized film is *Metropolis* (1926), a science fiction spectacle written, like most of his early movies, by his wife Thea von Harbou. The story is based in a city of the future where tremendous advances have been made possible by the toil of workers underground. They revolt, and the leader of the city floods their subterranean homes; but he finally relents and promises a new order. Some sensational scenery and the creation of a treacherous female robot are among the highlights of *Metropolis*, a movie that pleases the eye more than the intellect.

Many of these German films had limited distribution abroad because of the problems of wartime, but their innovations went a long way toward defining the ingredients and attitudes that were to become characteristic of the sinister cinema. And movies, during the silent era, had no real language barrier. Still, the great tradition of the horror film is largely an American phenomenon. The first prestige production there was yet another version of *Dr. Jekyll and Mr. Hyde* (1920), this one starring the distinguished actor John Barrymore. He played Hyde as a dirty old man with an elongated head. The screenplay by Clara Berenger elaborated on Stevenson's story by adding a pair of young women for him to threaten; no subsequent version was considered complete without them. Barrymore's most impressive scenes relied on his stage ability, which permitted him to contort his features sufficiently to portray the transformation without makeup or special

In many ways the first important American horror film was John Barrymore's *Dr. Jekyll and Mr. Hyde.* The accomplished actor is shown here in the more entertaining of the two roles.

photography. The film is not as good as its star, but it certainly surpasses the version released in the same year that featured Sheldon Lewis and seems to have been designed to confuse audiences into believing it was the Barrymore picture.

America finally produced the first full-fledged horror star in Lon Chaney, the "Man of a Thousand Faces," who more or less inaugurated the tradition of elaborate screen makeup, even becoming an authority on the subject for an edition of *The Encyclopaedia Britannica*. Chaney's parents were both deaf-mutes, and his gift for pantomime made him one of the most expressive actors of the silent screen. Although his macabre roles brought him his greatest fame, they constitute a distinct minority of his motion picture performances, which were largely character parts. He played villains of every stripe, using his skills as a makeup artist in several Oriental characterizations and contorting his limbs to portray an unlikely succession of amputees. His first fantastic role came in *A Blind Bargain* (1922), when he portrayed a low-browed ape-man, the victim of experiments in gland transplantations performed by a crackpot scientist, who was also played by Chaney. The film proved popular enough to lead to bigger and better things.

His next two films were his greatest, *The Hunchback of Notre Dame* (1923) and *The Phantom of the Opera* (1925), both made at Universal, a company that was well on its way to becoming the world's most productive monster factory. Both films were based on French novels, Victor Hugo's *Notre Dame de Paris* and Gaston Leroux's *Phantom of the Opera*; both were set in a Paris reconstructed on Hollywood back lots. The first featured Chaney as the deformed foundling who grows up to be the bell ringer of the greatest church in Paris, which he transforms into a fort to protect a Gypsy girl condemned to death. The story had been filmed before, but never on such a grand scale. Hugo's plot appears almost as twisted as Quasimodo's spine: Chaney saves Esmeralda at the cost of his own life, while in the book his efforts were frustrated and he survived the doomed heroine. The film thus avoids the tragedy and irony of Hugo's original conception, substituting for it a mood of pathos, the burden of which falls on Quasimodo's ungainly shoulders. Chaney rose to the occasion, infusing his role with a sense of suffering that was probably not all acting, since the disguise he designed for himself was extremely uncomfortable. He not only covered his face with putty, applied a fake blind eye, false teeth, and a fright wig, but he also constructed a rubber torso that made the hunchback convincing even when he was stripped to the waist for a whipping. Chaney's tortured air was to become stock-in-trade for later monsters, few of whom would achieve stardom unless they could evoke a little sympathy.

Hugo's novel was not really a horror story; but the film almost succeeded in turning it into one, and it is regarded today as something along those lines. Working with a plot that was frankly intended to raise goose bumps, Chaney enjoyed his greatest triumph as Erik, the mysterious figure who haunts the Paris Opera. A patron of the arts who extends his critic's prerogative to include the killing of unworthy performers and unappreciative audiences, the masked Phantom takes a young singer as his protégée and leads her to his home in the grottoes beneath the opera house. He releases her when she promises not to reveal his secret but kidnaps her after she betrays him. She is finally rescued by the bumbling hero and an intelligent detective; the Phantom is killed by an inexplicably incensed mob, who may perhaps have had relatives among the wealthy music lovers obliterated when Erik released a huge chandelier hanging over the heads of the opera audience.

The Phantom of the Opera suffers hardly at all from its weak motivation and shaky plotting; although the story is preposterous even by horror movie standards, its

Lon Chaney distorted his body as well as his face to portray Quasimodo in *The Hunchback of Notre Dame* (1923), a free adaptation of Hugo's novel directed by Wallace Worsley. *Courtesy of Universal Pictures.*

Rupert Julian's *Phantom of the Opera*, with Lon Chaney and Mary Philbin, was the film that launched Carl Laemmle's Universal studio as the primary producer of American horror movies, a position it retained for decades. *Courtesy of Universal Pictures.*

simple-mindedness conveys an irresistible charm. Later versions lost the magic mood when, for instance, they attempted to explain the Phantom's origin as a disfigured musician or a swindled composer. Chaney's Erik has no such pedestrian background; he simply is the Phantom and always has been. It is his career, and he is a professional. When the heroine creeps up behind him to remove his mask and he leaps up from his organ to reveal his hideous visage, Erik's life seems to have reached a peak. Certainly Chaney's had; the scene is remembered with mingled awe and affection as one of the great thrills in the annals of the cinema. The makeup is Chaney's masterpiece. A domed skull, hollow eyes, high cheekbones, distended nostrils, and jagged teeth make it the face of death itself. The beauty of later monsters was only skin deep, but Chaney probed beneath the surface of his own body, stretching his mouth with fish hooks, shoving lumps of celluloid high up into his cheeks and, according to some reports, using chemicals to distort the appearance of his eyes. The disguise was still flexible enough to permit some emoting, and the actor gave his all, shifting from the despair of the unloved to the bravado of the unremorseful. He has a wonderful last moment when he turns on his pursuers and holds them at bay with a threatening gesture, as if he were about to throw a bomb. As the mob cowers, he contemptuously opens his hand to reveal that it is empty.

By the time this movie was released, the genre had become sufficiently well established to be parodied; so Chaney appeared in *The Monster*, a haunted-house comedy in which he played a demented doctor defeated by a correspondence-school detective. His last great horror role came two years later in *London after Midnight* (1927), directed by Tod Browning, who was to be responsible for some of the best frightening features of the sound era. Chaney played a vampire who turns out to be a detective who scares a murderer into confessing. He was planning to play Dracula in Browning's film version when he died, in 1930.

Meanwhile, the popular success of recorded music preserved more than a few weird songs for posterity. Regional markets opened up as local performers were sought out, and shellac 78s recorded a number of morbid traditions in native ballads and blues, songs considerably less sentimental than their Tin Pan Alley counterparts. Nearby murders and disasters were frequently described in the lyrics of new songs, while many Elizabethan songs on supernatural subjects survived a transatlantic passage to emerge in new versions among Appalachian folk singers.

Certainly more influential than the new music market, at least as far as fearsome fantasies were concerned, was the extraordinary expansion of the press during the same period. Nobody guessed that electric devices were about to replace the printed word as the principal means for communicating ideas. Formal literary decorum was mislaid as mass public education led inevitably to mass-oriented periodicals. The most vivid and apparently reprehensible of these were known as "pulp" magazines, after the inexpensive, eminently biodegradable material on which they were printed. The pulps became the primary depository for lurid fantasies in the United States, unleashing dozens of apparently immortal characters like Tarzan, the Shadow, Buck Rogers, Doc Savage, and the Spider, thus initiating a pantheon of heroes into the mythology of a new but tenacious "lowbrow" culture.

In fact, the creation of a blatantly fraudulent mythology became the main concern of many of the writers associated with the most consistently literate of the pulps, *Weird Tales*, which began publication in 1923. Published by Jacob Clark Henneberger and edited—for its first few issues—by Edwin Baird, who was soon replaced by Farnsworth Wright, its editor for its formative years, *Weird Tales* was a labor of love that managed to stay afloat for more than thirty years even though it never showed a profit. Its most important author was Howard Phillips Lovecraft, who since his death in 1937 has become one of the most popular and imitated men in his field.

A sickly child prodigy who was writing a professional astronomy column while still a teenager, Lovecraft's mature work managed to combine ancient demonology with the recent Einsteinian theories of space, time, and relativity, which he apparently found fully intelligible. The result was what is now called the "Cthulhu Mythos," named for the most famous of the hideous entities which he portrays both as the monsters of yore and the masters of a fourth dimension which science has yet to reveal. Many of his stories have autobiographical overtones and are set in the history-haunted regions of New England that he knew so well. Both qualities appear in "The Silver Key," a nostalgic piece in which a family relic enables the protagonist to transcend chronology by returning to his own childhood, creating a closed cycle of growth and return without the intervening traumas of birth and death.

Lovecraft was a favorite not only with the readers of *Weird Tales*, but also with a sizable group of writers whom he encouraged to imitate the style and subjects that were his own. The most prominent members of this coterie were Robert E. Howard, Clark Ashton Smith, Robert Bloch, Frank Belknap Long, August Derleth, and Donald Wandrei. Wandrei and particularly Derleth did the most to establish their mentor's reputation through Arkham House, a publishing company started in 1939 for the express purpose of preserving Lovecraft's work in permanent form. Their first volume, *The Outsider and Others*, a fat book containing almost all of Lovecraft's important work, would be the ideal introduction to his strange world if not for the fact that this rare item now commands prices ranging upward from a hundred dollars.

There are several qualities that set Lovecraft apart from the average pulp magazine writer. His style is remarkably stately for the periodicals in which his stories appeared, his plots suggest a new source of strange atmosphere, and his eccentric but endearing personality has become almost legendary. In fact, one commentator called Lovecraft himself "his own most fantastic creation," which is quite an achievement for an author whose most famous character is a gigantic green glob of tentacled terror called Cthulhu.

It is as the creator of the Cthulhu mythos that Lovecraft is most widely recognized. The title refers to the group of stories he wrote toward the end of his life, creating implicitly if not deliberately a mythology in which beings from outside our universe wait on the edge of human experience for a chance to recapture the planet that was once their domain. These stories gain their power not so much from the descriptions or activities of the extraterrestrial monsters as from the implications to be drawn from their presence: that the universe is not essentially benign or humanistic and that mankind represents an accident rather than a triumph of nature. Lovecraft's terrors have little to do with the essentially egocentric topics of death and return from the grave. Although some of his early stories do involve these more traditional devices, a typical Lovecraft character is less likely to lose his life than his life-style, less in danger of a broken neck than a snapped mind. The emblem of the Lovecraft cosmos is the blind idiot-god Azathoth, king of creation, who cackles in chaos to the music of frantic flute players; and the ultimate shock in his tales comes from the unwelcome ability to see the universe through Azathoth's eyes. Lovecraft described his stories as attempts to create the effect of "dislocations in space and time," and his success in some efforts makes his work the literary equivalent of a psychedelic trip, which may in part account for his recent popularity with a new generation of readers.

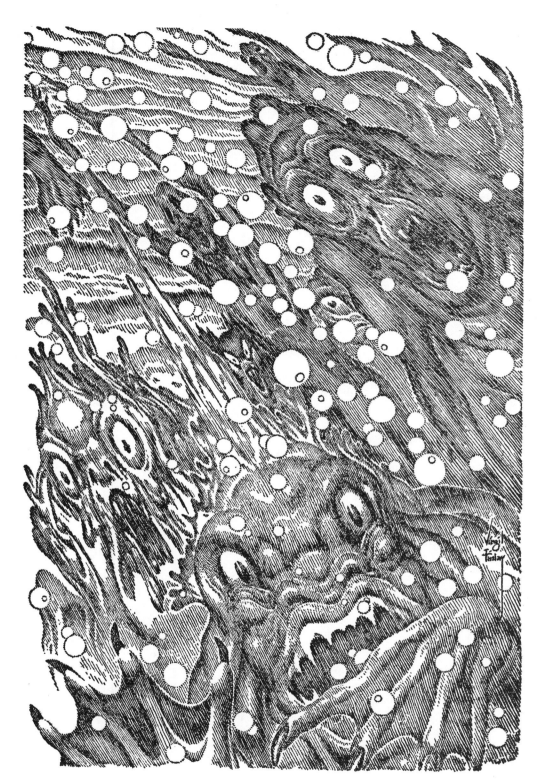

Virgil Finlay, the most renowned *Weird Tales* artist, began his career with the magazine shortly before death ended Lovecraft's, but Finlay later illustrated several Cthulhu stories, including "The House in the Valley" by Lovecraft's disciple August Derleth.

Lovecraft, however, denied any interest in drugs, although some of his characters take to opium to blot out intolerable memories. He even scorned the use of alcohol and tobacco, finding his greatest stimulation and inspiration in his own dreams, which were vivid and often organized enough to form the basis for some of his best stories. Dreams and darkness were his domain in life as well as in literature; he was a "night person" who roamed the streets after midnight and kept his shades drawn during the daylight hours to maintain an appropriately gloomy atmosphere.

Born in Providence, Rhode Island, in 1890, H. P. Lovecraft lived there all his life, excepting a few excursions and a short, ill-fated marriage that brought him briefly to New York. He grew up in a strange atmosphere amid the declining fortunes of a once distinguished family; both his parents died in a local mental hospital. Most of his adult life was spent in residence with his two elderly aunts. He was a recluse with relatively few personal contacts except those maintained through his huge correspondence by which he communicated with kindred spirits, mostly aspiring authors. His incredible letters, some of which have been published in several Arkham House volumes, accounted for an incredible amount of his time and energy. It was not unusual for one of these elaborate letters in his infinitesimal script to be the equivalent of one hundred typed pages, longer than almost any of his stories.

Equally demanding was his work in revising and ghostwriting, activities that provided most of his meager income. His most famous client was the magician Harry Houdini, but there were a number of lesser lights whose work might never have been published without Lovecraft's extensive efforts. One was Providence writer C. M. Eddy, Jr., whose scandalous story of an undertaking necrophile, "The Loved Dead," helped to make *Weird Tales* famous. But all of these activities restricted Lovecraft's own work and made him something less than a prolific writer. The list of his tales was expanded after his death in a somewhat grotesque manner, through a series of "posthumous collaborations" with August Derleth. These do not involve messages from beyond but are stories worked up by Derleth from notes and fragments left at Lovecraft's death. Unfortunately the stories are presented as Lovecraft's work despite the fact that in most cases his contribution consists of but one or two sentences or, in the case of the novel *The Lurker at the Threshold* (1945), a few pages. The essentially derivative nature of Derleth's writing in these tales makes them a poor introduction to Lovecraft.

Perhaps his most typical performance, and his most famous, is the story "The Call of Cthulhu," written in 1927. This tale of an elemental force rising out of the Pacific after eons of imprisonment was the first major exposition of the myth pattern that made Lovecraft's horrors unique. As usual, the tale is told in the first person by a narrator whose main characteristic is an overwhelming curiosity. His investigations into the legends and lore of the Cthulhu cult, conducted at a discreet scholarly distance, produce a body of information that leaves the hero stricken with horror from afar. The story begins with the line "The most merciful thing in the world, I think, is the inability of the human mind to correlate all its contents." This is a fair statement of Lovecraft's principal theme, a sophisticated prefiguration of the later monster movie cliché, "There are some things man was not meant to know." But his heroes are not mad scientists bent on unholy experiments so much as they are jaded intellectuals morbidly drawn to bizarre events already in progress.

The generally investigative form of Lovecraft's fiction often leads to a sort of shock ending that is not exactly a twist, but rather the logical culmination of suggestions scattered throughout the story. The tales are organized so that the final phrase, often in italics, reveals a detail that provides the cornerstone for a construction of events with staggering implications. This technique seems to be Lovecraft's interpretation of Poe's principle concerning unity of effect.

Utilizing what was essentially a nineteenth-century form to present his unnerving version of twentieth-century speculations about the cosmos, Lovecraft employed a prose style that was straight out of the eighteenth century. This was his favorite period in history, the era in which he felt he belonged. His preference for it was also expressed in his love for colonial architecture and in his frequently stated desire to dress in the costume of the period, which was apparently fulfilled only in his most famous portrait, by *Weird Tales* artist Virgil Finlay. Lovecraft's attachment to the eighteenth century was a result of a precocious childhood spent largely among the old books in his grandfather's library, where his interests in literature and escapism were encouraged by the formal prose of a bygone era.

Stylistically, Lovecraft's writing set him immediately apart from his contemporaries in pulp magazines, who with rare exceptions wrote in punchy phrases loaded with contemporary slang. Perhaps it was snob appeal that accounted for the respect he earned at *Weird Tales*. On the other hand, many critics have accused him of overwriting and of relying too heavily on adjectives. It is true that many of his stories seem stilted, and they are often more impressive when recalled than when they are being read. The best example of the way in which Lovecraft's stories retrospectively overcome their own faults

Finlay's whimsical portrait of Lovecraft shows the author in the attire of his beloved eighteenth century. Lovecraft never really used a quill pen, but his mentor, Lord Dunsany, did.

may be found in the case of Colin Wilson, the British critic who wrote a scathing attack on Lovecraft a few years ago, then turned around and wrote several stories and a novel as contributions to the Cthulhu mythos.

The whole business of this story cycle has some amusing aspects. Lovecraft and his followers were aware of the humor inherent in some of their extravagant visions and would occasionally include gags and in-jokes among their gruesome incidents. For instance, Lovecraft was fond of referring to nonexistent books that purportedly contained evil lore. One of these, the *Necronomicon* of Abdul Alhazred, was such a successful hoax that several collectors have offered astronomical prices for a copy. The frequently cited *Cultes des Ghouls* by the Comte d'Erlette was a tribute to August Derleth, and the dreaded high priest Klarkash-Ton, mentioned in several stories, was Lovecraft's California colleague Clark Ashton Smith. The most extravagant example of this kind of kidding around came about in 1934 when Robert Bloch, now most famous as the author of *Psycho*, wrote "The Shambler from the Stars," a story set in Providence which describes Lovecraft falling victim to one of his own demons. Lovecraft responded with "The Haunter of the Dark," in which a certain Robert Blake meets an equally grim fate while investigating a haunted church. This in turn set Bloch to work on "The Shadow from the Steeple."

Like Bloch, many of the writers Lovecraft inspired began when they were teenagers, but he himself did not write his first serious terror tale until the age of twenty-seven, when he produced "Dagon," a story of a sea monster suggestive of the later "Call of Cthulhu." The late-blooming author had a sickly constitution that prevented him from receiving a complete formal education; but his extensive reading made him the master of a number of historical and scientific subjects which stood him in good stead during a career that moved from brief, dreamlike fantasies to complex, lengthy tales bordering on science fiction. With a few exceptions, each story he wrote was longer than the last, as he progressively intensified his atmosphere and elaborated his plots. His work can be divided into three periods, of which the last was to prove the most popular and influential. His earliest tales, written in the manner of Lord Dunsany, were brief, slight, suggestive pieces only a few pages long, prose poems too vague for any real shock value, although some of them, like "Celephais" and "The Cats of Ulthar," do succeed in evoking the aura of imaginary ancient civilizations.

More important was a second group of stories, written in the early twenties, frequently set in New England, and often considered to have been inspired by the works of Poe, although the importance of this influence has been exaggerated. The best of these tales include "The Outsider," "The Rats in the Walls," "Pickman's Model," and "In the Vault." More effective than most of Lovecraft's more ambitious Cthulhu epics, "The Outsider" creates an authentic sense of dislocation as the amnesiac protagonist, lost in a tenantless structure with a haunting atmosphere, climbs an abandoned tower for a view of his surroundings and discovers, when he reaches the top, that he is not where he expected to be at all. This story, reprinted at the end of this chapter, is arguably the author's finest work. "Pickman's Model," which has been widely imitated, describes a Boston artist with a fondness for supernatural subjects who is discovered to be painting from life. The picture of ghouls at work in a subway sounds especially unnerving. "In the Vault" is the story of a degenerate New England undertaker who shortens a corpse to fit an undersized coffin and lives to regret it. This seems to have inspired a number of stories about reprehensible individuals in the same profession. The unusually gruesome "Rats in the Walls" features a hero who returns to his ancestral home where he discovers that his ancestors were cannibals. He immediately reverts to type.

This theme of inherited weirdness occurs in a number of Lovecraft's lesser tales like "Arthur Jermyn" and "The Lurking Fear." It also provided the plot for his finest novel, *The Case of Charles Dexter Ward*, in which a young man is possessed by the spirit of a deceased distant relative who was a black magician. This sort of treatment seems to express Lovecraft's views on evolution, which he presented not as a form of upward mobility so much as a proof that mankind has dark origins and impulses that can never be wholly eradicated.

His concept of inhuman forces at work in heredity was one manifestation of the general pattern that emerged during the last decade of his life to form the Cthulhu cycle. He wrote, "All my stories, unconnected as they may be, are based on the fundamental lore or legend that this world was inhabited at one time by another race who, in practicing black magic, lost their foothold and were expelled, yet live on outside ever ready to take possession of this earth again."

It should be made clear that this statement represents Lovecraft's fictional position and not a conscious personal belief. He claimed to be a skeptic, an atheist, and a materialist, and one of the most interesting features of his personality is the contrast between his philosophy and his fantasy life. It was his theory that people who believed in the supernatural would find it as dull as anything else they take for granted. Although Lovecraft never developed quite that attitude toward the inhuman entities he imagined, his last tales show the development of a strange kind of tolerance. His earlier portrayals of the Great Old Ones are uniformly ghastly, perhaps best exemplified by "The Colour Out of Space," in which a strange force blights the Massachusetts countryside, a tale remarkable for its anticipation of the horrors of radiation poisoning. His later, longer tales of the Cthulhu mythos begin to carry overtones of sympathy and even identification with the monsters, whose immortality and ability to range through space and time give them opportunities for scientific investigation, through which Lovecraft projects his own curiosity about the mysteries of the universe. The most obvious example of this kind of development occurs in *At the Mountains of Madness*, a short novel in which an Antarctic expedition uncovers the remnants of an ancient alien civilization. Lovecraft's delight with his own creations becomes so obvious that he has to drag in a new kind of monster at the last minute to alleviate an increasingly chummy atmosphere.

Perhaps the best effort among these later stories is "The Shadow Out of Time," in which an American scientist involuntarily trades bodies with an alien bent on an exchange of information. The man returns to normal with garbled memories and serious doubts about his sanity, finally realizing the appalling truth when an archaeological investigation uncovers proof of his own presence beneath mysterious ruins, left eons before his birth.

The sense of wonder that such a story can produce is Lovecraft's greatest achievement. He transformed the archaic conventions of the supernatural story into something approaching scientific speculation, achieving in his best tales a mood that exists nowhere else in literature, not even in the works of his imitators. Yet to dismiss the best of the *Weird Tales* authors as no more than pale imitations of Lovecraft would be unfair. Many of them made important contributions in their own right, and at least one has a following which today puts him in the unenviable position of being, like H. P. Lovecraft, a writer who lived close to poverty only to become a best-selling author decades after his death.

Such was the fate of Robert E. Howard, a young Texan who wrote a handful of tales in the Lovecraft manner but who specialized in combining horror with heroics. His fondness for stalwart characters who battle incredible menaces in a series of stories puts his work close to the mainstream of the pulp magazines; but his fascination with fear and

WEIRD TALES

SEPT.

25c

THE PEOPLE OF THE BLACK CIRCLE

a smashing weird novel of eery black magic

By ROBERT E. HOWARD

SEABURY QUINN   GREYE LA SPINA

his fondness for scenes of bloody conflict, combined with a raw talent for fast-paced storytelling, are more than enough to set him apart. One of Howard's most impressive heroes is Solomon Kane, a seventeenth-century Puritan swordsman who made his debut in 1928 with the story "Red Shadows." Kane, who contends with supernatural forces in a kind of one-man crusade, has some of his wildest adventures with black magic in Africa. He is almost completely overshadowed, though—as are such other Howard creations as King Kull and Bran Mak Morn—by the appearance in 1932 of Conan, a barbaric soldier of fortune struggling for spoils and survival in a world full of sorcery and seduction. Conan's wild adventures, which eventually bring him the crown of a mythical kingdom called Aquilonia, created a sensation in *Weird Tales* for three years, cut short by Howard's suicide in 1936. Like Lovecraft's Cthulhu cycle, the Conan epic proved irresistible to later writers, several of whom have carried on Conan's career with mixed results.

The only writer to vie consistently with Howard and Lovecraft for first place in the hearts of *Weird Tales* readers was Seabury Quinn, creator of the psychic detective Jules de Grandin. Virtually unknown today, de Grandin is a fast-talking Frenchman whose accent is somewhat more preposterous than his adventures. He appears in almost a hundred solidly plotted encounters with the uncanny, beginning in 1925 with "Terror on the Links," about an ape-man running amok on a golf course. Quinn may have acquired some background information for these tales while he was editor of a mortician's trade paper called *Casket and Sunnyside.*

Another *Weird Tales* giant was Clark Ashton Smith, a Californian who can be compared to Lovecraft for his reclusiveness and his fondness for elaborate prose. Smith was originally a poet, as well as an artist and a sculptor, whose macabre verse helped inspire Lovecraft to write professionally. He in turn introduced Smith to the magazine, and the result was a group of macabre stories dripping with florid prose. Smith's ornately worded tales are generally lightened by a sly sense of humor. Most are set in exotic worlds of the distant past or future, where immoral characters meet quaintly appropriate dooms. His style delights some readers as much as it dismays others. The florid prose suddenly stopped flowing when Smith decided to abandon fiction, cutting his *Weird Tales* career almost as short as Lovecraft's or Howard's, although he outlived them both by decades.

The longest-running career to begin in the magazine seems to have been that of Robert Bloch, now still hard at work twenty years after *Weird Tales* gave up the ghost in 1954. His first contribution was a grim medieval tale of cannibalistic monks called "The Feast in the Abbey." It took him a few years to come out from under Lovecraft's shadow, but he eventually emerged with a style and substance all his own, specializing in wry, ironic stories in which horror is mixed with screwball humor. Many of Bloch's best tales are narrated in a modern slang that far removes them from the sedate solemnity of his mentor.

Strangely enough, the one who stayed closest to Lovecraft was August Derleth. A serious writer of considerable ability who wrote a number of excellent novels outside the domain of the dreadful, Derleth continued to produce supernatural stories in the Lovecraftian manner throughout his long career, in an obvious tribute to the man who inspired him to try his hand at fiction. Lovecraft and his other colleagues were more than repaid by Derleth's indefatigable efforts on their behalf, especially through publication by Arkham House, which rescued their work from obscurity and made their reputations.

This *Weird Tales* cover illustrates one of Robert E. Howard's Conan tales. The artist, Margaret Brundage, used her daughters for models. Her fondness for the female form embarrassed H. P. Lovecraft, who used to remove the covers and dispose of them.

Clark Ashton Smith, best remembered for his stories, was also a poet and a self-taught sculptor and artist. This pencil drawing, which reflects some of the flavor of his prose, depicts the head of a magician hovering over a clawed demon.

The only pulp with an influence comparable to that of *Weird Tales* was *Black Mask*, which altered the flavor of the mystery story with the "hard-boiled," hardworking, nonintellectual detectives of Dashiell Hammett and Raymond Chandler. Still, the eerie and inexplicable crime found its greatest champion during this period in the person of the Anglo-American author John Dickson Carr. His specialty is the locked-room mystery, in which there seems to be no explanation for the method of the criminal except a supernatural one. He creates an effectively macabre atmosphere in novels like *The Three Coffins* and *Castle Skull*, and his solutions, while dissipating the uncanny overtones, are often as frightening as his puzzles. Ellery Queen, another major mystery author, handled creepy cases like *The Greek Coffin Mystery* and *The Egyptian Cross Mystery*, in which the crime proves especially puzzling because all of the victims have been decapitated. Thrillers like these helped to keep the tradition of the horror story alive while detective stories were well on their way to becoming the most popular type of novel in the English-speaking world.

By this time, mysteries and horror stories were becoming so well established that parodies and comedy treatments of the mode were developing into a separate genre. The classic stage examples include *The Bat* by Mary Roberts Rinehart and Avery Hopwood, and *The Cat and the Canary* by John Willard, which was made into an excellent silent film by Paul Leni in 1927. Both concern crazed killers with animal pseudonyms, and both are set in supposedly haunted houses where comic relief is provided by the exaggerated panic of potential victims. And in October 1927, Broadway audiences got a taste of something a little stronger when the stage version of *Dracula* opened at the Fulton Theater, where it ran for almost a year. Playing the title role was a Hungarian actor, Bela Lugosi. He would repeat the role in a talking motion picture four years later, when tales of terror were beginning to reach new heights of popularity as Hollywood created images and intonations to embody the fantasies of yesterday for generations yet unborn.

THE OUTSIDER

By H. P. Lovecraft

That night the Baron dreamt of many a wo;
And all his warrior-guests, with shade and form
Of witch, and demon, and large coffin-worm,
Were long be-nightmared.

—KEATS

Unhappy is he to whom the memories of childhood bring only fear and sadness. Wretched is he who looks back upon lone hours in vast and dismal chambers with brown hangings and maddening rows of antique books, or upon awed watches in twilight groves of grotesque, gigantic, and vine-encumbered trees that silently wave twisted branches far aloft. Such a lot the gods gave to me—to me, the dazed, the disappointed; the barren, the broken. And yet I am strangely content and cling desperately to those sere memories, when my mind momentarily threatens to reach beyond to *the other*.

I know not where I was born, save that the castle was infinitely old and infinitely horrible, full of dark passages and having high ceilings where the eye could find only cobwebs and shadows. The stones in the crumbling corridors seemed always hideously damp, and there was an accursed smell everywhere, as of the piled-up corpses of dead generations. It was never light, so that I used sometimes to light candles and gaze steadily at them for relief, nor was there any sun outdoors, since the terrible trees grew high above the topmost accessible tower. There was one black tower which reached above the trees into the unknown outer sky, but that was partly ruined and could not be ascended save by a well-nigh impossible climb up the sheer wall, stone by stone.

I must have lived years in this place, but I can not measure the time. Beings must have cared for my needs, yet I can not recall any person except myself, or anything alive but the noiseless rats and bats and spiders. I think that whoever nursed me must have been shockingly aged, since my first conception of a living person was that of something mockingly like myself, yet distorted, shriveled, and decaying like the castle. To me there was nothing grotesque in the bones and skeletons that strewed some of the stone crypts deep down among the foundations. I fantastically associated these things with everyday events, and thought them more natural than the colored pictures of living beings which I found in many of the moldy books. From such books I learned all that I know. No teacher urged or guided me, and I do not recall hearing any human voice in all those years—not even my own; for although I had read of speech, I had never thought to try to speak aloud. My aspect was a matter equally unthought of, for there were no mirrors in the castle, and I merely regarded myself by instinct as akin to the youthful figures I saw drawn and painted in the books. I felt conscious of youth because I remembered so little.

Outside, across the putrid moat and under the dark mute trees, I would often lie and dream for hours about what I read in the books; and would longingly picture myself amidst gay crowds in the sunny world beyond the endless forests. Once I tried to escape from the forest, but as I went farther from the castle the shade grew denser and the air more filled with brooding fear; so that I ran frantically back lest I lose my way in a labyrinth of nighted silence.

So through endless twilights I dreamed and waited, though I knew not what I waited for. Then in the shadowy solitude my longing for light grew so frantic that I could rest no more, and I lifted entreating hands to the single black ruined tower that reached above the forest into the unknown outer sky. And at last I resolved to scale that tower, fall though I might; since it were better to glimpse the sky and perish, than to live without ever beholding day.

In the dank twilight I climbed the worn and aged stone stairs till I reached the level where they ceased, and thereafter clung perilously to small footholds leading upward. Ghastly and terrible was that dead, stairless cylinder of rock; black, ruined, and deserted, and sinister with startled bats whose wings made no noise. But more ghastly and terrible still was the slowness of my progress; for climb as I might, the darkness overhead grew no thinner, and a new chill as of haunted and venerable mold assailed me. I shivered as I wondered why I did not reach the light, and would have looked down had I dared. I fancied that night had come suddenly upon me, and vainly groped with one free hand for a window embrasure, that I might peer out and above, and try to judge the height I had attained.

All at once, after an infinity of awesome, sightless crawling up that concave and desperate precipice, I felt my head touch a solid thing, and knew I must have gained the roof, or at least some kind of floor. In the darkness I raised my free hand and tested the barrier, finding it stone and immovable. Then came a deadly circuit of the tower, clinging to whatever holds the slimy wall could give; till finally my testing hand found the barrier yielding, and I turned upward again, pushing the slab or door with my head as I used both hands in my fearful ascent. There was no light revealed above, and as my hands went higher I knew that my climb was for the nonce ended; since the slab was the trap-door of an aperture leading to a level stone surface of greater circumference than the lower tower, no doubt the floor of some lofty and capacious observation chamber. I crawled through carefully, and tried to prevent the heavy slab from falling back into place, but failed in the latter attempt. As I lay exhausted on the stone floor I heard the eerie echoes of its fall, but hoped when necessary to pry it up again.

Believing I was now at prodigious height, far above the accursed branches of the wood, I dragged myself up from the floor and fumbled about for windows, that I might look for the first time upon the sky, and the moon and stars of which I had read. But on every hand I was disappointed; since all that I found were vast shelves of marble, bearing odious oblong boxes of disturbing size. More and more I reflected, and wondered what hoary secrets might abide in this high apartment so many eons cut off from the castle below. Then unexpectedly my hands came upon a doorway, where hung a portal of stone, rough with strange chiseling. Trying it, I found it locked; but with a supreme burst of strength I overcame all obstacles and dragged it open inward. As I did so there came to me the purest ecstasy I have ever known; for shining tranquilly through an ornate grating of iron, and down a short stone passageway of steps that ascended from the newly found doorway, was the radiant full moon, which I had never before seen save in dreams and in vague visions I dared not call memories.

Fancying now that I had attained the very pinnacle of the castle, I commenced to rush up the few steps beyond the door; but the sudden veiling of the moon by a cloud caused me to stumble, and I felt my way more slowly in the dark. It was still very dark when I reached the grating—which I tried carefully and found unlocked, but which I did not open for fear of falling from the amazing height to which I had climbed. Then the moon came out.

Most demoniacal of all shocks is that of the abysmally unexpected and grotesquely unbelievable. Nothing I had before undergone could compare in terror with what I now saw; with the bizarre marvels that sight implied. The sight itself was as simple as it was stupefying, for it was merely this: instead of a dizzying prospect of treetops seen from a lofty eminence, there stretched around me on the level through the grating nothing less than *the solid ground,* decked and diversified by marble slabs and columns, and overshadowed by an ancient stone church, whose ruined spire gleamed spectrally in the moonlight.

Half unconscious, I opened the grating and staggered out upon the white gravel path that stretched away in two directions. My mind, stunned and chaotic as it was, still held the frantic craving for light; and not even the fantastic wonder which had happened could stay my course. I neither knew nor cared whether my experience was insanity, dreaming, or magic; but was determined to gaze on brilliance and gayety at any cost. I knew not who I was or what I was, or what my surroundings might be; though as I continued to stumble along I became conscious of a kind of fearsome latent memory that made my progress not wholly fortuitous. I passed under an arch out of that region of slabs and columns, and wandered through the open country; sometimes following the visible road, but sometimes leaving it curiously to tread across meadows where only occasional ruins bespoke the ancient presence of a forgotten road. Once I swam across a swift river where crumbling, mossy masonry told of a bridge long vanished.

Over two hours must have passed before I reached what seemed to be my goal, a venerable ivied castle in a thickly wooded park, maddeningly familiar, yet full of perplexing strangeness to me. I saw that the moat was filled in, and that some of the well-known towers were demolished; whilst new wings existed to confuse the beholder. But what I observed with chief interest and delight were the open windows—gorgeously ablaze with light and sending forth sound of the gayest revelry. Advancing to one of these I looked in and saw an oddly dressed company, indeed; making merry, and speaking brightly to one another. I had never, seemingly, heard human speech before and could guess only vaguely what was said. Some of the faces seemed to hold expressions that brought up incredibly remote recollections, others were utterly alien.

I now stepped through the low window into the brilliantly lighted room, stepping as I did so from my single bright moment of hope to my blackest convulsion of despair and realization. The nightmare was quick to come, for as I entered, there occurred immediately one of the most terrifying demonstrations I had ever conceived. Scarcely had I crossed the sill when there descended upon the whole company a sudden and unheralded fear of hideous intensity, distorting every face and evoking the most horrible screams from nearly every throat. Flight was universal, and in the clamor and panic several fell in a swoon and were dragged away by their madly fleeing companions. Many covered their eyes with their hands, and plunged blindly and awkwardly in their race to escape, overturning furniture and stumbling against the walls before they managed to reach one of the many doors.

The cries were shocking; and as I stood in the brilliant apartment alone and dazed, listening to their vanishing echoes, I trembled at the thought of what might be lurking near me unseen. At a casual inspection the room seemed deserted, but when I moved toward one of the alcoves I thought I detected a presence there—a hint of motion beyond the golden-arched doorway leading to another and somewhat similar room. As I approached the arch I began to perceive the presence more clearly; and then, with the first and last sound I ever uttered—a ghastly ululation that revolted me almost as poignantly as its noxious cause—I beheld in full, frightful vividness the inconceivable, indescribable, and unmentionable monstrosity which had by its simple appearance changed a merry company to a herd of delirious fugitives.

I can not even hint what it was like, for it was a compound of all that is unclean, uncanny, unwelcome, abnormal, and detestable. It was the ghoulish shade of decay, antiquity, and dissolution; the putrid, dripping eidolon of unwholesome revelation, the awful baring of that which the merciful earth should always hide. God knows it was not of this world—or no longer of this world—yet to my horror I saw in its eaten-away and bone-revealing outlines a leering, abhorrent travesty on the human shape; and in its moldy, disintegrating apparel an unspeakable quality that chilled me even more.

I was almost paralyzed, but not too much so to make a feeble effort toward flight; a backward stumble which failed to break the spell in which the nameless, voiceless monster held me. My eyes, bewitched by the glassy orbs which stared loathsomely into them, refused to close; though they were mercifully blurred, and showed the terrible object but indistinctly after the first shock. I tried to raise my hand to shut out the sight, yet so stunned were my nerves that my arm could not fully obey my will. The attempt, however, was enough to disturb my balance; so that I had to stagger forward several steps to avoid falling. As I did so I became suddenly and agonizingly aware of the *nearness* of the carrion thing, whose hideous hollow breathing I half fancied I could hear. Nearly mad, I found myself yet able to throw out a hand to ward off the fetid apparition which pressed so close; when in one cataclysmic second of cosmic nightmarishness and hellish accident *my fingers touched the rotting outstretched paw of the monster beneath the golden arch.*

I did not shriek, but all the fiendish ghouls that ride the night wind shrieked for me as in that same second there crashed down upon my mind a single and fleeting avalanche of soul-annihilating memory. I knew in that second all that had been; I remembered beyond the frightful castle and the trees, and recognized the altered edifice in which I now stood; I recognized, most terrible of all, the unholy abomination that stood leering before me as I withdrew my sullied fingers from its own.

But in the cosmos there is balm as well as bitterness, and that balm is nepenthe. In the supreme horror of that second I forgot what had horrified me, and the burst of black memory vanished in a chaos of echoing images. In a dream I fled from that haunted and accursed pile, and ran swiftly and silently in the moonlight. When I returned to the churchyard place of marble and went down the steps I found the stone trap-door immovable; but I was not sorry, for I had hated the antique castle and the trees. Now I ride with the mocking and friendly ghouls on the night wind, and play by day amongst the catacombs of Nephren-Ka in the sealed and unknown valley of Hadoth by the Nile. I know that light is not for me, save that of the moon over the rock tombs of Neb, nor any gayety save the unnamed feasts of Nitokris beneath the Great Pyramid; yet in my new wildness and freedom I almost welcome the bitterness of alienage.

For although nepenthe has calmed me, I know always that I am an outsider; a stranger in this century and among those who are still men. This I have known ever since I stretched out my fingers to the abomination within that great gilded frame; stretched out my fingers and touched *a cold and unyielding surface of polished glass.*

·7·

THE INVISIBLE RAY: MASS MEDIA

The sound of terror brought a new dimension to worlds of weirdness in the third decade of the twentieth century, arriving just in time to startle a public weighted down by a massive worldwide depression. Films, at last able to speak and even to scream, unleashed a stream of horrors, and the "monster movie" became one of the safest investments in the cutthroat world called Hollywood. Simultaneously, the burgeoning business of radio broadcasting brought a new kind of drama into millions of homes, and sinister stories were among the most welcome additions to the family circle. Horror had found a voice at last.

Of course, deadly dialogue had been available for centuries to the fortunate minority that patronized the theater, but the new media were available on a mass scale. Motion pictures in particular provided strange sights and sounds that seem to have embedded themselves permanently in the modern consciousness. The first attempt to terrify moviegoers was entitled, appropriately enough, *The Terror*, a 1928 effort from Warner Brothers, which had released the first important talking picture, *The Jazz Singer*. Directed by Roy Del Ruth from a play by England's popular mystery author Edgar Wallace, the film was just another thriller about a masked murderer on the loose in an old house, and it failed to create a sensation. The real birth of talking terror was postponed until 1931, when Universal released its version of *Dracula*, a tremendous success that set the studio on the road to becoming the major producer of macabre motion pictures for the next quarter of a century.

Director Tod Browning apparently had originally planned to feature Lon Chaney in the title role, especially after Chaney's success in the talking remake of the mystery story *The Unholy Three* (1930); but the actor's unexpected death necessitated a change of plans. Eventually, Browning recruited Bela Lugosi, who had taken the part on Broadway, and thus a legend was born. Lugosi, with his slicked-back black hair, piercing eyes, predatory profile, and rich Hungarian accent, became permanently identified with the role, even though he played it only twice in films (and on one of these occasions, at that, in a comedy). He looked almost nothing like the white-haired, mustachioed old man described by Bram Stoker; but Lugosi's highly theatrical performance was so effective that his face has become Dracula's face and his voice, Dracula's voice. His stately, slightly overripe readings of lines like "I never drink . . . wine" and "I am taking with

130

me only three . . . boxes" come perilously close to comedy; but he makes an impressively sinister figure nonetheless.

Although there were a few slight changes, the film *Dracula* was closely based on actor Hamilton Deane's stage version. The unfortunate decision to use the play was understandable in view of its considerable success, but it made the movie less vivid than it should have been. As it was, the film coasted on the strength of its first few minutes, set amid the grim gray mountains of Transylvania. The script replaced the traveling real-estate salesman Jonathan Harker with Renfield, the madman who comes under Dracula's power in the book; he is here at least given a good reason for losing his grip on reality. His ride to Castle Dracula in a coach whose driver is suddenly replaced by a bat, his confrontation with the Count who passes through a giant spider web without disturbing it, and his climactic encounter with Dracula's three undead wives all build to an appropriately creepy crescendo. He travels with Dracula on the ship bound for

Bela Lugosi carries Helen Chandler into his lair in this scene from the climax of Tod Browning's 1931 film *Dracula. Courtesy of Universal Pictures.*

England and is completely batty by the time he is discovered as the only man alive among a crew of corpses. The lunatic laughter coming from the ship's hold remains one of the most haunting sounds in the history of horror movies. Renfield, who has some of the best moments later in the film as the man who knows more about Dracula than anybody wants to hear, was portrayed by Dwight Frye. This actor was subsequently cast in several famous films as a half-witted apprentice fiend, but *Dracula* gave him his meatiest role.

Another actor who had his work cut out for him after appearing in the film was Edward Van Sloan, who played the wise old enemy of evil, Dr. Van Helsing. Stern and inflexible, the white-haired gentleman with the wire-rimmed spectacles would return to do battle with many of Hollywood's most menacing monsters. His cat-and-mouse scenes with Lugosi provide most of the tension in the lackluster later portions of the film. The script seems to shy away from what should be its most shocking moments. The fact that Lucy has become a vampire is passed over in a few lines of limp dialogue, and Dracula's death scene is shown only in a shot of the heroine Mina (Helen Chandler) experiencing sympathy pains that look like a mild case of heartburn. The only blood in this film version of the bloodiest of all horror tales is the sample that Renfield squeezes out of his finger after cutting it accidentally on a paper clip. Still, Dracula's approving smile as Renfield sucks on the wounded finger is one of the film's best moments.

Dracula's merits for today's audiences may rest almost entirely on the performances of Lugosi, Frye, and Van Sloan; but it thrilled the public in 1931 and pointed the way for Universal to save itself from the hard times that threatened many major studios during the dark days of the early thirties, when economic chaos was complicated by the technical problem of transition to "talkies." The next obvious step was a follow-up film, which proved to be considerably better. In fact, it is the most famous film in its field, although admittedly *Dracula* remains a close second.

Frankenstein (1931) was a free, modernized adaptation of Mary Shelley's novel; it made a star of its monster, Boris Karloff (born William Henry Pratt). The plot of this picture, which leaves Frankenstein alive and explains his creation's hostility away as the result of an accidental "criminal brain" transplant, may leave something to be desired; but solid supporting players and sensitive direction by James Whale helped to save it. What makes it a classic, though, is the vivid yet understated performance of Karloff, who somehow infuses the character of the mute brute with a sensitive, almost poetic spirit. Another decisive factor is the shocking disguise designed for Karloff by Jack Pierce who, as Universal's makeup man, would create some of the world's most famous faces out of whole cloth. The square-skulled, bleary-eyed creature with the scar on his forehead and the electrodes in his throat has become a piece of visual folklore, although it remains protected by Universal's copyright. The face was very much designed for Karloff's features; it was considerably less effective in some of the numerous sequels when applied to other actors, among them, eventually, Bela Lugosi, who rejected this plum of a part in the original version either because he objected to the heavy makeup it would entail or because the monster had no lines. (Both explanations have been offered for his refusal to play the role; possibly it was the combination of drawbacks that convinced him it would hurt his career.)

Frankenstein himself was played with appropriate hysteria by Colin Clive; the screenplay by Garrett Fort and Francis Faragoh inexplicably changed his name to Henry and made his best friend Victor. Clive's most memorable scene occurs when the monster is vitalized after a pyrotechnical display of lightning flashes and electrical equipment. The monster is entirely swathed in bandages except for an indecently naked hand which twitches spasmodically as Clive screams "It's alive! It's alive!" His handiwork is revealed the next morning dressed in an undersized black suit; Karloff makes an unlikely entrance by backing through a door, apparently only so he can turn slowly to reveal his fearsome face. A skylight opens in the ceiling and the monster bathes himself in the light, raising his arms to the sun as though in worship; the scene recalls his creator's earlier lines about the discovery of a mysterious ray, the one that brought life into the world.

Dwight Frye and Edward Van Sloan returned in this film; Frye as Fritz, Frankenstein's hunchbacked assistant who so goads the monster by beating it that it finally murders him; and Van Sloan as Frankenstein's teacher, who becomes the second victim when he attempts to dissect the monster, rendered unconscious all too temporarily by a powerful drug. This leaves the monster free to roam the country, but his liberty is short. After murdering a few peasants and making a pass at Frankenstein's fiancée, he is chased back to Frankenstein's laboratory in an abandoned windmill by an army of torch-bearing villagers and is there consumed in flames. The combination of fire and an indignant population proved impressive; it was used again to end dozens of later films, including several more with the same monster. The final scene of *Frankenstein* shows the hero's relieved father preparing for his son's wedding with a toast: "Here's to a son to the house of Frankenstein!" He was to get his wish—and more. The film launched a series of seven sequels from Universal alone, to say nothing of the many others that emerged from other studios in later decades.

Universal's next effort was considerably less impressive. Directed by Robert Florey, who had almost been put in charge of *Frankenstein*, *The Murders in the Rue Morgue* (1932) starred Bela Lugosi as a nineteenth-century mad scientist who conducts a series of fruitless experiments having something to do with blood transfusions between people and his pet gorilla. Some evocative sets and a curly-headed Lugosi could hardly compensate for the fact that an actor in a monkey suit is rarely awe inspiring.

Karloff fared considerably better with his second effort into the uncanny, *The Mummy* (1932), a powerful tale of a reanimated Egyptian that had no direct literary source but was concocted out of nothing in particular by light humorist Nina Wilcox Putnam. This subtle film featured only a few minutes of Karloff as a half-decayed figure wrapped in bandages. After being resurrected by a foolhardy archaeologist reading an ancient scroll, the mummy Im-Ho-Tep disappears, showing up years later as a comparatively presentable modern Egyptian. Only extreme close-ups reveal his glowing eyes and dehydrated flesh. He plans to revive the ancient princess for whose love he had been buried alive thousands of years before; but her preserved body collapses in the museum where he finds it, and he is forced to seek out her reincarnation. The young lady in question responds by calling on an ancient goddess for protection from his unwelcome advances. A statue answers her plea with a beam of unearthly light, and Karloff disintegrates into dust in a pioneering piece of camera wizardry by Universal's special-effects artist, John P. Fulton. He was finally honored with an Academy Award in 1956 when, after years of brilliant work, he parted the Red Sea for Cecil B. De Mille's *Ten Commandments*. *The Mummy* was directed by Karl Freund, a cameraman who had photographed *Dracula* as well as most of Fritz Lang's silent fantasies in Germany. Featured in the cast as an expert on ancient curses was, not too surprisingly, Edward Van Sloan.

Universal had uncovered a box office bonanza with its horror films, and its rival studios were quick to get in on the action. None succeeded better than Paramount, which

Zita Johann confronts Boris Karloff who, despite his efforts to disguise his wizened visage, can only be _The Mummy_ (1932). _Courtesy of Universal Pictures._

scored a tremendous coup by releasing a monster movie that won an Oscar for its star, Fredric March, performing the dual role in the finest version of the frequently filmed _Dr. Jekyll and Mr. Hyde_ (1932). Director Rouben Mamoulian's version of the story remains the only film in the genre to have received such a major Academy Award, although March's performance is not really the best ever offered in a macabre motion picture. Nevertheless, March created quite an impression by overplaying both parts, making Jekyll cold and dull and Hyde a rambunctious brute whose outrageously ugly appearance created a new convention at odds with the literary source. This version continued the tradition of the 1920 Barrymore film, focusing on affairs with two women, one representing vice and the other, virtue. This emphasis served to provide a spurious sort of suspense involving the fate of the new characters while shifting attention away from the more complex topic of Jekyll's dilemma. The movie is most impressive in its visual effects. The transformations from Jekyll to Hyde surpassed anything ever seen on the screen in the way of technical wizardry, and the photography throughout conveys a feeling of menace and dislocation through a variety of unusual perspectives.

The same year saw the release of one of the most disturbing and controversial films ever made: _Freaks_, from Metro-Goldwyn-Mayer. It was directed by Tod Browning, fresh from his lucrative adaptation of _Dracula_; but it proved to be anything but a money-maker. Audiences proved as queasy as distributors when confronted with this bizarre look at the world of circus sideshows in which most of the cast consisted of actual freaks. The plot involves a physically normal performer named Cleopatra who seduces a midget into marriage to get her hands on his inheritance. The freaks accept her into their community, only to discover that she and her strong man lover plan to murder her little husband. The freaks take up arms, killing Cleopatra's confederate and turning her, improbably enough, into a chicken with the head of a woman. This transformation, which could hardly have been accomplished by any natural method, seems to imply that the freaks have supernatural powers; but it is introduced so abruptly that it appears merely absurd. The film's power lies in the way Browning manipulates audience reactions: pinheaded or limbless characters overcome the viewers' initial dismay and engage their sympathy; but as the freaks pursue the larcenous lovers through a thunderstorm they once again become sources of shock. One brief shot of an armless, legless man crawling rapidly through the mud with a knife in his teeth, emerging from under a circus wagon like a gigantic worm, is particularly dismaying. This sort of material puts *Freaks* in a very different category from the mainstream of horror films, which, however gruesome or depraved, are clearly works of the imagination.

The MGM studio was far better served, commercially speaking, by its second 1932 venture into the grotesque, a corny but engaging adaptation of Sax Rohmer's *Mask of Fu Manchu*, with Boris Karloff in the title role. In the same year, Karloff also appeared in Universal's *Old Dark House*, playing a brutish, bearded butler in this haunted-house thriller directed by James Whale.

Bela Lugosi, who generally chose his roles less carefully than his horror colleague, got a fairly good part for a preposterously small fee in the independently produced *White Zombie*. This tale of black magic in Haiti has a poetic charm generated in large measure by its unsophisticated melodramatics. It is, at least, the best of the low-budget productions that emanated from the minor Hollywood studios during the depression and the Second World War.

Among the other major studios that took a stab at scaring money out of their customers during 1932 were RKO, with *The Most Dangerous Game*; and Warner Brothers, with *Dr. X*. The former, based on a famous short story by Richard Connell, concerns a hunter (Leslie Banks) who stages shipwrecks to bring human prey to his island home; the latter depicts a series of stranglings committed by a one-armed scientist who has concocted a formula for building a new limb out of "synthetic flesh." *Dr. X* was the first horror film shot in color, although there had been a few color scenes in Lon Chaney's silent *Phantom of the Opera*. There was an unrelated "sequel," *The Return of Dr. X*, in 1939, interesting only because the role of the sinister scientist, who in this incarnation kept himself alive with constant blood transfusions, was played by Humphrey Bogart.

Warner Brothers followed *Dr. X* with another color film, *The Mystery of the Wax Museum* (1933). It featured the same heroine, Fay Wray, as well as Doctor X himself, Lionel Atwill. This sauve, sinister actor was to enliven many a morbid movie with his icy intensity. In the 1932 film he had been a red herring dragged across the trail of the real killer; but he is definitely up to no good in the wax museum as its crazed proprietor who makes dummies of all his victims. His antisocial behavior is attributed to a fire that destroyed an earlier exhibition as well as most of his face; the climax of the film comes when the struggling heroine punches Atwill in the nose, shattering the wax mask that has disguised him from her as well as the audience. The unexpected revelation of his disfigured features is still remembered as a moment of true terror by those who have seen *The Mystery of the Wax Museum*. Atwill reported an ironic result of his care in performing the part: having read the script and realizing that his face was supposed to be a mask, he was careful to keep his features as immobile as possible. The result was so effective that the producers, anxious to preserve their surprise ending, removed almost all his close-ups from the final print.

Fay Wray had already begun to establish a reputation as the screen's shrillest screamer; she was to have her finest hour in the hands of Hollywood's most lovable monster, a fifty-foot gorilla named Kong. The special effects in this 1933 RKO release have never been duplicated. Since *King Kong* appeared there have been dozens of films about oversized creatures wreaking havoc; but few have benefited from such time and care as technician Willis O'Brien expended, and none has been able to endow the central character with the vividly expressed personality that made Kong such a delight. O'Brien had begun his experiments with miniature models to be enlarged by double exposures back in the silent era, when he engineered a troupe of dinosaurs for the 1925 production *The Lost World.* Adapted from a novel by Arthur Conan Doyle, the plot of this film, in which prehistoric animals are discovered and brought back to civilization, is similar to that of *King Kong.* What the newer film provided was a sympathetic menace and a disheveled blond heroine whose tempestuous affair really deserved the publicity campaign that had described Browning's version of *Dracula* as the "Strangest Love Story of All." What Kong might have in mind for the lady can only be imagined; he seems to be content to carry her around clenched in his hairy fist—or so it seems, since the scene in which he curiously removes her clothes was eliminated by the studio censor. After all, she was a movie star (the expedition that uncovered Kong was a search for some spectacular film footage), and the giant ape may have been no more than the world's biggest Fay Wray fan. There are some interesting similarities between the roles assigned to the monster and the heroine; they first meet when she is trussed up as a sacrifice by the mob of savages who worship Kong, and his first appearance in Manhattan finds him in the same sort of predicament, displayed in chains for the benefit of a jaded theater audience. His sudden escape to wreak havoc upon the metropolis may well be what killed vaudeville. Kong's climactic battle against modern civilization is the most memorable portion of this famous film; audiences depressed by economic disaster were apparently delighted to watch a brute force assaulting their disappointing civilization. The great ape destroys an elevated train as if it were one of the hapless dinosaurs of his island home, and he meets his end when an attack by a squadron of biplanes with machine guns turns his last stand atop the Empire State Building into an aviator's shooting gallery. Kong's death scene, while a trifle hammy, is one of the most famous in the history of the cinema.

The popular success of the film led almost immediately to a sequel, *Son of Kong* (1933), a movie that must bear the responsibility for inaugurating the tradition of naming sequels after the relatives of successful monsters. Kong, Jr., proved to be a smaller but still impressive white gorilla named Kiko, considerably more sociable than his father. He watches over the crew who returns to Kong's island (including actor Robert Armstrong, who had discovered Junior's more impressive forebear) and eventually sacrifices his life to save his human acquaintances from a flood. Kong's son was the most altruistic monster ever presented on the screen, but that seems to have counted against him. The primary function of a fictional fiend is to express the audience's suppressed hostility; by this standard, *Son of Kong* was somewhat disappointing.

Universal retaliated in the same year with a more subtle but nevertheless impressive adaptation of H. G. Wells's novel *The Invisible Man.* The special effects by John P. Fulton were less spectacular than those in the *Kong* films; but they were still eerie and effective, especially when augmented by James Whale's witty direction and an intense vocal

Above, Kong battles a ptero-dactyl for the privilege of escorting Fay Wray around Skull Island in *King Kong*, a film enriched by Max Steiner's musical score, one of the first supplied for a sound horror film. *RKO Radio Pictures.*

Right, Claude Rains contem-plates his troubles in *The Invisible Man* (1933). The beautiful detail of the artificial nose poking out from the bandages was ignored in subsequent treatments of the subject. *Courtesy of Universal Pictures.*

performance by Claude Rains. The scene in which Rains unwraps the bandages around his head to reveal a visual vacancy is still amazing, especially because Fulton took the trouble to show the back of the wrapping encircling the invisible head—the kind of detail overlooked by later imitators. Rains became one of a number of performers who used fantasy films to establish themselves as serious actors.

The Invisible Man demonstrated the eminent adaptability of the short science fiction novels by Wells, many of which seem to have been written for the screen. Further proof was offered by Paramount's 1933 production *The Island of Lost Souls*, a version of his *Island of Dr. Moreau*. Charles Laughton plays the demented doctor whose jungle retreat is an experimental laboratory for attempts to turn beasts into human beings through surgery; Bela Lugosi plays the leader of the beast-men who turn on their creator when they realize that he is ignoring the commandments he has given them.

The fact that *The Island of Lost Souls* featured a whole menagerie of monsters may have inspired Universal to costar its two major menaces, Karloff and Lugosi, in the 1934 feature *The Black Cat*. Only the title was retained from a story by Poe; the new plot concerned a Hungarian Satanist (Karloff) tormenting a comparatively normal physician who finally goes mad when he realizes that his wife and daughter have been stuffed in his enemy's cellar. As the doctor, Lugosi finally proves himself to be more offensive by skinning the devil worshiper alive. The unlikely events are justified principally by the performances of the stars, whose scenes together communicate a convincing mood of mounting conflict.

The natural result of the successful collaboration was another effort along the same lines, complete with another spurious Poe title, *The Raven* (1935). Lugosi portrayed a plastic surgeon who seeks revenge when a young woman he has cured spurns his love. He coerces a fugitive killer (Karloff) into assisting him with an operation which turns the gangster into a revolting mutant, and he embarks on a preposterous course of vengeance based on a series of torture devices, most of them derived from Poe's story of the Spanish Inquisition, "The Pit and the Pendulum." The surgeon is a fairly incompetent fiend, since he fails to eliminate any of the victims he has invited to his house for a weekend of terror; but the film almost overcomes its own shortcomings by the entertainment value of its outrageous melodramatics.

The best of the Karloff-Lugosi features is *The Invisible Ray* (1936), directed by Lambert Hillyer. This was the first film to suggest the possibility of radiation poisoning, as a

Universal's top horror stars, Karloff and Lugosi, meet across a chessboard in their elegant but insubstantial first encounter, *The Black Cat*, stylishly directed by Edgar G. Ulmer.

Elsa Lanchester meets Boris Karloff and wishes she had never been built in this scene from the tragicomic *Bride of Frankenstein* (1935).
Courtesy of Universal Pictures.

scientist, portrayed by Karloff, is contaminated by a new element he discovers in a meteorite. As a result, he glows in the dark and his very touch is fatal. The ray has power for good as well as evil; it can kill, but it also cures blindness, and it seems to be closely allied with the mysterious force described in the 1931 *Frankenstein*. The film comes closer than most of its genre to a serious consideration of science's strange trials and temptations, although Karloff inevitably goes "mad" and eliminates a good portion of the cast, including a sympathetic colleague played by Lugosi. Eventually the protagonist meets one of the most ignominious ends in the history of film fiends: he is destroyed like a naughty child by his own mother, who deprives him of the formula that keeps his crazy chemistry in balance.

A year earlier, in 1935, Universal had released the first in a long string of sequels, James Whale's *Bride of Frankenstein*. Many consider it to be superior to the original, and it is a vastly entertaining film, but one that replaces the grim mood of *Frankenstein* with considerable amounts of comedy and pathos. The monster escapes from the burning windmill, but his awesome appearance is almost immediately undercut by the humorously exaggerated reactions of the old lady who witnesses his resurrection. Subsequent scenes of his flight through a forest reproduce the tone and some of the incidents of the original novel. The monster saves a shepherdess from drowning and is wounded by hunters for his pains, and he finds temporary refuge in the cottage of an old blind man, who welcomes him as a friend. The scenes with the hermit (O. P. Heggie) contain some embarrassingly sentimental moments as the old man thanks God for sending him a friend, weeping while his grotesque guest pats him on the back and strains of "Ave Maria" swell up on the sound track. He also teaches the creature a few words, and the unfortunate effect of the subsequent dialogue is that the monster seems more a stupid brute than the uncanny figure of his first appearances. Karloff delivers his clumsy lines as well as can be expected; only years after the film was made did he reveal his distress at the changes in the character that had brought him fame.

The real point of *The Bride of Frankenstein* is the creation of the monster's mate; but this is delayed until the last few minutes, while Frankenstein (again Colin Clive) teeters between terror and the temptation to try again. Providing most of the impetus is a crackpot old scientist named Dr. Praetorius, portrayed with sinister glee by Ernest Thesiger. Introduced as Frankenstein's former teacher, he sparks the young scientist's imagination with a display of his own handiwork, a group of miniature humans wearing fanciful costumes and living in bottles. This ludicrous collection is not as persuasive as the monster who, on orders from Dr. Praetorius, kidnaps Frankenstein's bride, thus ensuring the young man's cooperation in the creation of a female monster. One nasty-minded writer came up with the idea that parts of Mrs. Frankenstein might be used to manufacture the monster's mate; but this notion was Universally rejected. Instead, anonymous donors provide the raw material for film history's most famous femme fatale, who is spectacularly animated in a fantastic electrical laboratory designed by Kenneth Strickfaden. As played by Elsa Lanchester (who also portrayed Mary Shelley in the film's brief prologue), the monstress is considerably more presentable than her intended spouse. Looking almost human beneath a wild hairdo that still seems charged with lightning, she loses no time in expressing disgust for her pathetically eager suitor; he responds fatalistically by blowing up the laboratory with a switch conveniently, if improbably, designed for just that purpose. Mr. and Mrs. Frankenstein are allowed to escape, to provide the stock Hollywood ending and some offspring to populate future sequels.

The Bride of Frankenstein marked the climax of the depression's Hollywood horror cycle and the beginning of the end as well. Its horrors were too fully humanized, and while such a technique might work once, it became self-defeating when employed as standard operating procedure. A spate of similarly self-conscious productions left frightening films as dead as Dracula by 1936. Universal's *Werewolf of London* (1935) attempted without much success to capitalize on the legends of lycanthropy. It concentrated largely on the hero's efforts to cure his condition, and even in his bestial form Henry Hull seems incapable of much enthusiasm. Even the expert technicians seemed asleep at the switch: Jack Pierce's makeup job was sketchy, and John Fulton's shaky special effects required Hull to pass behind a row of pillars as each stage of the transformation from man to monster was revealed. The film did at least establish the motion picture tradition that werewolves are not men who turn into wolves, but men who turn into hairy men with fangs and claws.

Equally disappointing was MGM's *Mark of the Vampire* (1935), Tod Browning's remake of the silent *London after Midnight*. What makes the film so infuriating is that it contains a

Carol Borland yields to Bela Lugosi in a bloodsucking scene that turns out to be only playacting, from Tod Browning's tricky *Mark of the Vampire* (1935). *Courtesy of MGM.*

few minutes of the most eerie and evocative vampire scenes ever filmed, but they are interspersed with great stretches of dull exposition, and the conclusion of the film reveals that the supernatural manifestations are only a hoax. Bela Lugosi and Carol Borland are impressive in what are, unfortunately, no more than bit parts.

The last nail in the coffin of fearsome film fare was provided by Universal's 1936 offering, *Dracula's Daughter*. The plot was not really based, as the studio claimed, on Bram Stoker's short story "Dracula's Guest," which was an early portion of the original novel excised before the first printing. Rather, *Dracula's Daughter* was a sequel to the Lugosi film, in which the count's vampiric heiress appears in London to claim her father's body. The sequel makes up for the telescoped version of the novel by returning most of the characters to Transylvania for the climax, something its predecessor had failed to do; but it is, for the most part, an anemic effort. Perhaps out of misguided deference to the "weaker sex," the script depicts its title character (Gloria Holden) as a reluctant leech who spends most of her time bemoaning her condition and seeking medical advice. Her backsliding is so apparent that she is eliminated, not by the forces of good, but by a disgusted underling with a bow and arrow. This ingenious variation on the obligatory wooden stake passed almost unnoticed for decades, but it was to become a cliché of latter-day vampire epics.

For audiences of the depressing thirties, and perhaps for all followers of the genre, much of the pleasure to be derived from horror films depends on the presence of a purposeful menace, rather than one plagued by doubt and indecision or explained away as part of a rational plan as in *Mark of the Vampire*. And so in 1936 the movie monsters crawled back into their crypts, only to be resurrected three years later when a revival of the original *Dracula* and *Frankenstein* demonstrated that the right kind of macabre motion picture was more popular than ever.

Meanwhile, radio broadcasting had developed into a successful commercial enterprise. Just as the movies were discovering sound, the public discovered radio, and a new medium for drama was born, one that soon proved eminently suitable for the presentation of mysterious melodramas. The earliest and most successful radio series with a macabre theme was "The Shadow." Perhaps the best-remembered program in the history of radio drama, "The Shadow" was on the airwaves in one form or another for a quarter of a century, covering nearly all the years in which plays were broadcast. The program and the title character evolved gradually from a primitive effort in the late twenties called "Street and Smith's Detective Story Magazine Hour." Originally, the program consisted of no more than an actor reading stories from the popular pulp magazine, but writer Harry Charlot suggested that the narrator (James La Curto) should be called the Shadow, and a character gradually evolved to become the principal figure in the stories he had been designed to tell. He soon became so impressive that publishers Street and Smith inaugurated a new magazine named after him. The Shadow in print, however, was a different character than the one on the radio. In his magazine incarnation, as conceived by writer Walter Gibson under the pseudonym Maxwell Grant, the Shadow was a black-clad crime fighter whose principal weapons were a pair of huge revolvers. The radio Shadow was above such crude tactics, preferring to torment the wicked into betraying themselves through a more subtle use of supernatural powers. He had learned in the Orient how to "cloud men's minds" so that he was, in effect, invisible. Common criminals were obviously no match for him, so script writers frequently pitted him against more exotic menaces like werewolves, vampires, zombies, mad scientists, and even beings from outer space. Somehow, none of them was as frightening as the Shadow himself, even though he seemed perfectly personable in his secret identity as a wealthy playboy named Lamont Cranston. The Shadow's most popular lines were "The weed of crime bears bitter fruit" and "Who knows what evil lurks in the hearts of men? The Shadow knows!" They were followed by bursts of maniacal laughter which strongly suggested that his knowledge of evil was based on personal experiences never revealed to the public. Actors who assumed the role included Frank Readick, Robert Hardy Andrews, Bill Johnstone, Bret Morrison, and, for a two-year stretch beginning in 1937, a young actor named Orson Welles, who would soon be involved in a broadcast that must be counted as the most successful attempt to scare audiences in the history of mass communications.

A crew of less exotic heroes confronted a similar series of bizarre villains in a radio series called "I Love a Mystery." A trio of fun-loving adventurers operating out of a detective agency, Jack Packard, Doc Long, and Reggie York were the creations of Carlton E. Morse, a pioneer in radio drama whose offerings were usually a bit more sedate. The "I Love a Mystery" crew handled many a bizarre case, including one, "The Decapitation of Jefferson Monk," that was made into a movie. Their most notorious adventure, "The Temple of the Vampires," was frequently revived during the program's run from 1939 to 1952.

In addition to the weird adversaries that some of radio's popular heroes encountered, broadcasting unleashed on the public a plethora of preternatural personalities whose horrors went virtually unopposed. A surprising number of programs took to the air with no regular characters to sustain them, only the promise of a series of unrelated sinister stories. Yet the programs that were dramatic anthologies of terror tales enjoyed considerable success during the decades of radio's finest hours. Among them were "Inner Sanctum," "Suspense," "Superstition," "The Hermit's Cave," "The Haunting Hour," "The Weird Circle," "The Sealed Book," "The Witch's Tales," "Stay Tuned for Terror," "Starring Boris Karloff," "Lights Out," and even, briefly, the redundantly titled "The Strange Dr. Weird," starring Maurice Tarplin.

The most memorable of the group was "Inner Sanctum," which began in January 1941 under the more evocative title "The Squeaking Door." The original title contained the key to the program's success. The stories were frequently mechanical murder mysteries; but they basked in the uncanny aura created by a sound-effects man and the show's host, Raymond Edward Johnson, who introduced himself simply as Raymond. His slow, sardonic introductions invited the listeners into the dark room of their own imaginations, accompanied by the sound of a massive portal creaking on rusty hinges. When the door finally slammed shut at the end of the half-hour, cutting short Raymond's insincere farewell ("Good night, and pleasant dreams"), the audience was ready for nightmares. Johnson and his producer Himan Brown more or less created the tradition of the horror story hosted by a sinister, sarcastic spokesman; the technique was subsequently used in films, in comic books, and on television. Indeed, "Inner Sanctum" was one of the few radio programs of any type to make a successful transition to video, showing the squeaking door in all its splendor while Raymond remained modestly off camera.

Most of the other programs were pale imitations of these. "The Hermit's Cave" made more of an impression than most because its cantankerous caretaker came across as a convincing character and because most of his narratives eschewed simple or even complicated murder stories in favor of tales with a more uncanny flavor. "Lights Out," a spin-off from an earlier program called "Everyman's Theater," showcased the works of writer Arch Oboler, who had an unusual grasp of the techniques that could turn sounds and the spoken word into a compelling dramatic experience. Among his best efforts were

"Two" (with Joan Crawford and Raymond Edward Johnson), a play about the end of the earth; and "The Ugliest Man in the World," a surprisingly sentimental offering that was repeated five times by popular request. The most notorious "Lights Out" program concerned a scientist whose experiments with cell structure accidentally produce a chicken heart that grows until it threatens to absorb the entire planet.

Not as well known but equally skillful were the scripts prepared by Robert Bloch for "Stay Tuned for Terror." Bloch, a *Weird Tales* author who began as a disciple of Lovecraft, had found his own style in the years after his mentor's death. His specialty was a sort of gallows humor that bore some resemblance to that employed by Ambrose Bierce, but Bloch's work was distinguished by a particularly modern flavor, in which the skepticism and slang of twentieth-century life were contrasted with ancient terrors. His most famous story, "Yours Truly, Jack the Ripper," became the most renowned offering of "Stay Tuned for Terror." Virtually unrelieved by Bloch's usual comic touches, the script hypothesized that the murders perpetrated by the nineteenth century's notorious mass killer were part of a ritual by which he achieved immortality, forcing him to enact a similar series of crimes at regular intervals in his endless career. It seemed as reasonable a theory as any to account for the sporadic outbreaks of senseless slaughter that have plagued contemporary civilization.

Despite their merits, all these efforts to unnerve radio listeners pale beside what was achieved by "The Mercury Theater" on October 30, 1938. Its version of the H. G. Wells novel *The War of the Worlds* scared more people more thoroughly than any work of the imagination ever created. Most of the credit (or blame) must go to actor and coproducer Orson Welles, who conceived the plan to modernize the 1898 novel, shift the locale from England to the United States, and, most important, to present the story as a series of news announcements interrupting a musical program. Several announcements during the program explaining its fictional nature were missed or ignored by thousands of radio fans who became firmly convinced that their planet had in fact been attacked by monsters from Mars. The result was a mass panic, especially in New Jersey, where scriptwriter Howard Koch had decided the Martians would land first. The most common extreme reaction was to jump into a car and flee from the invaders. Fortunately no one was seriously injured, and within a few days the broadcast was accepted by most Americans as a great joke, while a few serious thinkers paused to analyze public impressionability to official-sounding statements. Welles and his coproducer John Houseman claimed that their intentions were perfectly innocent; but they were soon on their way, along with writer Howard Koch, to distinguished careers in the motion picture industry. If any of them had any idea of the sensation they would cause, they have never admitted it.

On a much more modest scale, pulp magazines continued their campaign to keep readers on the edges of their seats. *Weird Tales* struggled on, producing some excellent fiction and no profits; yet its grim financial condition failed to discourage competition. Inspired by the success of Hollywood horrors, several pulp publishers ventured into the domain of the macabre, usually with motives somewhat less lofty than those that kept *Weird Tales* afloat. An outfit modestly designated as Culture Publications started a new slant on the literature of terror with its magazine *Spicy Mystery*. This was just one of a whole line of "spicy" titles, dedicated to the proposition that sex, or as much of it as the censors would allow, could sell magazines. The term "mystery" was used here to designate uncanny events rather than criminal cases; but the principal emphasis was on the "spicy," and the thrust of the stories was toward sadism. Elements of this sort of eroticism are present, of course, in many artistically accomplished works of the macabre,

Weird Tales

is on the air . . . . in

STAY TUNED FOR TERROR

This programme is adapted by
ROBERT BLOCH from his stories
which have appeared in WEIRD
TALES, the narrator being Craig
Dennis.

STAY TUNED FOR TERROR is
produced by Neblett Radio Productions, with the active cooperation of
WEIRD TALES MAGAZINE . . .
for the enjoyment of fantasy fans
everywhere.

LOOK FOR ANNOUNCEMENTS
IN YOUR LOCAL NEWSPAPER
giving the broadcast time and dates
in your area.

~ ★ ~

And remember to . . . .

Stay Tuned for Terror!

Boris Dolgov designed
this ad to inform
Weird Tales readers
that Robert Bloch's
stories were also
available on the radio.

but the offerings in *Spicy Mystery* were crude and monotonous. The same sort of hackwork formula was repeated in *Dime Mystery*, *Horror Stories*, and *Terror Tales*, all the products of Popular Publications. Other publishers followed suit, and the slightly perverted horror pulps flourished for a decade, finally dying out during the Second World War when many of their producers began converting to comic books. This new type of magazine became a major factor in the decline and eventual disappearance of the pulps.

Bucking the tide was the one pulp magazine to rival the esteem in which aficionados of fantasy held *Weird Tales.* This was Street and Smith's *Unknown*, edited by John W. Campbell, Jr. *Unknown*, whose title was later changed to *Unknown Worlds*, appeared in the midst of a failing market and only lasted from 1939 until 1943. Yet in those few short years it managed to acquire a reputation that still survives. Regular *Unknown* authors developed a characteristically light, whimsical mood. There were darker moments; but the typical tale recognized the humorous incongruity of the supernatural in urban life and demonstrated that even magical intervention in the affairs of men was unlikely to relieve the frustration of the human condition. Wisecracks worked hand in hand with hexes, creating a hybrid horror style that juxtaposed legendary legerdemain with contemporary complications. Among the writers who helped to establish the flavor of this short-lived but influential publication was L. Sprague de Camp who specialized in novels like *Lest Darkness Fall*, a tale of a modern historian adrift in ancient Rome which owed something of its concept to Mark Twain's *Connecticut Yankee in King Arthur's Court.* Fritz Leiber, Jr., created a lighthearted variation on Robert E. Howard's sword-and-sorcery

Unknown World's chief artist, Edd Cartier, came up with this vision of Fritz Leiber's "Smoke Ghost," a sinister spirit of the sooty city. *Copyright © 1941 by Street and Smith Publications, Inc. Copyright © (renewed) 1969 by The Condé Nast Publications Inc.*

One of Edd Cartier's illustrations for Henry Kuttner's "A Gnome There Was," an apparently humorous story that, with typical *Unknown* duplicity, slips suddenly into stark horror. *Copyright © 1941 by Street and Smith Publications, Inc. Copyright © (renewed) 1969 by The Condé Nast Publications Inc.*

sagas with a series of stories about the ancient adventurers Fafhrd and the Gray Mouser; more characteristic of the *Unknown* forum were pieces like "Smoke Ghost," in which Leiber attempted with considerable success to conjure up a new sort of spirit, one that haunted the dark and dirty recesses of a modern metropolis. He also brought witchcraft to a modern college campus with his celebrated novel *Conjure Wife*.

Perhaps the best representative of the magazine was Theodore Sturgeon, who excelled in screwball conceptions such as "Yesterday Was Monday," in which the hero discovers a gang of little men whose strange task it is to shift scenery from one day to the next, preparing the stage for the drama of mortal existence. In a change of pace, Sturgeon penned the magazine's best-known horror tale, "It," about a mindless creature spontaneously formed on the skeleton of a murdered man. Another eminently successful chiller was "The Devil We Know," by Henry Kuttner, in which a man makes what seems to be a successful deal with a demon, only to discover that in the process he has inherited his demon's demon, a hideous entity totally beyond human comprehension. Perhaps the magazine's most celebrated contributor is L. Ron Hubbard, who wrote whimsical adventure fantasies like *Triton* and *Slaves of Sleep* years before he propounded the theories which brought him fame and fortune as the creator of the controversial self-improvement programs Dianetics and Scientology. All of these writers were later to achieve fame in the field of science fiction; after Lovecraft's experimental fusion of that genre with fantasy, it was not uncommon for authors to work in both fields. Some *Unknown* authors, like Fredric Brown and Anthony Boucher, were equally adept in the field of the detective story. Boucher's novelette *The Compleat Werewolf*, about a lovable lycanthrope who ends up working as an undercover investigator, is a classic example of the *Unknown* style. The magazine demonstrated the extent to which traditionally frightening fantasies had become commonplace and thus fair game for parodists.

Hollywood was discovering that its monsters, too, had become tolerable. Universal started off a new cycle of sinister cinema well enough in 1939 with *Son of Frankenstein*; in retrospect it was a transition point between the comparatively sincere efforts of the thirties and the more mechanical productions of the forties. Solidly directed by Rowland V. Lee, it featured Boris Karloff's last appearance in the role that had made him a star. The monster is silent again, but *Bride of Frankenstein* had established the precedent that he should be a tool in the hands of a superior intelligence, devoid of the unpredictability that had made him such a fascinating figure in the first film. On the other hand, Bela Lugosi got his best role since *Dracula*, portraying a homicidal peasant named Ygor who had survived the hangman's noose with a broken neck. Ygor discovers the monster, dormant but intact after the previous film's explosion, and convinces the original Frankenstein's son (Basil Rathbone) to revive his father's creation. The monster becomes Ygor's pawn in a plan of revenge against the men who had sent the depraved old codger to the gallows; the son of Frankenstein comes to regret his scientific curiosity and assuages his guilt by swinging Tarzan-style from a rope to kick the monster in a pool of boiling sulfur. Well acted and lavishly produced, *Son of Frankenstein* is an exciting film that nevertheless fails almost completely to evoke an aura of the uncanny. Even the addition of an extra menace in the person of the deformed Ygor failed to recall the eerie atmosphere of earlier efforts; but it was becoming apparent that the horror film was established as a genre that audiences were prepared to enjoy even when it failed to produce a strong emotional impact.

Universal was not the only studio to show a revived interest in horror in 1939; most of the other Hollywood studios sensed the trend. Paramount perhaps came closest to an assessment of the general trend by releasing a totally humorous version of that old standby *The Cat and the Canary*, designed as a vehicle for comedian Bob Hope. RKO remade *The Hunchback of Notre Dame* with Charles Laughton in the title role, playing down the frightening features of the story and, as in Lon Chaney's silent version, ignoring the novel's downbeat conclusion.

A series of slightly more thoughtful mad-scientist melodramas began to emerge from Columbia, including *The Man They Could Not Hang* (1939), *Before I Hang* (1940), and *The Man with Nine Lives* (1940). These were concocted from the formula of a well-meaning doctor whose experiments are interrupted by the authorities, resulting in the death of a volunteer subject, the doctor's execution for murder, and his return for revenge through the very device that had caused all the trouble. All starred Boris Karloff, and they are especially interesting today because so many of the outlandish devices he struggles with, such as artificial hearts and frozen patients, have become medical realities since the films were made.

Parody continued in 1940 with the Bob Hope feature *The Ghost Breakers*, successful enough to be remade in the next decade as a Dean Martin and Jerry Lewis feature, *Scared Stiff*. Meanwhile, Universal decided to revive two of its most successful unemployed monsters, the Mummy and the Invisible Man. Each suffered in comparison with the original conception. *The Mummy's Hand* was not a sequel to the 1932 film but a new story about a different mummy, Kharis, who was revived by Egyptian priests to guard a royal tomb. Tom Tyler played Kharis, reanimated by a brew of Tanna leaves, as an efficient but characterless killing machine. *The Invisible Man Returns* featured Vincent Price as an embattled hero who uses invisibility to track down a murderer. The role was a feeble version of the megalomaniac originally enacted by Claude Rains, noteworthy only because it gave Price his first opportunity in the sort of film that would, in later decades, provide him with his greatest fame.

A more immediate but shorter-lived success came to the actor who, beginning in 1941, was to carry Universal's horror films for the next five years, portraying most of their famous fiends and a few new ones besides. This was Lon Chaney, Jr. Born Creighton Chaney, the son of the silent film star had given a powerful performance in 1939 as a simpleminded killer in *Of Mice and Men*. His first Universal horror feature, *Man-Made Monster*, gave Chaney a similar role, as a bewildered circus performer who becomes supercharged with electric current.

Bewilderment became Chaney's principal expression in those performances in which his features were fairly free of makeup. Lacking the dynamic presence of his predecessors, he usually managed to carry his weight through his evident sincerity and dedication. He got his best part almost immediately in the 1941 feature *The Wolf Man* directed by George Waggner. As reluctant werewolf Larry Talbot, Chaney displayed his dismay within an appropriate context, and the role became a sort of minor classic which he would repeat in four more films (although never without the support of a more reliable monster). Curt Siodmak's screenplay for *The Wolf Man* established the Hollywood version of the werewolf myth, in which the lycanthrope must be killed with a silver weapon. The deathblow is finally delivered by Talbot's father (Claude Rains); the curse had originally

Lon Chaney, Jr., had his best and favorite role as Larry Talbot, the Wolf Man (1941), in the screen's most famous treatment of the lycanthropy legend. *Courtesy of Universal Pictures.*

been inflicted on him by another sort of father figure, Bela Lugosi, who plays the cameo role of a Gypsy werewolf. Jack Pierce and John Fulton came through with what they had failed to provide for *The Werewolf of London*: Pierce's makeup work was appropriately menacing, and Fulton handled the transformation scenes with a skill that would increase with each new Wolf Man saga.

The same year saw a more familiar series of transformations as *Dr. Jekyll and Mr. Hyde* was dragged out once again, this time by MGM. Spencer Tracy played the dual role with minimal makeup and considerable restraint, but this careful film is decidedly inferior to the occasionally ludicrous but always lively Fredric March version.

In 1942, RKO launched a new series of horror movies to be produced by Val Lewton, whose strong hand seems to have had more influence on the character of his films than the directors he employed. His productions included *The Cat People* (1942), *I Walked with a Zombie* (1943), *The Seventh Victim* (1943), *The Curse of the Cat People* (1944), *Isle of the Dead* (1945), *The Body Snatcher* (1945), and *Bedlam* (1946). As a group they were distinguished by subtlety and psychological overtones; they hint at the supernatural, while other motion pictures of the decade exploited its entertainment value. They are well liked by critics who deplore the usual movie of this type, being in this sense at least the cinematic equivalent of *The Turn of the Screw*. Unfortunately some of them seem only halfhearted attempts, more respectable than entertaining.

Perhaps the most widely known and praised of Lewton's movies is *The Cat People*, a variation on the werewolf theme in which a young woman (Simone Simon) is transformed into a black panther. Director Jacques Tourneur manages to sustain doubt about whether or not the changes are really taking place until the end of the film, when the woman dies after the unseen beast has been wounded by one of its victims. The ambiguity about the nature of the heroine's problem creates a kind of suspense, but it leaves open until the last moment the truly horrifying possibility that *The Cat People* may be, like *Mark of the Vampire*, one of those horror films that degenerate at the end into implausible murder mysteries. Even its devotees should have been disappointed by the movie's spurious sequel *The Curse of the Cat People*. This tale of a small girl and her imaginary playmates is totally devoid of terror and may well be the most inaccurately titled production in the history of the cinema.

Lewton's subsequent productions abandoned the uncanny element almost entirely. For instance, the "zombie" in *I Walked with a Zombie*, also directed by Tourneur, is not one of the resurrected corpses employed as slave laborers by Caribbean sorcerers but a woman whose unusual disease makes her look like a zombie to her superstitious neighbors. Yet even after a logical explanation is offered the ambiguity remains, providing most of the tension and a haunting mood most fully expressed when a backsliding nurse escorts the patient through the night to a forbidden voodoo ceremony.

Eventually Lewton acquired the services of a prominent performer in the field, Boris Karloff. Bigger budgets also allowed more elaborate productions, perhaps shown to best advantage in an adaptation of Stevenson's *Body Snatcher*. Nineteenth-century Edinburgh is convincingly evoked in this story of physicians and grave robbers, and Karloff's excellent performance as a body snatcher who graduates to murder is matched by that of Henry Daniell as a sanctimonious doctor whose quest for specimens leads him down the road to disaster. The conflict between the two makes the whole film grim and suspenseful; it achieves an authentic moment of supernatural shock when the doctor, driven to the murder of his unscrupulous supplier, visits a cemetery himself and discovers that he has carted off the corpse of his vengeful victim. Karloff's other features for Lewton, lacking the fine hand of director Robert Wise, were less successful. *Isle of the Dead* showed the unpleasant predicament of a group of war refugees quarantined by a plague that sends one of their number to a premature burial; *Bedlam* presented Karloff as the brutal proprietor of an insane asylum who is finally murdered by one of his charges.

A film with a similarly subtle approach to the supernatural was Paramount's *The Uninvited* (1944). This genteel ghost story featured Ray Milland and Ruth Hussey as the owners of a haunted house. Based on a popular novel by Dorothy Macardle, and directed by Lewis Allen, it was a capable effort which also made more money than most of the mainstream monster movies. It was, in fact, so far removed from the typical Hollywood treatment that it almost seems to belong to a different genre.

While these productions were making some impressive attempts to unnerve audiences, the mainstream efforts at Universal seemed less intent on frightening the fans than on providing them with a rousing good time. The tone of the studio's later films suggests that the intention was to let the viewers identify with the increasingly outrageous antics of their favorite monsters, most of them played by Lon Chaney, Jr. In 1942 he got his chance at the monster in *Ghost of Frankenstein*, probably the worst of the studio's series, lacking both the conviction of the first three films and the wild action of those that were to follow. It did at least establish a nice sense of continuity, for the monster is released from the now hardened sulfur pit where he had been in retirement since *Son of Frankenstein*. He is once again in the hands of Ygor (still Lugosi) who has overcome his apparent death in the previous episode with no explanation at all. Their adventures take them to visit another son of Frankenstein (Cedric Hardwicke), who is persuaded to replace the monster's objectionable criminal brain with that of a colleague. With the help of a corrupt assistant, Ygor succeeds in having his own brain placed in the gigantic body, and he enjoys a brief moment of triumph before succumbing to the inevitable conflagration. No mention is made of this startling transformation in later sequels, although the monster was played in the next film by none other than Bela Lugosi.

In the same year, Chaney made a somewhat overweight Kharis in *The Mummy's Tomb*, searching America without much success for the reincarnation of his lost Egyptian love. The 1944 sequel, *The Mummy's Ghost*, seemed to be cut from the same moldy bandage, as Kharis discovers a familiar face (Ramsay Ames) on a college campus and makes several attempts to carry her off. Incredibly, he finally gets away with it, slinking off into a swamp with the heroine who tacitly admits the wisdom of his choice as her hair turns white and she is transformed into an ancient mummified crone. It took three writers, Griffin Jay, Henry Sucher, and Brenda Weisberg, to come up with this downbeat ending, apparently the first in the history of the commercial horror film. Unfortunately the series did not end on this surprising note but concluded in the same year with still another sequel, *The Mummy's Curse*, in which Kharis and his lady love are dredged out of the swamp (mysteriously transported from New England to Louisiana) and put through their paces one more time.

Chaney inherited another set of antisocial characteristics in 1943 when he appeared as *Son of Dracula*. He made a rather too solid and stolid vampire, but the film provided a field day for John Fulton by elaborating on some of the more obscure powers of the undead. For the first time a man was shown changing himself into a bat (always photographed from the rear, so that the long black cloak could be transformed by animation), and Chaney also appeared as a mobile cloud of mist. In one particularly impressive scene, the vampire floats across a lake standing upright on his coffin. The film also must bear the responsibility for firmly establishing the cinematic tradition (contrary to most previously published accounts, but also present in the silent film *Nosferatu*) that sunlight is poison to Dracula and his descendants.

The Mummy's Tomb (1942) featured Lon Chaney, Jr., as the walking mass of mold and bandages, Kharis, whose adventures filled four films. *Courtesy of Universal Pictures.*

This imaginative outing was overshadowed, though, by 1943's spectacular social event, *Frankenstein Meets the Wolf Man*. Chaney returned to his best role as Larry Talbot, carrying most of the movie's weight as he inexplicably returns from the dead, complete with his curious affliction. Seeking expert medical advice from Dr. Frankenstein, he encounters the monster (Bela Lugosi) instead. After decorous maneuvering, Talbot becomes the Wolf Man just as the monster receives his annual dose of electricity, and the two engage in a fight to the finish, staged with less relish than might be desired. Before a winner can be declared, civic-minded villagers blow up a dam, flooding the castle where the monsters are earning their keep and slowing them down for several months.

They were back in 1944, along with Count Dracula and other assorted fiends; the film was *House of Frankenstein*. Boris Karloff and J. Carrol Naish were featured as a mad scientist and a hunchback awaiting execution when a fortuitous lightning bolt demolishes their prison. On their journey back to the doctor's abandoned laboratory, they join a traveling chamber of horrors whose chief attraction is the skeleton of Dracula, a stake still planted in its ribs. Karloff removes the stake and, contrary to all traditional lore, revives the vampire. Appearing in a rather mechanical series of double exposures which includes the formation of a dress suit, Dracula is incarnated in the person of John Carradine, a fine actor whose tall, gaunt appearance, complete with white hair and moustache, duplicates the description in the original novel more accurately than any other performer. Unfortunately, he has only a few minutes of screen time before he is eliminated by the rays of the sun. The two linking characters continue their journey, discovering the Wolf Man and the Frankenstein monster encased in ice after the previous film's flood. Chaney emerges in human form and enlists the doctor's help in ending his affliction; but the unconscious monster captures Karloff's interest, and the Wolf Man is eliminated with a silver bullet. The monster is finally revived in the film's climax, hardly getting on his feet before he is driven into a pool of quicksand by the inevitable band of torch-bearing villagers. A former wrestler named Glenn Strange portrayed Hollywood's most famous horror. Coached by Karloff, he was to play the role three times, duplicating his master's record, if not his artistic accomplishment. Still, his brief appearance did not allow for a very profound performance. *House of Frankenstein* strained credibility, even by the standards of its genre; but the story by Curt Siodmak made for an entertaining free-for-all, demonstrating that the monsters were now stars in their own right who had only to appear and take a bow to satisfy their clearly unfrightened followers.

Inevitably, 1945 brought a new house party, *House of Dracula*. Another scientist (Onslow Stevens), provided the focal point as he is visited by the Wolf Man (still Chaney) and Dracula (again Carradine), both seeking a cure for their conditions. The doctor tries transfusions on the vampire, but he ends up infected himself and decides to shove the count's coffin out into the daylight. The Wolf Man, on one of his rampages, finds his old friend the monster unconscious in a cavern, apparently beneath the last film's quicksand. The doctor, of course, is anxious to give Glenn Strange another dose of voltage, but he finds time to cure Larry Talbot by altering the shape of his skull. The monster walks again, for just long enough to go up in flames with the doctor. As a variation on the previous film, *House of Dracula* has a female hunchback as the scientist's assistant. Nonetheless, the movie signaled the end of the line for the long cycle of Hollywood horrors.

Numerous other movies of less consequence were released during the same period, many by poverty-row studios like Monogram and P.R.C. Occasionally good performers like John Carradine and Bela Lugosi ended up in deadly productions from these outfits such as *Revenge of the Zombies* or *The Devil Bat*; the best actor to emerge from this school was bald, beady-eyed George Zucco, a threatening thespian who eventually graduated to supporting roles in some of Universal's later productions. In some ways the most remarkable star of the sinister cinema was Rondo Hatton, whose total lack of acting ability found cruel compensation in his naturally distorted features. He appeared in second-rate efforts like *The Brute Man* and *House of Horrors*, in which he played a creature called the Creeper. Universal kept a bad concept going for three films (to allow for double features), in a series begun when a demented doctor creates an ape-woman in *Captive Wild Woman* (1943), *Jungle Woman* (1944), and *Jungle Captive* (1945).

While Hollywood was running out of steam, England came up with one of the most accomplished films on supernatural subjects, *Dead of Night* (1945). Several directors were involved in this project, which was a compendium of six stories told by guests at a house and linked together by the story of a visitor who had dreamed that he would arrive there. Some of the sequences are light in tone or sketchy in execution, but they provide a sense of the range of uncanny effects which the standard "monster" movies had ignored. The most morbid of the lot involves a schizophrenic ventriloquist (Michael Redgrave) whose dummy acquires a life of its own; variations on this plot became a stock device in various media.

In general, fearsome films were a rare occurrence in Europe during the same period when they flourished most fantastically in the United States. One exception was Carl Dreyer's unrecognizably free adaptation of Le Fanu's "Carmilla" entitled *Vampyr* (1932). This moody, impressionistic film, shot entirely through gauze and available in several versions, has proved to be of more interest to the critics than to the public. The increasingly Kafkaesque air of depression Germany is captured in Fritz Lang's *M* (1931), in which criminals supplant the regular police force to unearth a homicidal maniac. The director and his star, Peter Lorre, soon emigrated to the United States, where their melancholy talents were well employed. Lorre shaved his head to appear in MGM's *Mad Love* (1935), directed by Karl Freund, as a surgeon who grafts a murderer's hands onto a crippled musician. In one remarkably bizarre scene, he attempts to prove his skill by masquerading as a guillotined killer whose head has been replaced with the aid of a grotesque steel brace. Lorre also had the distinction of starring in the last serious Hollywood horror film of the forties, the Warner Brothers adaptation of William Fryer Harvey's story, *The Beast with Five Fingers* (1947).

Universal finally threw in the towel in 1948 with its last monster rally, which might have been entitled *House of the Wolf Man*; instead, it was *Abbott and Costello Meet Frankenstein.* Sometimes very funny, and never as bad as purists might imagine, this was the film in which Bela Lugosi donned his famous cape again for his second and last portrayal of the bloodthirsty Dracula, although he had played a similar role in Columbia's 1944 *Return of the Vampire.* The popular comedy team of Abbott and Costello made expository scenes more entertaining than many more serious performers had been able to do, and the Wolf Man (Chaney), the Frankenstein monster (Strange), and Count Dracula were all allowed to play it straight. This time Dracula is in charge, planning to make the monster more malleable by giving him Costello's addled brain. The Wolf Man is something of a hero when in human form, and he even sacrifices his life to destroy Dracula by jumping over a ledge to crush the vampire bat in his hairy paws. It was the end of the line for Larry Talbot and for the Universal version of the monster as well. Sizzling in the fourth fire of his seventeen-year career, Frankenstein's brainchild decided to retire permanently. There was one brief moment of hope: having destroyed the three

Comedians Bud and Lou in *Abbott and Costello Meet Frankenstein* **(Glenn Strange),
to say nothing of Dracula (Bela Lugosi) and the Wolf Man (Lon Chaney, Jr.).** *Courtesy
of Universal Pictures.*

most durable demons in Hollywood history, the heroes had only a moment's peace at the
end of the movie before the voice of Vincent Price informed them that the Invisible Man
was on the job.

It was a prophetic moment; Price was one of the few movie menaces to survive the
next decade with his credentials intact. The huge harvest of horrors unleashed in the
thirties and forties seemed to have exhausted both creators and consumers, and the fortunes of fiends were failing. There were, however, a few keepers of the flame who worked
unacknowledged wonders while waiting for lightning to strike again.

·8·

SLIME: THE RETREAT TO REALITY

The Second World War, climaxing with the explosion of nuclear weapons and capped by the hideous revelations unearthed in a beaten Germany, had temporarily exhausted the public's appetite for horrors of any kind. The continuing series of Abbott and Costello parodies were all that remained of the frightening films that had resurrected so many fictional fiends; the comedy team went on to *Meet Dr. Jekyll and Mr. Hyde* and *Meet the Invisible Man* in 1953 and *Meet the Mummy* in 1954. None of them could hold a candle to the duo's original encounter with the uncanny in 1948.

By 1950, however, there were a few signs of new blood. Viewed historically, these were temporary phenomena, highlights of a low period for fearsome fantasies. Some significant creations emerged, though; in fact, two different art forms came up with innovative structures for raising the hair of the mass audience, each to have a significant effect during the few years of its existence. In the cinema, monster movies got a new lease on life through a transfusion of "science fiction," which came to mean that mutation and invasion from outer space were the sources for new horrors constructed around old plot outlines. The apparently greater plausibility of the "scientific" over the supernatural served to keep the genre alive until a new generation of out-and-out thrill seekers could grow into an economic bloc. More extraordinary and unexpected was the brutally graphic and remarkably literate group of comic books that helped to turn a commercial enterprise into a budding art form, one whose importance has only begun to be appreciated.

The comic book publisher was William Gaines, a fear fancier who inherited Entertaining Comics with some misgivings, then decided to promote horror material as a serious proposition. The resulting E.C. comic books were *Tales from the Crypt*, *The Vault of Horror*, and *The Haunt of Fear*. They were not exactly the first in their field to play on the emotion of fear, but they concentrated on it with new intensity, building on a tradition that stretched back for years.

The comic book was an outgrowth of the newspaper comic strips which were close to half a century old before they began to appear successfully in magazine form. The original newspaper strips were predominantly humorous, but they grew grimmer with the advent of the depression. Adventure material began to appear, and there were occasional touches of terror in works like *Tarzan* (adapted from the Edgar Rice Burroughs sagas by Hal Foster, later by Burne Hogarth), *Buck Rogers* (by Phil Nowland

156

and Dick Calkins), *Flash Gordon* (by Alex Raymond), and *Dick Tracy* (by Chester Gould). Gould's detective strip was the grimmest of the lot, more than once running into censorship problems because of the creator's insistence on violent deaths and grotesquely deformed villains. Writer Lee Falk came up with two characters with subdued supernatural suggestions: Mandrake the Magician, who used hocus-pocus to right wrongs; and the Phantom, a masked hero who preserved the illusion that he was immortal by training successive generations of offspring to inherit his disguise.

Comic books began by reprinting newspaper material, but they came into their own in 1938 when the debut of Superman in *Action Comics* demonstrated that new characters could be even more successful. Amid the wide variety of costumed heroes that sprang up to follow this example, there were several whose demeanor had macabre overtones. The most popular came from Superman's publishers, National Periodicals. This was Batman, a creation of Bob Kane, Jerry Robinson, and Bill Finger who bowed in 1939 in *Detective Comics*. An enemy of crime who was inspired by the murder of his mother and father, Bruce Wayne adopted the grotesque gray guise of a bat to frighten superstitious felons. His early adventures depicted the Batman as a merciless menace; but he was gradually humanized, and the uncanny atmosphere of the original stories was dissipated. Another major character with a weird background was Will Eisner's Spirit, who got his start in 1940. Another masked avenger, though considerably less flamboyant, the Spirit was a detective who faked his own death to solve a case and enjoyed his new role as a mystery man so much that he adopted it permanently, setting up headquarters in Wildwood Cemetery. Drawn and written with unusual flair, *The Spirit* did not really emphasize its hero's supposedly supernatural origin; Eisner achieved most of his effects through wit and an unusual degree of naturalism.

There was a comic book policeman who was actually killed but managed to come back anyway as the Spectre. Written by Jerry Siegel, the author of the original Superman stories, *The Spectre*'s title character had powers surpassing those of every other comic book hero. In fact, the forbidding white figure wrapped in a green cloak was absolutely omnipotent, battling felonious plots with a limitless array of sensational stunts. One of his favorite tricks was scaring his adversaries to death. Most of his adventures took place in National's *More Fun Comics*, where he lasted for five years despite his lack of human warmth and weaknesses. Slightly less spectacular magicians were a commonplace in the early days of comic books; most of them, like Fred Guardineer's Zatara, were similar to Lee Falk's Mandrake. The exception, who lasted longer than any of his rivals, was Fawcett Publications' Ibis the Invincible, who began his thirteen-year career in 1940. Ibis, a resurrected Egyptian prince, woke up from a four-thousand-year sleep to discover himself in twentieth-century America. He wore a turban instead of a top hat and performed his miracles with the aid of a magic wand called the Ibistick. Created by Bill Parker and drawn during his best period by Mac Raboy, Ibis distinguished himself during his *Whiz Comics* appearances by battling not the usual crew of gangsters, but a series of bloodcurdling supernatural fiends. For a decade, this feature was as close as comic books came to creating an authentically macabre atmosphere.

The search for bizarre superheroes in the early days of comic books unleashed a number of short-lived characters who were more or less monsters in their own right. Among the strangest was Russ Cochran's Eye, who was just what his name implied; his appearance inspired the Hand, who appeared with the slogan "The hand is quicker than the eye." Other unattractive heroes included the Hunchback, the Black Dwarf, the Banshee, and Blackout, who fought crime even after having been burned to a crisp. None of them became a great popular favorite, but monsters of almost every description were commonplace as opponents for almost every comic book character. Throughout the 1940s, the whole medium featured healthy doses of blood and thunder. Inevitably, the best box office attraction of all the monsters became a comic book star in his own right when Dick Briefer's version of Frankenstein began in a 1941 issue of *Prize Comics*. In this incarnation, the well-intentioned monster soon became a pawn of Nazi masterminds. After the war, Briefer began a new *Frankenstein* comic book, a comedy treatment in which the monster was a lovable lout. A few years later he reverted back to his antisocial habits, doubtless inspired by the success of William Gaines and his E.C. horror comic books.

A similar series of personality changes was undergone by the most outlandish of comic book creatures, the Heap. A downed German ace from the First World War, he rose again to aid the Nazis, his body fused by some odd osmosis with a vast mass of grass. The gigantic green walking vegetable started his career as a villain for the heroic Sky Wolf in Hillman Publications' *Air Fighters*. He was soon converted into an aid to the Allies, then set loose on the civilian population as the star of his own series. Always menacing, the Heap still did his share of good deeds, at least by efficiently eliminating more mortal evildoers. He was the creation of writer Harry Stein and artist Mort Leav.

Any one of these characters from the golden age of comic books was capable of creating nightmares, but they all paled beside the gruesome graphics of E.C.'s *Tales from the Crypt*, *Vault of Horror*, and *Haunt of Fear*. These three titles were launched in 1950, as part of what publisher Gaines called a "new trend," different from what had been attempted before because the magazines featured short stories related only by theme, without the crutch of continuing characters. As a result, the basically optimistic outcome of the traditional comic book tale was no longer required. In fact, E.C. specialized in unhappy endings. Editor Albert Feldstein, who wrote the scripts from the publisher's suggestions, brought a new level of sophistication to comic book stories in vocabulary, mood, tone, and plot. His skill was matched by the witchcraft of the artists. The chief chefs around this cauldron of ink were Jack Davis, Johnny Craig, and Graham Ingels, each identified with one of the terror titles by virtue of his skill in depicting its master of ceremonies. These were, respectively, the Crypt-Keeper *(Tales from the Crypt)*, the Vault-Keeper *(The Vault of Horror)*, and the Old Witch *(The Haunt of Fear)*. They functioned like the horror hosts of earlier radio shows, opening and closing the stories with lurid leers and pungent puns.

Occasionally, the artists appeared in their stories, as in the case of an early effort that purported to explain the origin of the comic books themselves. Publisher Gaines and editor Feldstein were depicted as a pair of innocent young fellows with a fondness for love comics who were kidnapped by the terrible trio. They saved their lives by signing contracts promising permanent employment to the sinister storytellers. Other tales in the same ludicrous vein offered origins for the nasty narrators: "A Little Stranger" depicted the Old Witch as the daughter of a werewolf and a vampire, while "Lower Berth" revealed that the Crypt-Keeper was the offspring of an elopement by two sideshow exhibits, an ancient mummy and a two-headed man who climbed out of a jar of formaldehyde to express his love. The scurrilous sexual suggestions inherent in these tales were just an example of the outrages against decorum of which the E.C. horror line made a specialty.

These publications were most outrageous, however, in their graphically detailed depiction of the gruesome and the grotesque. Revenge from beyond the grave was the most standard plot device, and those who returned were not the pale and dignified ghosts so common in literature but half-decayed corpses, dragging themselves from their coffins to enact their ghastly retribution. The vividly rendered features of the walking dead

Ibis the Invincible and his companion, Taia, fend off the forces of evil on this dramatic comic book cover by Mac Raboy.

Dick Briefer's humorous treatment of Frankenstein, referred to during this comic book incarnation as "the merry monster."

Editor and writer Al Feldstein also did artwork for the early E.C. comics, as in the case of this cover for a 1951 *Haunt of Fear*. © *1975 William M. Gaines.*

Graham Ingels, known to his fans as "Ghastly," did this cover, illustrating a scene from the story "Nobody There." There is also a notice that E.C. had acquired the services of the distinguished fantasy author Ray Bradbury. © *1975 William M. Gaines.*

surpassed anything seen before in the mass media. Among the astounding variations employed on this theme was a story in which the vengeful rotten remnants were those of a circus elephant, lovingly depicted by the most morbid of the staff artists, "Ghastly" Graham Ingels. Such bizarre extensions of more or less traditional plots were a specialty at E.C., where the fine line between horror and hilarity was crossed with impunity. Many of the best tales had the quality of "shaggy dog" stories, and it was apparent that many readers were not only willing to suspend their disbelief, but actually were beyond being frightened. Producers and their public alike took a fiendish glee in each new atrocity, abetting the advancement of a new aesthetic of artistic terror. Audiences with a palate for this sort of fare were recognizing the implausibility of the whole genre, were quite aware that it was concocted for their amusement, and were impressed by ingenuity and technical expertise rather than by their own emotional reactions. This sort of attitude, which distinguishes the hardened horror fan from the ordinary citizen, may have been encouraged by the obvious overkill in some of the multimonster movies like *Frankenstein Meets the Wolf Man*; but it was never more evident than in *Tales from the Crypt*, *Vault of Horror*, and *Haunt of Fear*.

Exposed to this sort of material without previous conditioning, serious thinkers were apt to be appalled, especially when the giddy ghoulishness appeared in a format that was presumed to be intended for young children. The final result was a carefully orchestrated demand for comic book censorship, which succeeded in driving horror comics out of business and at the same time inaugurated the whole concept of sociological dismay over macabre themes in the popular arts. Fuel for the flames of moral indignation was provided by the countless imitations of E.C. that flooded the market. Without exception they were inferior to the originals, but the dozens of miscellaneous titles made horror comics a bigger target and justified critical disdain with their crude scripts and artwork.

Still, E.C. had five years to build a reputation that has grown steadily since the company was forced into its untimely retreat from the world of the weird. Considerable credit should go to artist Johnny Craig, whose clean-cut characters ended up in messy situations that were only the more gruesome because of the vivid contrast. Craig began early to work on his own scripts, and ended up writing all the stories for *Vault of Horror*. At the opposite end of the spectrum was Graham Ingels, whose every line seemed touched with corruption, producing a powerful cumulative effect by a process of progressive putrefaction. Somewhere between the two was Jack Davis, whose speed and incisiveness have since made him one of the most popular commercial artists in the United States. His work now appears on the covers of wholesome middle-class magazines, but he got his start committing atrocities in ink as introduced by the Crypt-Keeper. Somehow he seemed to end up with the wildest scripts, perhaps best exemplified by the notorious "Foul Play" from the June 1953 *Haunt of Fear*. This tale about a murderous baseball player ended with the killer's indignant colleagues dismembering him and using his remains as equipment for a night game, shown in gory detail. Stories like this seem to have been designed to further offend those already critical of comic books, and indeed, the last page of "Foul Play" was reprinted in Dr. Frederic Wertham's *Seduction of the Innocent*, a 1954 book that sealed the doom of horror comics, at least for the foreseeable future. Davis himself seems to have preferred something a bit more subtle. His favorite tale from the crypt was "Country Clubbing," a bloodless and humorous 1954 tall tale from the South which, according to editor Al Feldstein, was the artist's own idea. In keeping with his choice of restrained treatment, but considerably more chilling, is the Davis story reproduced at the end of this chapter. "Model Nephew," from *Haunt of Fear*,

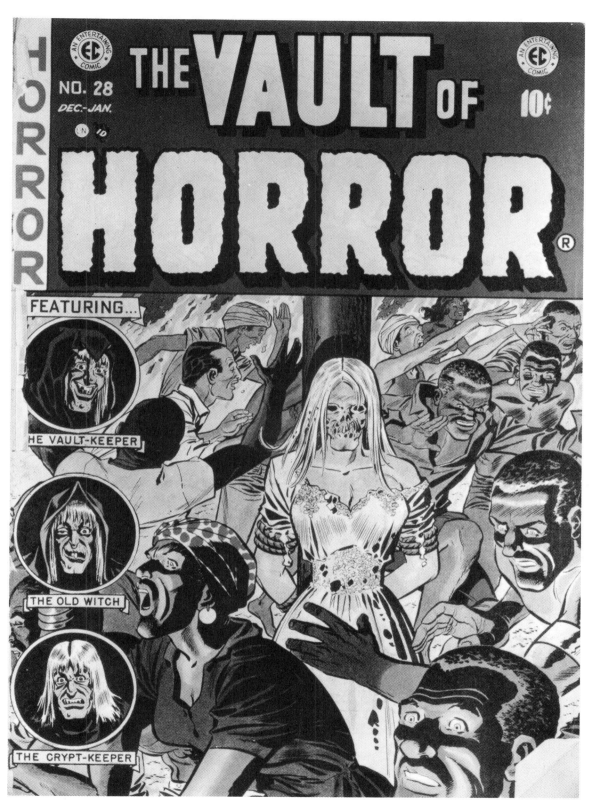

This cover by Johnny Craig, who also wrote and edited *Vault of Horror*, shows a highlight from his wrenching little epic "Till Death" about a man who revives his beloved wife with voodoo but cannot prevent her decomposition. © *1975 William M. Gaines.*

number 22, is one of the ingenious and infinite variations on the theme of supernatural vengeance which were the E.C. specialty.

Although Davis, Ingels, and Craig were the artists most consistently identified with the E.C. horror line, there were a number of others, including Feldstein, who drew the original versions of the hosts before overwork kicked him upstairs into the editor's chair. Two talented realists, Reed Crandall and George Evans, and a controversial impressionist, Bernie Krigstein, helped enliven the later issues. The generally grim attitude of the trend-setting terror offerings spilled over into other E.C. publications, such as *Shock Suspenstories* and *Crime Suspenstories*, and took some spectacular new directions with the monstrous aliens depicted by Al Williamson, Wallace Wood, and Joe Orlando for the science fiction comic books *Weird Science* and *Weird Fantasy*.

All of them were abandoned simultaneously in 1954 as the result of the Comics Code Authority. This censorship body, created with mixed disgust and delight by comic book publishers of various persuasions, made it impossible to get distribution without a seal of approval. Getting the seal meant eliminating anything that might prove objectionable to almost anyone. The most telling charge against comic books, promulgated with debatable logic in *Seduction of the Innocent* and adopted by hordes of self-righteous citizens, was that the depiction of crime was contributing to juvenile delinquency. Macabre material was banned almost as an afterthought but in such specific terms that it became impossible to market. Crime and criminals, on the other hand, continued to be involved in the plots of most publications, simply because the standard superheroes had to have somebody to fight. Nobody ever seriously suggested that fictional werewolves had led to even a slight increase in the werewolf population, but stories along these lines stood accused of the more nebulous transgression of warping minds. Perhaps for the first time in human history, tales of terror were being declared unfit for human consumption, slimy throwbacks from an ignorant past that could be jettisoned without remorse from a scientific, psychoanalyzed civilization.

The last of the pulp magazines was wiped out in the same magazine distribution cleanup of 1954–55. A few of these publications survived by converting to the more sedate digest format; but none of these was a terror title, although there had been dozens in the previous decade. Fantasy became a poor relation, occasionally admitted out of pity into the sanctified pages of the science fiction magazines, which had begun to enjoy a new prestige after the appearance of such astounding devices as the atomic bomb.

The pulps had been twice betrayed by comic books, which first had absorbed much of their audience and then had become involved in a scandalous situation that made the sale of any magazine with a lurid cover just about impossible. The venerable *Weird Tales* was one of the last to go, in September 1954, shortly after converting to a smaller size. Yet the last years of the magazine were far from vacant. It provided early opportunities for the considerable talents of Ray Bradbury, the first American science fiction writer to receive wide recognition from conservative critics. Bradbury began his career with a group of gruesome and remarkably original weird tales, and many of them were adapted with his consent by the E.C. comic book men. His first book, *Dark Carnival* (1947), was a collection of horror stories, and all of his subsequent collections have included something stranger than science fiction. His *October Country* is a revised and amended version of *Dark Carnival*, and the novel *Something Wicked This Way Comes* is a supernatural story about a sinister circus. As an avowed fan, Bradbury was driven to new heights by his dismay at the simultaneous destruction of both pulp magazines and the most imaginative comic book lines. The result was the novel *Fahrenheit 451*, in which the "firemen" of the future are sanitary-minded book burners. The same scorn for suppressors was expressed in stories like "Usher II," in which a lunatic builds a replica of Poe's fancied mansion on Mars and invites a party of censors there to be destroyed in a mechanical chamber of horrors. "The Exiles," a poignant variation on the same theme, depicts the saddened spirits of all earth's fantasy authors, each disintegrating in turn as the last volume of his works is consigned to the flames.

Such proselytizing aside, Bradbury brought a distinctively personal touch to his stories, delivering them in an effusively rhapsodic style that has been a subject of much controversy. Among his most memorable offerings is "The Handler," in which a disgruntled undertaker avenges snubs by playing grim practical jokes with the bodies of his customers. The heroine of "There Was an Old Woman" rises out of her coffin, consumed with righteous indignation, and goes home to finish her knitting. Like this one, many of his best tales seem to be told from the viewpoint of a naïve and fascinated child. A counterpoint is offered by "The Small Assassin," in which an infant expresses his resentment at being born by engineering the death of his parents.

Among the most significant stories printed in the twilight of *Weird Tales* was Joseph Payne Brennan's "Slime," a fantasy of living, growing, moving, omnivorous protoplasm. The structure is so solid and the description so vivid that this tale, reprinted at the end of this chapter, became the inspiration for many fictions and films, some of them shameless plagiarisms. Yet because the copyright holder, *Weird Tales*, was legally defunct, the author has gone virtually unrewarded. "Slime" in fact epitomized, if it did not single-handedly imagine, the plot that became a formula for fifties monster movies, in which a titanic creature threatens to destroy civilization. Instead of expressing human aberrations, monsters became symbols of impersonal forces; the conflict would be not between good and evil, but between survival and annihilation. Brennan has written many other memorable terror tales, including the haunting short-short story "Levitation," about a hypnotist's demonstration gone awry, and several adventures of a psychic detective collected in *The Casebook of Lucius Leffing*. Yet he is most concerned with his work as a poet; many of his best poems in the vein of the macabre appeared in the volume *Nightmare Need* (1964).

Macabre fiction did survive in the United States, largely because of the presence of two new magazines, both discreetly of digest size to distinguish them from the moribund pulps. The first was *The Magazine of Fantasy*, which first appeared in 1949, edited by Anthony Boucher and J. Francis McComas. This was a sincere effort to establish the literary credentials of fantastic fiction, relying for its selections on writers from the past as well as on new contributors. The stories were well chosen, and the magazine avoided the lurid graphics that so often characterized pulp magazines and comic books; but it survived only by changing its title and contents to *The Magazine of Fantasy and Science Fiction*, with a distinct emphasis on the latter. Nevertheless, the fantasy element was not entirely abandoned, and some fine stories of the supernatural have appeared from this source, especially welcome during the era when science fiction enthusiasts had only sneers for that genre's ancient ancestor. *Fantasy and Science Fiction* scored an especially impressive blow by publishing Robert Bloch's ingenious tale "That Hell Bound Train," which was good enough to win a best-short-story award from science fiction professionals, despite the fact that it was an unscientific variation on the deal-with-the-devil theme.

The other principal market for supernatural fiction was provided by *Fantastic*, which began promisingly in 1952 under the editorship of Howard Browne. Among the features that established the magazine's lineage were a series of beautifully rendered drawings by Virgil Finlay, who had established a reputation in *Weird Tales* as the most proficient American illustrator in fantasy periodicals. One of the finest of his remarkably detailed

Fantastic employed Virgil Finlay to create this scene for "The Lighthouse,"
a fragmentary Poe tale completed for the magazine by the prolific Robert Bloch.

and painstaking pieces appeared in conjunction with a unique posthumous collaboration, when Robert Bloch completed an unfinished Edgar Allan Poe tale, "The Lighthouse," for a 1953 issue of *Fantastic*. The magazine has also provided a home for further adventures of Fritz Leiber's *Unknown* characters, Fafhrd and the Gray Mouser. A series of changes in editors and publishers has varied the quality of *Fantastic* over the years, but it has published many fine stories in the supernatural tradition. Recently, the increasingly popular Robert E. Howard character, Conan, has been revived in its pages by Howard enthusiasts L. Sprague de Camp and Lin Carter. Still, science fiction dominated the magazine, as it did virtually all of the Hollywood horror films released in the decade between 1947 and 1957.

Actual events provided the inspiration for the new breed of monsters, which were generally by-products of atomic energy or the pilots of "flying saucers." Unidentified flying objects were sighted with increasing frequency in the postwar world; it was only a matter of time before they showed up on the motion picture screen. The first and in many respects the most impressive of the alien invaders was the parasitic vegetable man who, eulogized in song by Phil Harris, became the most famous monster of the decade: *The Thing* (1951). It lands near the North Pole, where its spaceship is discovered by a group of American soldiers. Perhaps the most telling scene in this Howard Hawks production is the first appearance of this strange object buried in the ice; as the men fan out on its perimeter to determine its shape and size, they and the audience realize simultaneously that they are standing around a huge disk, the dreaded flying saucer. Once its ice-covered passenger is moved to an Arctic station and thawed out, the action becomes very familiar, as the Thing stalks its victims in the approved monster tradition. Electricity eliminates the menace and presumably ends the threat of alien invasion, thus establishing the cost-conscious concept that invaders from space usually show up as solo scouts whose defeat will forestall a mass attack. The space being's appearance is far from exotic; he is just an oversized man with a vaguely featureless face, a far cry from the creature originally described in the source story, John W. Campbell's "Who Goes There?" In fact, the film has just about nothing to do with this much more subtle and complex piece of fiction.

Serious followers of literary science fiction found little satisfaction in most of the movies that followed in the wake of *The Thing*. The rare exceptions included monsterless movies like George Pal's documentary-style *Destination Moon* (1950) and the evangelistic *Day the Earth Stood Still* (1951). There were a few minutes of cataclysmic horror in Pal's serious-minded follow-up, *When Worlds Collide* (1952). The story by Philip Wylie and Edwin Balmer, already twenty years old, is about a rocket-powered attempt to escape from the title's astronomical catastrophe. There are some spectacular scenes of destruction, but the most frightening aspect of the film is the sanctimonious air radiating from the small band of self-appointed survivors.

Still, a more typical example of things to come was provided by *The Man from Planet X* (1951), a lackluster invader who is content to sit in his spaceship sending out menacing thought waves. Some extremely inept and childish films followed the early entries; the worst of the lot, which shall remain nameless here but was actually shown under several titles, features an alien dressed in the prop department's old gorilla suit, topped with a comical toy space helmet. He demonstrates his scientific sophistication with a machine that blows soap bubbles.

By 1953 at least a few efforts were being made to produce a quality product. The most obvious triumph was George Pal's production of *War of the Worlds*, featuring some spectacular special effects and, at last, a full-scale attack by the men from Mars. It was less convincing than the 1938 radio version, but it was more entertaining because the audience could watch. Apparently audiences took a real delight in seeing urban sprawl crumbling under the onslaught of a hostile intelligence. Actors, writers, and directors all played second fiddle to the technicians who engineered the destruction. One of the best, Ray Harryhausen, breathed life into *The Beast from 20,000 Fathoms*, a city-crushing dinosaur revived by nuclear experiments. This was based on Ray Bradbury's comparatively nonviolent short story "The Foghorn," in which a lonely sea monster falls in love with a lighthouse. Bradbury was perhaps more accurately represented by *It Came from Outer Space*, depicting a hideous visitor who panics the population but turns out to be, as the hero has insisted, just a tourist. This comparatively thoughtful approach unfortunately made for a dull film, and the screenplay adapted from Bradbury's original story failed to approach the style that is his essence.

Probably the most entertaining thing about *It Came from Outer Space* (and a dozen other films of 1953) is that it was made in a new three-dimensional process. Polaroid glasses made it possible for patrons of the arts to enjoy a convincing illusion of depth, but they also doomed the process because nobody wanted to wear them after the novelty had worn off. The first 3-D feature, a jungle adventure called *Bwana Devil*, was produced by radio writer Arch Oboler. Films of every identifiable genre were made in 3-D, which even temporarily revived the old-school horror film. The best of the bunch, in fact the best deep drama of all, was *House of Wax*, a new version of the old Warner Brothers thriller *Mystery of the Wax Museum*. Vincent Price played the artist in wax who turns to murder after he is disfigured in a fire; his enthusiastic performance made him a star of the sinister cinema, although his real reputation came later, when morbid melodramas were more firmly back in fashion. *House of Wax* itself was engagingly corny, with a restrained use of color and photographic gimmicks. The same studio got its monkey suit out of mothballs for *The Phantom of the Rue Morgue*, with Karl Malden; then Price was put through his paces again as *The Mad Magician*. Neither of these 1954 features would have been especially impressive in only two dimensions.

Universal finally got back into monster movies the same year with their 3-D black-and-white film *The Creature from the Black Lagoon*. This proved to be a prehistoric fish-man discovered by a scientific expedition to the tropics. This rather ordinary little film, directed in pedestrian style by Jack Arnold, remains lodged in the memory solely because of the beautifully designed creature whose sleek, finny structure was a joy to behold. He proved to be a winner and was annually revived in *Revenge of the Creature* and *The Creature Walks among Us*, the first of his breed in a decade to be so honored. In the former film he is shipped to the United States with predictable results; in the latter a team of surgeons alter his appearance to emphasize his human characteristics. He lost his good looks, and was so chagrined that he retired.

Warner Brothers came up with a new kind of mutant, the giant insect, with 1954's *Them!* Named by a horrified child who is the first surviving witness to their might, "Them" are several colonies of oversized ants. They are only about twice as tall as a man, but there are hundreds of them. They perform their share of mean feats in the streets; yet the film is most impressive in the claustrophobic scenes underground, where armed men seek to destroy the nests of the mutants.

One of the heroes of *Them* had also been the portrayer of the Thing. The heavily disguised actor was James Arness, whose towering strength found a more expressive range when he became the star of television's perennial western program "Gunsmoke." The new stature he gained on the picture tube typified what was in many ways the definitive trend of the fifties. Television conquered all, with terrible economic effects on

Vincent Price goes up in flames along with his museum in Andre deToth's *House of Wax*, the best of the three-dimensional movies and one that gave a big boost to the actor's career as a film fiend. *Courtesy of Warner Bros. Inc. Copyright © 1953.*

The Creature from the Black Lagoon, portrayed by Ricou Browning, was an aquatic menace with the usual crush on a human heroine. *Courtesy of Universal Pictures.*

Intrepid investigators go underground to discover a nest of oversized, atomically mutated ants in this scene from the pioneering insect adventure *Them! Courtesy of Warner Bros. Inc. Copyright © 1954.*

every other means of communication. Advertising deserted big-time radio, which in turn abandoned drama for a format of news and recorded music. Even those publishers in no immediate danger of being censored out of existence felt the pinch, and several major magazines folded, although there was some reassurance in the burgeoning sales of paperback novels. The motion picture, which had held its own against radio, seemed in danger of complete extinction, or at least absorption, by TV. Once proud studios like Warner Brothers and Universal found themselves reduced to producing film footage for the new medium. The talents of "quickie" or "B" movie artists were particularly appropriate for feeding the ravenous "idiot box," and a whole new pantheon of culture heroes appeared. The overkill effect of TV's embarrassment of tarnished riches soon altered almost everyone's concepts of art and entertainment.

The dark muse soon found her niche in this new black-and-white world, with shows like "Inner Sanctum" and "Suspense," transferred from radio, and a number of "mystery" anthology programs like "Climax." There were also numerous lurid literary adaptations on the more high-minded dramatic programs like "Studio One" and "Lux Video Theater." Still, most fantasy came packaged as science fiction. Purportedly plausible menaces were standard fare on the late-night series "Tales of Tomorrow" and its juvenile equivalents "Captain Video," "Space Patrol," and "Tom Corbett, Space Cadet." Nevertheless, the most forward-looking program in the field got most of its material from the past. It was a local effort, in which a slinky California actress donned a fright wig and dubbed herself Vampira. She hosted the presentation of the few horror films already released to television. Few of them were very good, but Vampira pioneered a style of programming that would become wildly popular a few years later, when Hollywood's major monsters were unleashed on the home screen.

Meanwhile, the mutants marched on across theater screens. 1955 brought *It Came from Beneath the Sea*, which introduced a mammoth octopus whose construction proved so expensive that it was only equipped with five tentacles. Universal's *Tarantula* featured a giant spider, with a couple of mutant men thrown in for good measure. The same studio's *This Island Earth* was a bit more imaginative, involving a planned invasion of earth that fails to come off when the alien agent of a doomed planet takes pity on the human race. Despite the reprieve, there are some frightening minutes for the people who become guests on the dying world of Metaluna, as they barely escape the climax of an atomic war and the loathsome monstrosities it has already spawned.

The most significant filmed fantasies of 1955, however, were a pair of films from abroad. They came from England and Japan, two countries that would soon be major producers in the field. The Japanese entry was *Godzilla*, another atomically reactivated lizard. He stood out from the competition, however, by being bigger than any of his rivals and also more destructive. King Kong had punched a train, but Godzilla could eat one. He also breathed fire and appeared to be totally invulnerable. The average monster got stopped before he had inflicted more than token damage, but Godzilla virtually wiped

The bugs kept getting bigger, as in the mutated *Tarantula* (1955). The film also featured the usually dignified Leo G. Carroll as a mad scientist whose experiments leave him almost as ugly as the overgrown spider. *Courtesy of Universal Pictures.*

The best of the giant monsters made in Japan was the first, Godzilla. Not
a puppet animated by stop-motion techniques, Godzilla was a man in a lizard
suit stomping miniature sets. *Courtesy of Jewell Enterprises.*

Tokyo off the map. The plots of movies of this school generally revolved around attempts to stop the monster; Godzilla was overpowering enough to demand a new invention, explained in appropriately "scientific" gibberish, which reduced him to a skeleton. A bit of footage featuring American actor Raymond Burr was added to increase audience identification in the United States, and the film made a killing. Godzilla, billed as "King of the Monsters," pretty well capped the trend toward giant monsters. The costs of technical effects were skyrocketing, and the comparatively small expenses at the Japanese studio Toho would soon make them the principal producers of mammoth menaces.

The Creeping Unknown was one of the earliest efforts from a studio that soon became extremely influential in the production of horror movies, England's Hammer Films. This movie, atypical of Hammer's later work, concerns a rocket pilot who returns to earth infected with a fungus. It covers his whole body, turning him into the title character who is electrocuted for his antisocial behavior. Originally titled *The Quatermass Experiment*, this was the first of a series about the cantankerous scientist Quatermass, played by Brian Donlevy. As in the case of *Godzilla*, an American actor seems to have been used to encourage exportation. Donlevy is the major incongruity in a generally plausible, low-key production, although the astronaut's wife, who continually refers to the murderous fungoid mass as "Victor," is equally dispensable.

In 1956 the science fiction sweepstakes included only two major entries, but they were among the best of the breed. MGM's *Forbidden Planet* was a lavish look at another world, embellished by special effects from Walt Disney Studios. The tone was predominantly light, with a good deal of comic relief provided by the sophisticated Robbie the Robot; but there was a monster too, its presence explained by an engaging premise. The civilization that had inhabited Altair-4 had created a technology that would instantly embody its conscious desires and, in the process, had destroyed itself with an invisible embodiment of the id. At the other end of the spectrum from this colorful, slick production was *Invasion of the Body Snatchers*, directed by Don Siegel from a story by Jack Finney. There were no titanic terrors here, but something far more insidious. These invaders are inert vegetable forms that have the power to reduplicate human beings while their victims sleep; the plan is not to wipe out the human race but to replace it. There is something a bit illogical about this plot, but it comes off with all the conviction of a nightmare, as the horrified inhabitants of a small town discover half-formed effigies of themselves lying in their homes and gradually succumb to sleep and supplantation. Only one exhausted man (Kevin McCarthy) escapes. Far from destroying the duplicators, he achieves his most triumphant moment at the film's end when he finally convinces the stolid authorities of a nearby city that the peril may indeed exist.

In the same year, there were some signs of renewed interest in the more traditional type of horror film, but they appeared within a depressing context. Three movies appeared featuring Bela Lugosi; one was none too good, and the other two were truly terrible. Lugosi's star had sunk almost steadily since his initial portrayal of Dracula. In 1955 he voluntarily committed himself to a hospital to be treated for a medically induced narcotics problem that had plagued him for twenty years. Having cured himself by a tremendous act of will at the age of seventy-three, he played a small part in United Artists' *Black Sleep*, a film about a nineteenth-century surgeon (Basil Rathbone) who makes monsters almost accidentally while searching for a miracle cure. Lugosi is his butler. His next two outings were probably the two worst horror films made up to that time, *Bride of the Monster* and *Plan 9 from Outer Space (Grave Robbers from Outer Space)*. Incredibly cheap and incompetent, featuring cardboard sets and wooden dialogue, they were significantly inferior to even the worst quickies of the previous decade. Lugosi died during the filming of *Plan 9*, which depicted aliens raising the dead to form an army, and his role was completed by a nameless extra holding a black cloak over his face.

Lugosi's death seemed to symbolize the end of an era. Science fiction-style horrors seemed to have gone about as far as they could, and old-school efforts like *Bride of the Monster* indicated that the genre was as dead as Dracula. Horror comics had come and gone, the pulps were finished, and it looked very much like the fictional fiends who had plagued humanity since the dawn of time were ready to call it a night. There was definite need for new blood.

SLIME

By Joseph Payne Brennan

It was a great gray-black hood of horror moving over the floor of the sea. It slid through the soft ooze like a monstrous mantle of slime obscenely animated with questing life. It was by turns viscid and fluid. At times it flattened out and flowed through the carpet of mud like an inky pool; occasionally it paused, seeming to shrink in upon itself, and reared up out of the ooze until it resembled an irregular cone or a gigantic hood. Although it possessed no eyes, it had a marvelously developed sense of touch, and it possessed a sensitivity to minute vibrations which was almost akin to telepathy. It was plastic, essentially shapeless. It could shoot out long tentacles, until it bore a resemblance to a nightmare squid or a huge starfish; it could retract itself into a round flattened disc, or squeeze into an irregular hunched shape so that it looked like a black boulder sunk on the bottom of the sea.

It had prowled the black water endlessly. It had been formed when the earth and the seas were young; it was almost as old as the ocean itself. It moved through a night which had no beginning and no dissolution. The black sea basin where it lurked had been dark since the world began—an environment only a little less inimical than the stupendous gulfs of interplanetary space.

It was animated by a single, unceasing, never-satisfied drive: a voracious, insatiable hunger. It could survive for months without food, but minutes after eating it was as ravenous as ever. Its appetite was appalling and incalculable.

On the icy ink-black floor of the sea the battle for survival was savage, hideous—and usually brief. But for the shape of moving slime there was no battle. It ate whatever came its way, regardless of size, shape or disposition. It absorbed microscopic plankton and giant squid with equal assurance. Had its surface been less fluid, it might have retained the circular scars left by the grappling suckers of the wildly threshing deep-water squid, or the jagged toothmarks of the anachronistic frillshark, but as it was, neither left any evidence of its absorption. When the lifting curtain of living slime swayed out of the mud and closed upon them, their fiercest death throes came to nothing.

The horror did not know fear. There was nothing to be afraid of. It ate whatever moved, or tried not to move, and it had never encountered anything which could in turn eat it. If a squid's sucker, or a shark's tooth, tore into the mass of its viscosity, the rent flowed in upon itself and immediately closed. If a segment was detached, it could be retrieved and absorbed back into the whole.

The black mantle reigned supreme in its savage world of slime and silence. It groped greedily and endlessly through the mud, eating and never sleeping, never resting. If it lay still, it was only to trap food which might otherwise be lost. If it rushed with terrifying speed across the slimy bottom, it was never to escape an enemy, but always to flop its hideous fluidity upon its sole and inevitable quarry—food.

It had evolved out of the muck and slime of the primitive sea floor, and it was as alien to ordinary terrestrial life as the weird denizens of some wild planet in a distant galaxy. It was an anachronistic experiment of nature compared to which the saber-toothed tiger, the woolly mammoth and even Tyrannosaurus, the slashing, murderous king of the great earth reptiles, were as tame, weak entities.

Had it not been for a vast volcanic upheaval on the bottom of the ocean basin, the black horror would have crept out its entire existence on the silent sea ooze without ever manifesting its hideous powers to mankind.

Fate, in the form of a violent subterranean explosion, covering huge areas of the ocean's floor, hurled it out of its black slime world and sent it spinning towards the surface.

Had it been an ordinary deep-water fish, it never would have survived the experience. The explosion itself, or the drastic lessening of water pressure as it shot towards the surface, would have destroyed it. But it was no ordinary fish. Its viscosity, or plasticity, or whatever it was that constituted its essentially amoebic structure, permitted it to survive.

It reached the surface slightly stunned and flopped on the surging waters like a great blob of black blubber. Immense waves stirred up by the subterranean explosion swept it swiftly towards shore, and because it was somewhat stunned it did not try to resist the roaring mountains of water.

Along with scattered ash, pumice, and the puffed bodies of dead fish, the black horror was hurled towards a beach. The huge waves carried it more than a mile inland, far beyond the strip of sandy shore, and deposited it in the midst of a deep brackish swamp area.

As luck would have it, the submarine explosion and subsequent tidal wave took place at night, and therefore the slime horror was not immediately subjected to a new and hateful experience—light.

Although the midnight darkness of the storm-lashed swamp did not begin to compare with the stygian blackness of the sea bottom where even violet rays of the spectrum could not penetrate, the marsh darkness was nevertheless deep and intense.

As the water of the great wave receded, sluicing through the thorn jungle and back out to sea, the black horror clung to a mudbank surrounded by a rank growth of cattails. It was aware of the sudden, startling change in its environment, and for some time it lay motionless, concentrating its attention on obscure internal readjustment which the absence of crushing pressure and a surrounding cloak of frigid sea water demanded. Its adaptability was incredible and horrifying. It achieved in a few hours what an ordinary creature could have attained only through a process of gradual evolution. Three hours after the titanic wave flopped it onto the mudbank, it had undergone swift organic changes which left it relatively at ease in its new environment.

In fact, it felt lighter and more mobile than it ever had before in its sea basin existence.

As it flung out feelers and attuned itself to the minutest vibrations and emanations of the swamp area, its pristine hunger drive reasserted itself with overwhelming urgency. And the tale which its sensory apparatus returned to the monstrous something which served it as a brain, excited it tremendously. It sensed at once that the swamp was filled with luscious tidbits of quivering food—more food, and food of a greater variety than it had ever encountered on the cold floor of the sea.

Its savage, incessant hunger seemed unbearable. Its slimy mass was swept by a shuddering wave of anticipation.

Sliding off the mudbank, it slithered over the cattails into an adjacent area consisting of deep black pools interspersed with waterlogged tussocks. Weed stalks stuck up out of the water and the decayed trunks of fallen trees floated half-submerged in the larger pools.

Ravenous with hunger, it sloshed into the bog area, flicking its tentacles about. Within minutes it had snatched up several fat frogs and a number of small fish. These, however, merely titillated its appetite. Its hunger turned into a kind of ecstatic fury. It commenced a systematic hunt, plunging to the bottom of each pool and quickly but carefully exploring every inch of its oozy bottom. The first creature of any size which it encountered was a muskrat. An immense curtain of adhesive slime suddenly swept out of the darkness, closed upon it—and squeezed.

Heartened and whetted by its find, the hood of horror rummaged the rank pools with renewed zeal. When it surfaced, it carefully probed the tussocks for anything that might have escaped it in the water. Once it snatched up a small bird nesting in some swamp grass. Occasionally it slithered up the crisscrossed trunks of fallen trees, bearing them down with its unspeakable slimy bulk, and hung briefly suspended like a great dripping curtain of black marsh mud.

It was approaching a somewhat less swampy and more deeply wooded area when it gradually became aware of a subtle change in its new environment. It paused, hesitating, and remained half in and half out of a small pond near the edge of the nearest trees.

Although it had absorbed twenty-five or thirty pounds of food in the form of frogs, fish, water snakes, the muskrat, and a few smaller creatures, its fierce hunger had not left it. Its monstrous appetite urged it on, and yet something held it anchored in the pond.

What it sensed, but could not literally see, was the rising sun spreading a gray light over the swamp. The horror had never encountered any illumination except that generated by the grotesque phosphorescent appendages of various deep-sea fishes. Natural light was totally unknown to it.

As the dawn light strengthened, breaking through the scattering storm clouds, the black slime monster fresh from the inky floor of the sea sensed that something utterly unknown was flooding in upon it. Light was hateful to it. It cast out quick feelers, hoping to catch and crush the light. But the more frenzied its efforts became, the more intense became the abhorred aura surrounding it.

At length, as the sun rose visibly above the trees, the horror, in baffled rage rather than in fear, grudgingly slid back into the pond and burrowed into the soft ooze of its bottom. There it remained while the sun shone and the small creatures of the swamp ventured forth on furtive errands.

A few miles away from Wharton's Swamp, in the small town of Clinton Center, Henry Hossing sleepily crawled out of the improvised alley shack which had afforded him a degree of shelter for the night and stumbled into the street. Passing a hand across his rheumy eyes, he scratched the stubble on his cheek and blinked listlessly at the rising sun. He had not slept well; the storm of the night before had kept him awake. Besides, he had gone to bed hungry, and that never agreed with him.

Glancing furtively along the street, he walked slouched forward, with his head bent down, and most of the time he kept his eyes on the walk or on the gutter in the hopes of spotting a chance coin.

Clinton Center had not been kind to him. The handouts were sparse, and only yesterday he had been warned out of town by one of the local policemen.

Grumbling to himself, he reached the end of the street and started to cross. Suddenly he stooped quickly and snatched up something from the edge of the pavement.

It was a crumpled green bill, and as he frantically unfolded it, a look of stupefied rapture spread across his bristly face. Ten dollars! More money than he had possessed at any one time in months!

Stowing it carefully in the one good pocket of his seedy gray jacket, he crossed the street with a swift stride. Instead of sweeping the sidewalks, his eyes now darted along the rows of stores and restaurants.

He paused at one restaurant, hesitated, and finally went on until he found another less pretentious one a few blocks away.

When he sat down, the counterman shook his head. "Get goin', bud. No free coffee today."

With a wide grin, the hobo produced his ten-dollar bill and spread it on the counter. "That covers a good breakfast here, pardner?"

The counterman seemed irritated. "Okay, okay. What'll you have?" He eyed the bill suspiciously.

Henry Hossing ordered orange juice, toast, ham and eggs, oatmeal, melon and coffee.

When it appeared, he ate every bit of it, ordered three additional cups of coffee, paid the check as if two-dollar breakfasts were customary with him, and then sauntered back to the street.

Shortly after noon, after his three-dollar lunch, he saw the liquor store. For a few minutes he stood across the street from it, fingering his five-dollar bill. Finally he crossed with an abstracted smile, entered and bought a quart of rye.

He hesitated on the sidewalk, debating whether or not he should return to the little shack in the side alley. After a minute or two of indecision, he decided against it and struck out instead for Wharton's Swamp. The local police were far less likely to disturb him there, and since the skies were clearing and the weather mild, there was little immediate need of shelter.

Angling off the highway which skirted the swamp several miles from town, he crossed a marshy meadow, pushed through a fringe of bush, and sat down under a sweet gum tree which bordered a deeply wooded area.

By late afternoon he had achieved a quite cheerful glow, and he had little inclination to return to Clinton Center. Rousing himself from reverie, he stumbled about collecting enough wood for a small fire and went back to his sylvan seat under the sweet gum.

He slept briefly as dusk descended, but finally bestirred himself again to build a fire, as deeper shadows fell over the swamp. Then he returned to his swiftly diminishing bottle. He was suspended in a warm net of inflamed fantasy when something abruptly broke the spell and brought him back to earth.

The flickering flames of his fire had dwindled down until now only a dim eerie glow illuminated the immediate area under the sweet gum. He saw nothing and at the moment heard nothing, and yet he was filled with a sudden and profound sense of lurking menace.

He stood up, staggering, leaned back against the sweet gum and peered fearfully into the shadows. In the deep darkness beyond the waning arc of firelight he could distinguish nothing that had any discernible form or color.

Then he detected the stench and shuddered. In spite of the reek of cheap whiskey which clung around him, the smell was overpowering. It was heavy, fulsome, fetid, alien, and utterly repellent. It was vaguely fishlike, but otherwise beyond any known comparison.

As he stood trembling under the sweet gum, Henry Hossing thought of something dead which had lain for long ages at the bottom of the sea.

Filled with mounting alarm, he looked around for some wood which he might add to the dying fire. All he could find nearby, however, were a few twigs. He threw these on and the flames licked up briefly and subsided.

He listened and heard—or imagined he heard—an odd sort of slithering sound in the nearby bushes. It seemed to retreat slightly as the flames shot up.

Genuine terror took possession of him. He knew that he was in no condition to flee—and now he came to the horrifying conclusion that whatever unspeakable menace waited in the surrounding darkness was temporarily held at bay only by the failing gleam of his little fire.

Frantically he looked around for more wood. But there was none. None, that is, within the faint glow of firelight. And he dared not venture beyond.

He began to tremble uncontrollably. He tried to scream, but no sound came out of his tightened throat.

The ghastly stench became stronger, and now he was sure that he could hear a strange sliding, slithering sound in the black shadows beyond the remaining spark of firelight.

He stood frozen in absolute helpless panic as the tiny fire smoldered down into darkness.

At the last instant a charred bit of wood broke apart, sending up a few sparks, and in that flicker of final light he glimpsed the horror.

It had already glided out of the bushes, and now it rushed across the small clearing with nightmare speed. It was a final incarnation of all the fears, shuddering apprehensions, and bad dreams which Henry Hossing had ever known in his life. It was a fiend from the pit of Hell come to claim him at last.

A terrible ringing scream burst from his throat, but it was smothered before it was finished as the black shape of slime fastened upon him with irresistible force.

Giles Gowse—"Old Man" Gowse—got out of bed after eight hours of fitful tossing and intermittent nightmares and grouchily brewed coffee in the kitchen of his dilapidated farmhouse on the edge of Wharton's Swamp. Half the night, it seemed, the stench of stale seawater had permeated the house. His interrupted sleep had been full of foreboding, full of shadowy and evil portents.

Muttering to himself, he finished breakfast, took a milk pail from the pantry, and started for the barn where he kept his single cow.

As he approached the barn, the strange offensive odor which had plagued him during the night assailed his nostrils anew.

"Wharton's Swamp! That's what it is!" he told himself. And he shook his fist at it.

When he entered the barn the stench was stronger than ever. Scowling, he strode towards the rickety stall where he kept the cow, Sarey.

Then he stood still and stared. Sarey was gone. The stall was empty.

He reentered the barnyard. "Sarey!" he called.

Rushing back into the barn, he inspected the stall. The rancid reek of the sea was strong here, and now he noticed a kind of shine on the floor. Bending closer, he saw that it was a slick coat of glistening slime, as if some unspeakable creature covered with ooze had crept in and out of the stall.

This discovery, coupled with the weird disappearance of Sarey, was too much for his jangled nerves. With a wild yell he ran out of the barn and started for Clinton Center, two miles away.

His reception in the town enraged him. When he tried to tell people about the disappearance of his cow, Sarey, about the reek of sea and ooze in his barn the night before, they laughed at him. The more impolite ones, that is. Most of the others patiently heard him out—and then winked and touched their heads significantly when he was out of sight.

One man, the druggist, Jim Jelinson, seemed mildly interested. He said that as he was coming through his backyard from the garage late the previous evening, he had heard a fearful shriek somewhere in the distant darkness. It might, he averred, have come from the direction of Wharton's Swamp. But it had not been repeated and eventually he had dismissed it from his mind.

When Old Man Gowse started for home late in the afternoon he was filled with sullen, resentful bitterness. They thought he was crazy, eh? Well, Sarey *was* gone; they couldn't explain *that* away, could they? They explained the smell by saying it was dead fish cast up by the big wave which had washed into the swamp during the storm. Well—maybe. And the slime on his barn floor they said was snails. *Snails!* As if any he'd ever seen could cause that much slime!

As he was nearing home, he met Rupert Barnaby, his nearest neighbor. Rupert was carrying a rifle and he was accompanied by Jibbe, his hound.

Although there had been an element of bad blood between the two bachelor neighbors for some time, Old Man Gowse, much to Barnaby's surprise, nodded and stopped.

"Evenin' hunt, neighbor?"

Barnaby nodded. "Thought Jibbe might start up a coon. Moon later, likely."

"My cow's gone," Old Man Gowse said abruptly. "If you should see her—" He paused. "But I don't think you will. . . ."

Barnaby, bewildered, stared at him. "What you gettin' at?"

Old Man Gowse repeated what he had been telling all day in Clinton Center.

He shook his head when he finished, adding, "I wouldn't go huntin' in that swamp tonight fur—ten thousand dollars!"

Rupert Barnaby threw back his head and laughed. He was a big man, muscular, resourceful, and levelheaded—little given to even mild flights of the imagination.

"Gowse," he laughed, "no use you givin' me those spook stories! Your cow got loose and wandered off. Why, I ain't even seen a bobcat in that swamp for over a year!"

Old Man Gowse set his lips in a grim line. "Maybe," he said, as he turned away, "you'll see suthin' worse than a wildcat in that swamp tonight!"

Shaking his head, Barnaby took after his impatient hound. Old Man Gowse was getting queer all right. One of these days he'd probably go off altogether and have to be locked up.

Jibbe ran ahead, sniffing, darting from one ditch to another. As twilight closed in, Barnaby angled off the main road onto a twisting path which led into Wharton's Swamp.

He loved hunting. He would rather tramp through the brush than sit home in an easy chair. And even if an evening's foray turned up nothing, he didn't particularly mind.

Actually he made out quite well; at least half his meat supply consisted of the rabbits, racoons, and occasional deer which he brought down in Wharton's Swamp.

When the moon rose, he was deep in the swamp. Twice Jibbe started off after rabbits, but both times he returned quickly, looking somewhat sheepish.

Something about his actions began to puzzle Barnaby. The dog seemed reluctant to move ahead; he hung directly in front of the hunter. Once Barnaby tripped over him and nearly fell headlong.

The hunter paused finally, frowning, and looked ahead. The swamp appeared no different than usual. True, a rather offensive stench hung over it, but that was merely the result of the big waves which had splashed far inland during the recent storm. Probably an accumulation of seaweed and the decaying bodies of some dead fish lay rotting in the stagnant pools of the swamp.

Barnaby spoke sharply to the dog. "What ails you, boy? Git, now! You trip me again, you'll get a boot!"

The dog started ahead some distance, but with an air of reluctance. He sniffed the clumps of marsh grass in a perfunctory manner and seemed to have lost interest in the hunt.

Barnaby grew exasperated. Even when they discovered the fresh track of a racoon in the soft mud near a little pool, Jibbe manifested only slight interest.

He did run on ahead a little further, however, and Barnaby began to hope that, as they closed in, he would regain his customary enthusiasm.

In this he was mistaken. As they approached a thickly wooded area, latticed with tree thorns and covered with a heavy growth of cattails, the dog suddenly crouched in the shadows and refused to budge.

Barnaby was sure that the racoon had taken refuge in the nearby thickets. The dog's unheard-of conduct infuriated him.

After a number of sharp cuffs, Jibbe arose stiffly and moved ahead, the hair on his neck bristled up like a lion's mane.

Swearing to himself, Barnaby pushed into the darkened thickets after him.

It was quite black under the trees, in spite of the moonlight, and he moved cautiously in order to avoid stepping into a pool.

Suddenly, with a frantic yelp of terror, Jibbe literally darted between his legs and shot out of the thickets. He ran on, howling weirdly as he went.

For the first time that evening Barnaby experienced a thrill of fear. In all his previous experience, Jibbe had never turned tail. On one occasion he had even plunged in after a sizeable bear.

Scowling into the deep darkness, Barnaby could see nothing. There were no baleful eyes glaring at him.

As his own eyes tried to penetrate the surrounding blackness, he recalled Old Man Gowse's warning with a bitter grimace. If the old fool happened to spot Jibbe streaking out of the swamp, Barnaby would never hear the end of it.

The thought of this angered him. He pushed ahead now with a feeling of sullen rage for whatever had terrified the dog. A good rifle shot would solve the mystery.

All at once he stopped and listened. From the darkness immediately ahead, he detected an odd sound, as if a large bulk were being dragged over the cattails.

He hesitated, unable to see anything, stoutly resisting an idiotic impulse to flee. The black darkness and the slimy stench of stagnant pools here in the thickets seemed to be suffocating him.

His heart began to pound as the slithering noise came closer. Every instinct told him to turn and run, but a kind of desperate stubbornness held him rooted to the spot.

The sound grew louder, and suddenly he was positive that something deadly and formidable was rushing towards him through the thickets with accelerated speed.

Throwing up his rifle, he pointed at the direction of the sound and fired.

In the brief flash of the rifle he saw something black and enormous and glistening, like a great flapping hood, break through the final thicket. It seemed to be *rolling* towards him, and it was moving with nightmare swiftness.

He wanted to scream and run, but even as the horror rushed forward, he understood that flight at this point would be futile. Even though the blood seemed to have congealed in his veins, he held the rifle pointed up and kept on firing.

The shots had no more visible effect than so many pebbles launched from a slingshot. At the last instant his nerve broke and he tried to escape, but the monstrous hood lunged upon him, flapped over him, and squeezed, and his attempt at a scream turned into a tiny gurgle in his throat.

Old Man Gowse got up early, after another uneasy night, and walked out to inspect the barnyard area. Nothing further seemed amiss, but there was still no sign of Sarey. And that detestable odor arose from the direction of Wharton's Swamp when the wind was right.

After breakfast, Gowse set out for Rupert Barnaby's place, a mile or so distant along the road. He wasn't sure himself what he expected to find.

When he reached Barnaby's small but neat frame house, all was quiet. Too quiet. Usually Barnaby was up and about soon after sunrise.

On a sudden impulse, Gowse walked up the path and rapped on the front door. He waited and there was no reply. He knocked again, and after another pause, stepped off the porch.

Jibbe, Barnaby's hound, slunk around the side of the house. Ordinarily he would bound about and bark. But today he stood motionless—or nearly so—he was trembling—and stared at Gowse. The dog had a cowed, frightened, guilty air which was entirely alien to him.

"Where's Rup?" Gowse called to him. "Go get Rup!"

Instead of starting off, the dog threw back his head and emitted an eerie, long-drawn howl.

Gowse shivered. With a backward glance at the silent house, he started off down the road.

Now maybe they'd listen to him, he thought grimly. The day before they had laughed about the disappearance of Sarey. Maybe they wouldn't laugh so easily when he told them that Rupert Barnaby had gone into Wharton's Swamp with his dog—and that the dog had come back alone!

When Police Chief Miles Underbeck saw Old Man Gowse come into headquarters in Clinton Center, he sat back and sighed heavily. He was busy this morning and undoubtedly Old Man Gowse was coming in to inquire about the infernal cow of his that had wandered off.

The old eccentric had a new and startling report, however. He claimed that Rupert Barnaby was missing. He'd gone into the swamp the night before, Gowse insisted, and had not returned.

When Chief Underbeck questioned him closely, Gowse admitted that he wasn't *positive* Barnaby hadn't returned. It was barely possible that he had returned home very early in the morning and then left again before Gowse arrived.

But Gowse fixed his flashing eyes on the chief and shook his head. "He never came out, I tell ye! That dog of his knows! Howled, he did, like a dog howls for the dead! Whatever come took Sarey—got Barnaby in the swamp last night!"

Chief Underbeck was not an excitable man. Gowse's burst of melodrama irritated him and left him unimpressed.

Somewhat gruffly he promised to look into the matter if Barnaby had not turned up by evening. Barnaby, he pointed out, knew the swamp better than anyone else in the county. And he was perfectly capable of taking care of himself. Probably, the chief suggested, he had sent the dog home and gone elsewhere after finishing his hunt the evening before. The chances were he'd be back by suppertime.

Old Man Gowse shook his head with a kind of fatalistic skepticism. Vouching that events would soon prove his fears well founded, he shambled grouchily out of the station.

The day passed and there was no sign of Rupert Barnaby. At six o'clock, Old Man Gowse grimly marched into the Crown, Clinton Center's second-rung hotel, and registered for a room. At seven o'clock Chief Underbeck dispatched a prowl car to Barnaby's place. He waited impatiently for its return, drumming on the desk, disinterestedly shuffling through a sheaf of reports which had accumulated during the day.

The prowl car returned shortly before eight. Sergeant Grimes made his report. "Nobody there, sir. Place locked up tight. Searched the grounds. All we saw was Barnaby's dog. Howled and ran off as if the devil were on his tail!"

Chief Underbeck was troubled. If Barnaby *was* missing, a search should be started at once. But it was already getting dark, and portions of Wharton's Swamp were very nearly impassable even during the day. Besides, there was no proof that Barnaby had not gone off for a visit, perhaps to nearby Stantonville, for instance, to call on a crony and stay overnight.

By nine o'clock he had decided to postpone any action till morning. A search now would probably be futile in any case. The swamp offered too many obstacles. If Barnaby had not turned up by morning, and there was no report that he had been seen elsewhere, a systematic search of the marsh could begin.

Not long after he had arrived at this decision, and as he was somewhat wearily preparing to leave headquarters and go home, a new and genuinely alarming interruption took place.

Shortly before nine thirty, a car braked to a sudden stop outside headquarters. An elderly man hurried in, supporting by the arm a sobbing, hysterical young girl. Her skirt and stockings were torn and there were a number of scratches on her face.

After assisting her to a chair, the man turned to Chief Underbeck and the other officers who gathered around.

"Picked her up on the highway out near Wharton's Swamp. Screaming at the top of her lungs!" He wiped his forehead. "She ran right in front of my car. Missed her by a miracle. She was so crazy with fear I couldn't make sense out of what she said. Seems like something grabbed her boyfriend in the bushes out there. Anyway, I got her in the car without much trouble and I guess I broke a speed law getting here."

Chief Underbeck surveyed the man keenly. He was obviously shaken himself, and since he did not appear to be concealing anything, the chief turned to the girl.

He spoke soothingly, doing his best to reassure her, and at length she composed herself sufficiently to tell her story.

Her name was Dolores Rell and she lived in nearby Stantonville. Earlier in the evening she had gone riding with her fiancé, Jason Bukmeist of Clinton Center. As Jason was driving along the highway adjacent to Wharton's Swamp, she had remarked that the early evening moonlight looked very romantic over the marsh. Jason had stopped the car, and after they had surveyed the scene for some minutes, he suggested that, since the evening was warm, a brief "stroll in the moonlight" might be fun.

Dolores had been reluctant to leave the car, but at length had been persuaded to take a short walk along the edge of the marsh where the terrain was relatively firm.

As the couple were walking along under the trees, perhaps twenty yards or so from the car, Dolores became aware of an unpleasant odor and wanted to turn back. Jason, however, told her she only imagined it and insisted on going farther. As the trees grew closer together, they walked Indian file, Jason taking the lead.

Suddenly, she said, they both heard something swishing through the brush towards them. Jason told her not to be frightened, that it was probably someone's cow. As it came closer, however, it seemed to be moving with incredible speed. And it didn't seem to be making the kind of noise a cow would make.

At the last second Jason whirled with a cry of fear and told her to run. Before she could move, she saw a monstrous something rushing under the trees in the dim moonlight. For an instant she stood rooted with horror; then she turned and ran. She thought she heard Jason running behind her. She couldn't be sure. But immediately after she heard him scream.

In spite of her terror, she turned and looked behind her.

At this point in her story she became hysterical again, and several minutes passed before she could go on.

She could not describe exactly what she had seen as she looked over her shoulder. The thing which she had glimpsed rushing under the trees had caught up with Jason. It almost completely covered him. All she could see of him was his agonized face and part of one arm, low near the ground, as if the thing were squatting astride him. She could not say what it was. It was black, formless, bestial and yet not bestial. It was the dark gliding kind of indescribable horror which she had shuddered at when she was a little girl alone in the nursery at night.

She shuddered now and covered her eyes as she tried to picture what she had seen. "O God—*the darkness came alive! The darkness came alive!*"

Somehow, she went on presently, she had stumbled through the trees into the road. She was so terrified she hardly noticed the approaching car. There could be no doubt that Dolores Rell was in the grip of a genuine terror. Chief Underbeck acted with alacrity. After the white-faced girl had been driven to a nearby hospital for treatment of her scratches and the administration of a sedative, Underbeck rounded up all available men on the force, equipped them with shotguns, rifles, and flashlights, hurried them into four prowl cars, and started off for Wharton's Swamp.

Jason Bukmeist's car was found where he had parked it. It had not been disturbed. A search of the nearby swamp area, conducted in the glare of flashlights, proved fruitless. Whatever had attacked Bukmeist had apparently carried him off into the farthest recesses of the sprawling swamp.

After two futile hours of brush breaking and marsh sloshing, Chief Underbeck wearily rounded up his men and called off the hunt until morning.

As the first faint streaks of dawn appeared in the sky over Wharton's Swamp, the search began again. Reinforcements, including civilian volunteers from Clinton Center, had arrived, and a systematic combing of the entire swamp commenced.

By noon, the search had proved fruitless—or nearly so. One of the searchers brought in a battered hat and a rye whiskey bottle which he had discovered on the edge of the marsh under a sweet gum tree. The shapeless felt hat was old and worn, but it was dry. It had, therefore, apparently been discarded in the swamp since the storm of a few days ago. The whiskey bottle looked new; in fact, a few drops of rye remained in it. The searcher reported that the remains of a small campfire were also found under the sweet gum.

In the hope that this evidence might have some bearing on the disappearance of Jason Bukmeist, Chief Underbeck ordered a canvass of every liquor store in Clinton Center in an attempt to learn the names of everyone who had recently purchased a bottle of the particular brand of rye found under the tree.

The search went on, and midafternoon brought another, more ominous discovery. A diligent searcher, investigating a trampled area in a large growth of cattails, picked a rifle out of the mud.

After the slime and dirt had been wiped away, two of the searchers vouched that it belonged to Rupert Barnaby. One of them had hunted with him and remembered a bit of scrollwork on the rifle stock.

While Chief Underbeck was weighing this unpalatable bit of evidence, a report of the liquor store canvass in Clinton Center arrived. Every recent purchaser of a quart bottle of the particular brand in question had been investigated. Only one could not be located—a tramp who had hung around the town for several days and had been ordered out.

By evening most of the exhausted searching party were convinced that the tramp, probably in a state of homicidal viciousness brought on by drink, had murdered both Rupert Barnaby and Jason and secreted their bodies in one of the deep pools of the swamp. The chances were the murderer was still sleeping off the effects of drink somewhere in the tangled thickets of the marsh.

Most of the searchers regarded Dolores Rell's melodramatic story with a great deal of skepticism. In the dim moonlight, they pointed out, a frenzied, wild-eyed tramp bent on imminent murder might very well have resembled some kind of monster. And the girl's hysteria had probably magnified what she had seen.

As night closed over the dismal morass, Chief Underbeck reluctantly suspended the hunt. In view of the fact that the murderer probably still lurked in the woods, however, he decided to establish a system of night-long patrols along the highway which paralleled the swamp. If the quarry lay hidden in the treacherous tangle of trees and brush, he would not be able to escape onto the highway without running into one of the patrols. The only other means of egress from the swamp lay miles across the mire where the open sea washed against a reedy beach. And it was quite unlikely that the fugitive would even attempt escape in that direction.

The patrols were established in three-hour shifts, two men to a patrol, both heavily armed, and both equipped with powerful searchlights. They were ordered to investigate every sound or movement which they detected in the brush bordering the highway. After a single command to halt, they were to shoot to kill. Any curious motorists who stopped to inquire about the hunt were to be swiftly waved on their way, after being warned not to give rides to anyone and to report all hitchhikers.

Fred Storr and Luke Matson, on the midnight to three o'clock patrol, passed an uneventful two hours on their particular stretch of the highway. Matson finally sat down on a fallen tree stump a few yards from the edge of the road.

"Legs givin' out," he commented wryly, resting his rifle on the stump. "Might as well sit a few minutes."

Fred Storr lingered nearby. "Guess so, Luke. Don't look like—" Suddenly he scowled into the black fringes of the swamp. "You hear something, Luke?"

Luke listened, twisting around on the stump. "Well, maybe," he said finally, "kind of a little scratchy sound like."

He got up, retrieving his rifle.

"Let's take a look," Fred suggested in a low voice. He stepped over the stump and Luke followed him towards the tangle of brush which marked the border of the swamp jungle.

Several yards farther along they stopped again. The sound became more audible. It was a kind of slithering, scraping sound, such as might be produced by a heavy body dragging itself over uneven ground.

"Sounds like—a snake," Luke ventured. "A damn big snake!"

"We'll get a little closer," Fred whispered. "You be ready with that gun when I switch on my light!"

They moved ahead a few more yards. Then a powerful yellow ray stabbed into the thickets ahead as Fred switched on his flashlight. The ray searched the darkness, probing in one direction and then another.

Luke lowered his rifle a little, frowning. "Don't see a thing," he said. "Nothing but a big pool of black scum up ahead there."

Before Fred had time to reply, the pool of black scum reared up into horrible life. In one hideous second it hunched itself into an unspeakable glistening hood and rolled forward with fearful speed.

Luke Matson screamed and fired simultaneously as the monstrous scarf of slime shot forward. A moment later it swayed above him. He fired again and the thing fell upon him.

In avoiding the initial rush of the horror, Fred Storr lost his footing. He fell headlong—and turned just in time to witness a sight which slowed the blood in his veins.

The monster had pounced upon Luke Matson. Now, as Fred watched, literally paralyzed with horror, it spread itself over and around the form of Luke until he was completely enveloped. The faint writhing of his limbs could still be seen. Then the thing squeezed, swelling into a hood and flattening itself again, and the writhing ceased.

As soon as the thing lifted and swung forward in his direction, Fred Storr, goaded by frantic fear, overcame the paralysis of horror which had frozen him.

Grabbing the rifle which had fallen beside him, he aimed it at the shape of living slime and started firing. Pure terror possessed him as he saw that the shots were having no effect. The thing lunged towards him, to all visible appearances entirely oblivious to the rifle slugs tearing into its loathsome viscid mass.

Acting out of some instinct which he himself could not have named, Fred Storr dropped the rifle and seized his flashlight, playing its powerful beam directly upon the onrushing horror.

The thing stopped, scant feet away, and appeared to hesitate. It slid quickly aside at an angle, but he followed it immediately with the cone of light. It backed up finally and flattened out, as if trying by that means to avoid the light, but he trained the beam on it steadily, sensing with every primitive fiber which he possessed that the yellow shaft of light was the one thing which held off hideous death.

Now there were shouts in the nearby darkness and other lights began stabbing the shadows. Members of the adjacent patrols, alarmed by the sound of rifle fire, had come running to investigate.

Suddenly the nameless horror squirmed quickly out of the flashlight's beam and rushed away in the darkness.

In the leaden light of early dawn Chief Underbeck climbed into a police car waiting on the highway near Wharton's Swamp and headed back for Clinton Center. He had made a decision and he was grimly determined to act on it at once.

When he reached headquarters, he made two telephone calls in quick succession, one to the governor of the state and the other to the commander of the nearby Camp Evans Military Reservation.

The horror in Wharton's Swamp—he had decided—could not be coped with by the limited men and resources at his command.

Rupert Barnaby, Jason Bukmeist, and Luke Matson had without any doubt perished in the swamp. The anonymous tramp, it now began to appear, far from being the murderer, had been only one more victim. And Fred Storr—well, he hadn't disappeared. But the other patrol members had found him sitting on the ground near the edge of the swamp in the clutches of a mind-warping fear which had, temporarily at least, reduced him to near idiocy. Hours after he had been taken home and put to bed, he had refused to loosen his grip on a flashlight which he squeezed in one hand. When they switched the flashlight off, he screamed, and they had to switch it on again. His story was so wildly melodramatic it could scarcely be accepted by rational minds. And yet—they had said as much about Dolores Rell's hysterical account. And Fred Storr was no excitable young girl; he had a reputation for levelheadedness, stolidity, and verbal honesty which was touched with understatement rather than exaggeration. As Chief Underbeck arose and walked out to his car in order to start back to Wharton's Swamp, he noticed Old Man Gowse coming down the block.

With a sudden thrill of horror he remembered the eccentric's missing cow. Before the old man came abreast, he slammed the car door and issued crisp directions to the waiting driver. As the car sped away, he glanced in the rearview mirror.

Old Man Gowse stood grimly motionless on the walk in front of Police Headquarters.

"Old Man Cassandra," Chief Underbeck muttered. The driver shot a swift glance at him and stepped on the gas.

Less than two hours after Chief Underbeck arrived back at Wharton's Swamp, the adjacent highway was crowded with cars—state police patrol cars, cars of the local curious, and Army trucks from Camp Evans.

Promptly at nine o'clock over three hundred soldiers, police, and citizen volunteers, all armed, swung into the swamp to begin a careful search.

Shortly before dusk most of them had arrived at the sea on the far side of the swamp. Their exhaustive efforts had netted nothing. One soldier, noticing fierce eyes glaring out of a tree, had bagged an owl, and one of the state policemen had flushed a young bobcat. Someone else had stepped on a copperhead and been treated for snakebite. But there was no sign of a monster, a murderous tramp, nor any of the missing men.

In the face of mounting skepticism, Chief Underbeck stood firm. Pointing out that, so far as they knew to date, the murderer prowled only at night, he ordered that after a four-hour rest and meal period the search should continue.

A number of helicopters which had hovered over the area during the afternoon landed on the strip of shore, bringing food and supplies. At Chief Underbeck's insistence, barriers were set up on the beach. Guards were stationed along the entire length of the highway; powerful searchlights were brought up. Another truck from Camp Evans arrived with a portable machine gun and several flamethrowers.

By eleven o'clock that night the stage was set. The beach barriers were in place, guards were at station, and huge searchlights, erected near the highway, swept the dismal marsh with probing cones of light.

At eleven fifteen the night patrols, each consisting of ten strongly-armed men, struck into the swamp again.

Ravenous with hunger, the hood of horror reared out of the mud at the bottom of a rancid pool and rose towards the surface. Flopping ashore in the darkness, it slid quickly away over the clumps of scattered swamp grass. It was impelled, as always, by a savage and enormous hunger.

Although hunting in its new environment had been good, its immense appetite knew no appeasement. The more food it consumed, the more it seemed to require.

As it rushed off, alert to the minute vibrations which indicated food, it became aware of various disturbing emanations. Although it was the time of darkness in this strange world, the darkness at this usual hunting period was oddly pierced by the monster's hated enemy—light. The food vibrations were stronger than the shape of slime had ever experienced. They were on all sides, powerful, purposeful, moving in many directions all through the lower layers of puzzling, light-riven darkness.

Lifting out of the ooze, the hood of horror flowed up a latticework of gnarled swamp snags and hung motionless, while drops of muddy water rolled off its glistening surface and dripped below. The thing's sensory apparatus told it that the maddening streaks of lack of darkness were everywhere.

Even as it hung suspended on the snags like a great filthy carpet coated with slime, a terrible touch of light slashed through the surrounding darkness and burned against it.

It immediately loosened its hold on the snags and fell back into the ooze with a mighty *plop*. Nearby, the vibrations suddenly increased in intensity. The maddening streamers of light shot through the darkness on all sides.

Baffled and savage, the thing plunged into the ooze and propelled itself in the opposite direction.

But this proved to be only a temporary respite. The vibrations redoubled in intensity. The darkness almost disappeared, riven and pierced by bolts and rivers of light.

For the first time in its incalculable existence, the thing experienced something vaguely akin to fear. The light could not be snatched up and squeezed and smothered to death. It was an alien enemy against which the hood of horror had learned only one defence—flight, hiding.

And now as its world of darkness was torn apart by sudden floods and streamers of light, the monster instinctively sought the refuge afforded by that vast black cradle from which it had climbed.

Flinging itself through the swamp, it headed back for sea.

The guard patrols stationed along the beach, roused by the sound of gunfire and urgent shouts of warning from the interior of the swamp, stood or knelt with ready weapons as the clamor swiftly approached the sea.

The dismal reedy beach lay fully exposed in the harsh glare of searchlights. Waves rolled in towards shore, splashing white crests of foam far up the sands. In the searchlights' illumination the dark waters glistened with an oily iridescence.

The shrill cries increased. The watchers tensed, waiting. And suddenly across the long dreary flats clotted with weed stalks and sunken drifts there burst into view a nightmare shape which froze the shore patrols in their tracks.

A thing of slimy blackness, a thing which had no essential shape, no discernible earthly features, rushed through the thorn thickets and onto the flats. It was a shape of utter darkness, one second a great flapping hood, the next a black viscid pool of living ooze which flowed upon itself, sliding forward with incredible speed.

Some of the guards remained rooted where they stood, too overcome with horror to pull the triggers of their weapons. Others broke the spell of terror and began firing. Bullets from half a dozen rifles tore into the black monster speeding across the mud flats.

As the thing neared the end of the flats and approached the first sand dunes of the open beach, the patrol guards who had flushed it from the swamp broke into the open.

One of them paused, bellowing at the beach guards. "It's heading for sea! For God's sake don't let it escape!"

The beach guards redoubled their firing, suddenly realizing with a kind of sick horror that the monster was apparently unaffected by the rifle slugs. Without a single pause, it rolled through the last fringe of cattails and flopped onto the sands.

As in a hideous nightmare, the guards saw it flap over the nearest sand dune and slide towards the sea. A moment later, however, they remembered the barbed wire beach barrier which Chief Underbeck had stubbornly insisted on their erecting.

Gaining heart, they closed in, running over the dunes towards the spot where the black horror would strike the wire.

Someone in the lead yelled in sudden triumph. "It's caught! It's stuck on the wire!"

The searchlights concentrated swaths of light on the barrier.

The thing had reached the barbed wire fence and apparently flung itself against the twisted strands. Now it appeared to be hopelessly caught; it twisted and flopped and squirmed like some unspeakable giant jellyfish snared in a fisherman's net.

The guards ran forward, sure of their victory. All at once, however, the guard in the lead screamed a wild warning. "It's squeezing through! It's getting away!"

In the glare of light they saw with consternation that the monster appeared to be *flowing* through the wire, like a blob of liquescent ooze.

Ahead lay a few yards of downward slanting beach and, beyond that, rolling breakers of the open sea.

There was a collective gasp of horrified dismay as the monster, with a quick forward lurch, squeezed through the barrier. It tilted there briefly, twisting, as if a few last threads of itself might still be entangled in the wire.

As it moved to disengage itself and rush down the wet sand into the black sea, one of the guards hurled himself forward until he was almost abreast of the barrier. Sliding to his knees, he aimed at the escaping hood of horror.

A second later a great searing spout of flame shot from his weapon and burst in a smoky red blossom against the thing on the opposite side of the wire.

Black oily smoke billowed into the night. A ghastly stench flowed over the beach. The guards saw a flaming mass of horror grope away from the barrier. The soldier who aimed the flamethrower held it remorselessly steady.

There was a hideous bubbling, hissing sound. Vast gouts of thick, greasy smoke swirled into the night air. The indescribable stench became almost unbearable.

When the soldier finally shut off the flamethrower, there was nothing in sight except the white-hot glowing wires of the barrier and a big patch of blackened sand.

With good reason the mantle of slime had hated light, for its ultimate source was fire—the final unknown enemy which even the black hood could not drag down and devour.

MODEL NEPHEW

By Jack Davis, Albert Feldstein, and William M. Gaines

UNCLE'S HANDS BEGIN TO SHAKE SO THAT HE DROPS THE TINY MIZZEN MAST HE HOLDS WITH THE LONG SLENDER TWEEZERS...

YOU'LL *GET* IT ALL, SIDNEY... WHEN I'M *DEAD!* BUT NOT *ONE* MINUTE BEFORE...

I *KNOW*, UNCLE...

HE TURNS TO ME, AND THERE IS A FEAR IN HIS OLD EYES... THE FEAR OF A MAN WHO HAS SUDDENLY REALIZED THAT HE IS FACE TO FACE WITH DEATH. I MOVE TOWARD HIM...

YOU *WOULDN'T*...

OH, *WOULDN'T* I, UNCLE....?

HIS JAW DROPS OPEN AND HE STARTS TO CRY OUT. I CLAP MY HAND OVER HIS MOUTH...HIS NOSE... CUTTING OFF HIS AIR...

DON'T STRUGGLE, UNCLE. IT WILL *ALL* BE OVER IN A MOMENT...

G-G-G-GH...

I WATCH AS UNCLE'S FACE TURNS RED...THEN BLUE... AND HIS EYES FAIRLY POP FROM HIS HEAD AS THE LAST DROP OF OXYGEN IN HIS BLOODSTREAM IS ABSORBED...

SUFFOCATION CAN LOOK *SO MUCH* LIKE A *HEART ATTACK*, UNCLE! ONE CAN *RARELY* TELL THE *DIFFERENCE*... *ESPECIALLY* IN AN *AGED PERSON*...

UNCLE STIFFENS AS HIS LIFE EBBS AND DISSOLVES. AS HE DIES, HE SWINGS HIS ARMS BEFORE HIM, SWEEPING THE BOTTLE CONTAINING THE SHIP MODEL HE'D BEEN WORKING ON FROM HIS DESK...

DRAT IT...

THE BOTTLE SMASHES INTO A THOUSAND JAGGED FRAGMENTS WITH A SPLITTING CRASH AND THE TINY SHIP SPLINTERS INTO A SMALL PILE OF STRING AND TOOTHPICKS AND BALSA WOOD...

THAT'S *SURE* TO BRING THE *SERVANTS*. I'VE GOT TO GET *OUT* OF HERE.

I RELEASE MY UNCLE'S LIFELESS BODY, AND I DART FROM THE LIBRARY, OUT OF THE FRENCH DOORS, CLOSING THEM BEHIND ME. FROM A SAFE HIDING-PLACE AMONG THE BUSHES BEYOND THE PATIO, I WATCH THE SERVANT ENTER AND STAND DUMBFOUNDED AS HE VIEWS UNCLE'S CORPSE...

2

A FEW DAYS LATER, AT THE LAWYER'S OFFICE, MY LATE UNCLE'S WILL IS READ AND I LISTEN TO THE WORDS THAT MAKE ME A WEALTHY MAN...

...AND SO, TO MY *NEPHEW SIDNEY*, I LEAVE MY *ENTIRE ESTATE*, SAVE THOSE POSSESSIONS THAT ARE *NEAR* AND *DEAR* TO ME...MY *OLD SEA CAPTAIN'S UNIFORM* AND MY COLLECTION OF *SHIPS-IN-BOTTLES*. *THESE*, I REQUEST, BE *INTERRED* WITH MY *BONES*...

UNCLE'D MADE HIS FORTUNE WITH SHIPS. HE'D STARTED AS A SAILOR, WORKED HIS WAY UP TO SHIP'S CAPTAIN, AND EVENTUALLY BOUGHT HIS OWN FREIGHTER. FROM THERE, A WHOLE SHIPPING LINE HAD GROWN. WHEN UNCLE RETIRED, HE'D SOLD EVERYTHING. BUT HE NEVER COULD FORGET THE SEA ENTIRELY. I REMEMBER, AS A BOY, HIS TELLING ME STORIES OF HIS SEA ADVENTURES...

SHE WAS THE *SWEETEST* FOUR-MASTER THAT *EVER SAILED THE SEA*, SIDNEY.

AND THIS IS WHAT SHE *LOOKED* LIKE, UNCLE?

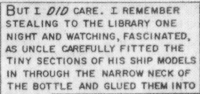

YEP, SIDNEY. *THAT'S HER*...EVERY *SPAR* AND *LANYARD*. MADE THAT MODEL *MYSELF*.

HOW'D YOU GET IT *IN THE BOTTLE*, UNCLE?

HEH, HEH. THAT'S A *SECRET*, BOY! A *SECRET*.

AW, *I DON'T CARE, ANYWAY!*

BUT I *DID* CARE. I REMEMBER STEALING TO THE LIBRARY ONE NIGHT AND WATCHING, FASCINATED, AS UNCLE CAREFULLY FITTED THE TINY SECTIONS OF HIS SHIP MODELS IN THROUGH THE NARROW NECK OF THE BOTTLE AND GLUED THEM INTO PLACE...

AND AS I GREW INTO MATURITY, AND I DISCOVERED HOBBIES OF MY OWN...CARS, AND WOMEN, AND HORSE RACES...THINGS THAT REQUIRED MONEY...I REMEMBER COMING TO MY UNCLE, AND BEGGING FOR A HANDOUT, AND HIM WORKING ON THOSE MISERABLE SHIP MODELS...

UNCLE, I...

SH-H-H-H! NOT NOW! THIS IS A TICKLISH PART...

BUT NOW ALL THAT IS OVER. I WILL NEVER HAVE TO BEG FOR ANOTHER CENT. IT IS ALL MINE...EVERYTHING. THE LAWYER, READING THE WILL, TELLS ME THAT...

...AND-THAT I BE PLACED IN THE MAUSOLEUM I HAVE BUILT FOR MYSELF IN FAIRHAVEN CEMETERY, ALONG WITH THESE NEAR AND DEAR POSSESSIONS...

GOOD RIDDANCE...

3

THE FUNERAL IS A SIMPLE AFFAIR. I HAVE SEEN TO THAT. AFTER ALL, WHY WASTE MONEY ON THE DEAD OLD GOAT, BUT I HAVE TO KEEP MYSELF FROM LAUGHING, AS THE SERVANTS FILE INTO THE MAUSOLEUM AND PLACE HIS STUPID SHIP-MODELS BESIDE HIS COFFIN...

ASHES TO ASHES... DUST TO DUST...

...AND DRAPE HIS MOTH-EATEN OLD UNIFORM AND CAP OVER THE SILENT SOMBER COFFIN...

AS SOON AS MY LATE UNCLE'S AFFAIRS ARE PUT IN ORDER AND HIS ESTATE IS TURNED OVER TO ME, I GO ON A WILD SPENDING BINGE...NO HOLDS BARRED. I GET RID OF ALL MY INHIBITIONS IN ONE MAD CONTINUOUS SPREE OF WINE, WOMEN, AND SONG...

ONE NIGHT, RETURNING HOME FROM MY LATEST FUN-SEEKING ESCAPADE, I FIND MYSELF DOWN BY THE WATER-FRONT, A LITTLE HIGH, WALKING DOWN A DESERTED, WINDING, FOG-BLANKETED, COBBLE-STONED STREET. AS I STAGGER ALONG, I HEAR A VOICE...

SIDNEY! I'VE BEEN *LOOKING* FOR YOU!

HUH?

A FIGURE STANDS BEFORE ME, SILHOUETTED IN THE HAZY LIGHT FROM A DISTANT STREET LAMP...A FIGURE IN A SEA-CAPTAIN'S UNIFORM...

COME, SIDNEY! I NEED A *CREW*. MY SHIP IS *WAITING*. COME...

WHO...WHO *IS* IT?

I TRY TO PEER INTO THE GLOOM, TO MAKE OUT THE FEATURES OF THE STOOPED FIGURE STANDING BEFORE ME, BUT THE LIQUOR I HAVE CONSUMED DULLS MY SENSES...

WE MUST *HURRY*, SIDNEY!

KEEP AWAY FROM ME! KEEP AWAY...

HE COMES TOWARD ME, SHAMBLING OVER THE COBBLESTONES. SUDDENLY AN ICY FEAR GRIPS MY HEART. THERE IS SOMETHING *FAMILIAR* ABOUT THAT FIGURE. HIS *WALK*. HIS *VOICE*...

WHO...WHO *ARE* YOU?

DON'T YOU *KNOW*, SIDNEY?

I BEGIN TO RUN. I AM TERRORIZED. MY HEART BEATS IN MY CHEST LIKE A TRIP HAMMER RUN WILD. HE STUMBLES AFTER ME...

NO! *NO! STAY AWAY...*

I RUN THROUGH THE DESERTED WATERFRONT ALLEYS, THE PERSPIRATION POURING FROM MY FACE. BUT NO MATTER HOW FAST I RUN, THE SHUFFLING FIGURE BEHIND GAINS ON ME. AND THEN, SUDDENLY, THE ROAD ENDS. I HAVE RUN OUT ONTO A PIER...

OUR *SHIP* IS *WAITING*, SIDNEY!

OH, LORD...

HE IS ALMOST UPON ME. I STAND, FROZEN, BENEATH THE DIM LAMP AT THE PIER'S END. AND THEN I SMELL IT...THE ODOR...THE ODOR OF DRIFTWOOD AND ROTTING SEAWEED...THE VILE AND NAUSEATING STENCH OF DECAY...

HE REACHES OUT TO ME, AND I INHALE THE FOULNESS OF HIS AURA, THE PUTRID REEK OF HIS FETOR. AND THEN THE LIGHT ABOVE US FALLS UPON HIS FACE...

CHOKE.. *UNCLE..*

THE FOG CLOSES IN ABOUT ME...FIRST GREY, THEN BLACK... AND I SLIP INTO THE MERCIFUL ESCAPE OF UNCONSCIOUSNESS, FALLING TO THE ROTTED BRINE-IMPREGNATED PIER BOARDS...

5

THE SOUND OF THE SEA AWAKENS ME. IT IS A HOLLOW ROARING SOUND, LIKE THE SOUND YOU HEAR WHEN YOU PLACE A SEA SHELL TO YOUR EAR. I STIR, SIT UP, AND LOOK ABOUT ME...

GOOD LORD! I'M ON A *SHIP!*

THE SKY ABOVE ME AS BLACK AS TAR, AND AN INKY GREEN SEA, CALM AND STILL, STRETCHES AWAY TOWARD IT. I STAND ON THE DECK AND I CALL...

YOU'VE GOT TO TAKE ME BACK! *HELP ME...* SOMEBODY. YOU'VE GOT TO TAKE ME BACK TO LAND! I'LL *PAY*...I'LL PAY *ANYTHING!*

I LISTEN. NO SOUND. ONLY THE EMPTY FAR AWAY ROAR, ECHOING. I STAGGER ACROSS THE DECK TO THE CABIN DOOR, SCREAMING...

ANYBODY ON BOARD? ANYBODY?

I PULL AT THE DOOR LATCH. THE DOOR STICKS FAST. AND THEN I SEE THAT IT'S NO DOOR AT ALL, BUT MERELY A DOOR PAINTED ON THE CABIN WALL...

WHAT *IS* THIS? WHAT KIND OF *SHIP* IS THIS?

I PEER INTO THE BLACK PORT HOLES...

ANYBODY *IN* THERE?

AND THEN I REALIZE THAT THEY ARE MERELY BLACK CIRCLES PAINTED TO RESEMBLE PORTHOLES...

GOOD LORD!

I AM *ALONE*... ALONE ON A *DERELICT SHIP*...A SHIP FLOATING IN THE MIDDLE OF *NOWHERE*... WITH *FAKE CABINS* AND *PAINTED PORT HOLES* AND *DUMMY DOORS.* OH, GOD...*SAVE ME!*

6

MY CRIES OF ANGUISH DRIFT INTO THE NIGHT, AND THEIR ECHOES COME BACK, TAUNTING, LAUGHING AT ME. FRANTICALLY, I PEER OUT ACROSS THE STILL SEA TO THE GLOW IN THE EAST THAT IS THE COMING DAWN...

DAYLIGHT! PERHAPS... PERHAPS...

AND THEN I SEE THAT THE OCEAN BELOW ME DOES NOT MOVE. ITS CALM SWELLS HANG FROZEN, PARALYZED, A MOTIONLESS MASS THAT STRETCHES AWAY SILENTLY TO THE...THE...

THE HORIZON! IT'S ONLY A SHORT DISTANCE AWAY!

SUDDENLY MY BLOOD FREEZES. I SWING DOWN THE SHIP'S SIDE, BURNING MY HANDS AS I SLIDE DOWN THE HEAVY ROPE...

OH, LORD! NO! NO!

...I DASH MADLY ACROSS THE SOLID SEA, STAMPING OVER THE FROZEN WAVES...

IT CAN'T BE...

AND I REACH THE WALL...THE WALL OF GLASS THAT RISES UPWARD AROUND AND OVER MY DERELICT SHIP AND DOWN TO THE DISTANT OPPOSITE HORIZON...

GLASS! IT'S GLASS! OH, GOD...

I STARE OUT OF MY BOTTLE PRISON AT THE DISTANT COFFIN LOOMING IN THE DAWN LIGHT FILTERING THROUGH THE MAUSOLEUM WINDOW. AND I SEE THE STILL-DAMP CAPTAIN'S UNIFORM DRAPED UPON IT...STILL DAMP FROM THE FOG OF THE NIGHT BEFORE. AND I KNOW THAT I AM DOOMED...DOOMED TO SPEND ETERNITY ON THE DECKS OF THIS SHAM VESSEL...THIS SHIP-IN-A-BOTTLE FOREVER LOCKED BESIDE ITS MAKER'S BIER...

CHOKE...

HEH, HEH. WELL, HIDIOTS! THAT ABOUT CORKS UP O.W.'S MORBID MESS-MAG FOR THIS ISSUE. WE'LL ALL SEE YOU NEXT IN MY HUMBLE HORROR HEDITION OF TALES FROM THE CRYPT. IN THE MEANTIME, IF YOU WANT TO MEET MORE FIENDS LIKE YOURSELF, CORRESPOND WITH OTHER CREEPS, WEAR PINS AND PATCHES, CARRY IDENTIFICATION CARDS, FRAME CERTIFICATES, AND GENERALLY ACT THE FOOL, THEN JOIN THE E.C. FAN-ADDICT CLUB! IF YOU WANT TO REMAIN REASONABLY SANE, DON'T DO IT! 'BYE, NOW.

·9·

BLOOD SONS:
A RUTHLESS REVIVAL

The onslaught of fearsome fantasies which constituted a definable and still viable horror revival may be dated at 1957, a year in which the sensitive and knowing might reasonably have expected the last monster to retire. The idea of expressing supernatural terror in works of the imagination had been so generally condemned that its exorcism was taken for granted. Moralists and do-gooders soon found new targets in television and in electronically amplified music, which soon replaced the comic book as the whipping boy of the arts. The flames of indignation were stoked by the morbid lyrics of the many popular songs like "Teen Angel" and "Endless Sleep," now classified by humorous historians as "death rock." Meanwhile, less sentimental images of mortality waited in the shadows.

It was a two-pronged attack. Two new film companies simultaneously rediscovered the commercial value of traditional terror tales; in the same year television unleashed a horde of Hollywood's hoary horrors. Screen Gems acquired the rights to the backlog of Universal's monster movie classics (and their numerous sequels), which were released to the public in a financial and cultural coup known to the trade as "Shock Theater." Syndicated to local stations throughout the United States for late-night viewing, these films introduced to a new generation such figures as Dracula, Frankenstein, the Wolf Man, the Mummy, and the Invisible Man, to say nothing of their offspring. The package proved to be eminently marketable, and it was followed in 1958 by more of the same, offered under the whimsical banner "Son of Shock."

The motion picture outfits that contributed most dramatically to the horror revival were Hammer Films of England and American International Pictures in the United States. Their rise to prominence foreshadowed forthcoming trends in the commercial cinema. This was most immediately obvious in the case of American International, whose first important release in the genre was *I Was a Teenage Werewolf* (1957). The title alone, by combining the dreaded blood lust of the monster movie with the equally menacing and relentless rhythm of "teenage" rock-and-roll music, jolted middle-aged taste makers and jaded adolescents as well, thus contributing in a small way to the contemporary generation gap. As the millions of kids from the war and postwar baby booms grew into a measure of financial freedom, they began to repaint the face of the entertainment industry. Mass communication made them infuriatingly sophisticated at an early age, and, raised in the shadow of nuclear annihilation, they began to look on

193

society-smashing monstrosities as heroic rebels. The undead villains of an earlier day were transformed mirthfully into immortal monsters, as youth attempted to forge an ethic out of iconoclasm. The aesthetics of "camp" and "pop" are based on a similar awareness of the ironies inherent in the projections of another era's mentality.

In short, *I Was a Teenage Werewolf* seemed as absurd to its devotees as to its detractors, but the absurdity in no way interfered with their enjoyment. The story introduced a variation on legendary lycanthropy, as the title character was converted into his bestial form by a scientific experiment in regression. This plot device emphasized the film's slight but self-evident vein of social significance, with the monster emerging as a victim of an indifferent establishment, his troubles increased by the malevolent authority figure who offers to relieve them. There were also less esoteric elements of adolescent fantasy, such as the scene in which the protagonist unleashes his animal passions in the girl's gymnasium of his high school. Although clearly never intended as a serious work of art, the film had more energy and momentum than many of its more pretentious competitors. The teenage terror was portrayed by Michael Landon who, like James Arness, later achieved less ephemeral fame as the star of a western television series ("Bonanza").

The concept of the awesome adolescent was the work of producer Herman Cohen, who concluded after a demographic survey that such a subject could hardly fail at the box office. The movie did indeed make an impressive profit on a small investment and was rapidly followed by *I Was a Teenage Frankenstein*, another 1957 Cohen production for American International. Whit Bissell played the sinister scientist, as he had in the previous outing, and Gary Conway was his creature, decked out in makeup so improbably putrescent that he looked as if he had just been hit in the face with a pie. More intentionally outrageous than its predecessor, this effort emphasized the humor and incongruity in the plot, becoming paradoxically less amusing because of its self-conscious efforts to transcend itself. Still, the image of the monster being irresistibly drawn to a rock-and-roll party remains etched in the memory. Cohen completed a trilogy in the same year with the release of *Blood of Dracula*, which really should have been called *I Was a Teenage Vampire*, since it features a heroine at a school for problem girls who is transformed into a bloodsucking monster by one of her treacherous teachers. Once again, traditional terrors were modified to accommodate the theme of puberty betrayed. Although a few other motion pictures were to appear in the same vein *(Teenage Caveman, Teenage Monster, Teenage Zombies),* a longer-lasting theme was inaugurated in American International's *Invasion of the Saucermen.* Here the kids are the heroes, defeating a menace that their obtuse elders have insisted on ignoring.

A somewhat more dignified but equally controversial approach was adopted by England's Hammer Films. Rather than updating the classic stories, Hammer restored them to their nineteenth-century settings, filming them in color with casts of excellent if unknown performers. Ingenuity and the English economy made it possible to produce impressively mounted movies at minimal cost, and the use of color film helped to give some old bodies a new lease on life.

Transformed by time and television, Karloff and Lugosi had begun to take on the aura of lovable father figures; a new menace was discovered just in the nick of time when a gaunt character actor named Christopher Lee was cast as both monsters in the Hammer remakes of *Frankenstein* and *Dracula.* Lee's classical training, comparative youth, and commanding physical presence produced the great horror star of the day. At one point he was reported to be receiving more fan letters from women than any other actor in Europe, indicating that his portrayals were flavored with a perverse sort of sex appeal. A

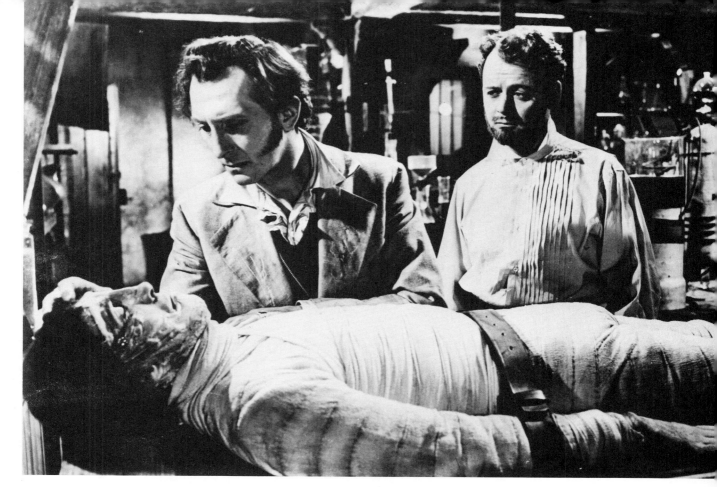

Peter Cushing goes to work on his creation, Christopher Lee, while Robert
Urquhart looks on skeptically. The trend-setting Hammer film *The Curse of
Frankenstein* was the first of a series following the career of the creator
rather than his creature. *Courtesy of Warner Bros. Inc. Copyright © 1957.*

perfect foil for Lee's grim vitality was found in the cool, intellectual performances of
Peter Cushing, who played the scientists responsible for creating the first monster and
destroying the second. Sequels and spin-offs followed like flies, for Hammer had
discovered a formula for converting crimson carnage into the long green. Their first color
horror film, *The Curse of Frankenstein* (1957), grossed millions of pounds worldwide on a
budget of a mere hundred thousand. The follow-up, released in America as *Horror of
Dracula* (1958), was equally successful, and no thing from this organization has finished in
the red.

The most identifiable ingredient in this bubbling vat of viciousness was its frankness.
The demonic, sometimes sadistic strain of the true Gothic found in authors like Walpole,
Maturin, and especially "Monk" Lewis was here in full flower. While the 1931 *Dracula*
had featured a virginal heroine and only as much blood as could be drawn from a cut
finger, the Hammer version offered a superfluity of statuesque starlets and gallons of gore
flowing from torn throats and transfixed hearts. Some critics carped and cringed; but the
public had no such reservations, and, within a decade, Hammer's ruddy realism had
become a cinema standard. Equally important as an indicator of future trends was the
company's financial position. An independent producer, Hammer released through a

Christopher Lee achieved stardom with Hammer Films' version of *Dracula*, released in the United States as *Horror of Dracula* (1958). In the opinion of some observers, his intense performance overshadowed that of Bela Lugosi. *Courtesy of Universal Pictures.*

variety of American studios which, caught in a cross fire between TV and the maverick menace mongers, were on their way to conversion into holding companies, video producers, or distribution directors.

The Curse of Frankenstein was no more faithful to the novel than previous adaptations, but the screenplay by Jimmy Sangster offered some new variations. Frankenstein is portrayed as a ruthless monomaniac, committing murders to obtain organs for his creation, which he deliberately uses for further crimes after bringing it to life. The sympathetic side of the original character is represented by a more scrupulous assistant who attempts to destroy the monster, only to discover that Frankenstein has revived it again. Billed as "the creature," Christopher Lee was a shambling, scarred, green-faced wreck who gives the unpleasant impression that he may fall apart at any moment. He is finally dissolved in a vat of acid, and Frankenstein, unable to prove that any such being has ever existed, is condemned to death for the monster's crimes.

Horror of Dracula, despite its cumbersome title, was a distinct improvement. Almost certainly Hammer's finest film, its adherents cite it as one of the genre's finest moments, while dissidents curse it for inaugurating a tradition in which subtlety and atmosphere counted less than shock and action. Director Terence Fisher was in this, as in the previous film, a very direct storyteller, abandoning the elaborate photographic tricks that can create a mood of mystery and concentrating instead on detailed scenes of sheer physical horror. Decked out in oversized canine teeth and crimson contact lenses, Christopher Lee makes Dracula a ferocious figure, far removed from the stately stalkers in earlier screen versions. His performance is effective enough to overshadow many of Bela Lugosi's most memorable mannerisms, and Lee went on to play the vampire in half a dozen sequels, becoming the premier interpreter of this most durable of horror roles. *Horror of Dracula* has an especially gruesome climax. The vampire's disintegration in the sunlight is not depicted in the usual series of sedate double exposures but in a rapid succession of violent action shots that make the transformation more effective than any amount of careful process photography.

Emboldened by the success of his compressed adaptations of the original novels, screenwriter Jimmy Sangster concocted a new story for Hammer's next effort, a sequel called *Revenge of Frankenstein* (1958). This witty little black comedy inaugurated a series that concentrated on the further adventures of the mad scientist, in contrast to the old Universal series that had considered his monster to be a much more marketable commodity. The film depicts Dr. Frankenstein (still Peter Cushing) escaping from a condemned cell to resume his experiments under an alias. Work in a charity hospital provides an endless supply of spare parts, and a new creature is soon under construction, its brain volunteered by a cripple who is anxious for a new lease on life. The result is an eminently presentable young man, at least until the brain begins to reproduce symptoms of paralysis in its new body. Frustration drives the creature to murder, and Frankenstein's identity is exposed. Before he can flee, he is attacked by his resentful charity patients and beaten to a pulp. Dying, Frankenstein instructs his assistant to take appropriate measures, and he is wheeled into a laboratory where a new host body is waiting for its creator's brain. An epilogue depicts a resurrected Dr. Frankenstein, with a new name and a new body, arranging his hair to hide a slight scar as he prepares to embark on a new experiment.

Released on the same program with *Revenge of Frankenstein* was one of the better horror films of the decade, a modest black-and-white non-Hammer offering entitled *Curse of the*

The gruesome climax of *Horror of Dracula,* in which Christopher Lee disintegrates into dust, exemplified director Terence Fisher's decision to provide maximum shock value. *Courtesy of Universal Pictures.*

Demon. Directed by Jacques Tourneur, *Curse of the Demon* retained much of the eerie atmosphere he had conjured up for the Val Lewton productions of an earlier era. Based on the M. R. James short story "Casting the Runes," the elaborated screenplay came closer to themes described by H. P. Lovecraft, especially in the appearance of a titanic entity from beyond. Despite a brief visit from this overpowering individual, the prevalent tone was tense and intimate, and the film came closer than most of its contemporaries to evoking an authentic sense of the supernatural.

The resurgence of interest in the macabre represented by these films and others of less importance was also reflected by broadcasters. Televised terrors began to come into their own. A leader in the field was Columbia Broadcasting System's "Alfred Hitchcock Presents," which bowed late in 1956. The famous motion picture director's fame was based on mystery and suspense films of a comparatively normal sort, but the television program rapidly acquired a somewhat ghoulish character. Amid stories of more common crimes, there appeared tales like Stanley Ellin's "Speciality of the House," in which an exclusive club for gourmets is revealed to be feeding its members human flesh; and John Keir Cross's "The Glass Eye," in which a spinster conceives an affection for a reclusive ventriloquist, only to discover that he is a life-sized dummy manipulated by a dwarf sitting on his knee. Occasionally the tales were frankly supernatural. In "Banquo's Chair," a detective plans to make a murderer confess by arranging for an actor to impersonate the victim's ghost. The actor is delayed, but the ghost appears right on cue. This episode and a few others were directed by Hitchcock himself, but for the most part he was content to serve as a sardonic master of ceremonies. In this capacity alone he broke a number of precedents. The rotund Englishman invariably introduced commercial messages with cutting remarks about his sponsor, a remarkably tolerant manufacturer of patent medicines. Furthermore, he subverted a cherished broadcasting rule which insisted that criminals should be punished for their misdeeds. More often than not, the teleplays left the villains triumphant, and Hitchcock would appear at the end of the program to reassure his viewers, with obvious insincerity, that justice had eventually triumphed.

The same network offered another program that intermittently touched on the macabre: Rod Serling's "Twilight Zone." Serling, a television writer who made his reputation with several social problem dramas like "Patterns" and "Requiem for a Heavyweight," was the host and chief scriptwriter for this series of dramas on fantasy themes. Although whimsy and science fiction were featured more frequently than tales of terror, "Twilight Zone" pioneered the concept of imaginative drama on prime-time television, making material of its type available on a wider scale than ever before. The themes were sometimes a trifle familiar to those already conversant with the literature in the field, but Serling's undeniable skill in dramatic construction provided considerable compensation. Perhaps his most frightening conception was "The Monsters Are Due on Maple Street," which depicted a small town degenerating into mass madness and murder under the threat of an invasion from outer space. A final twist suggests that spreading such panic is the form an actual invasion would take. A minor tour de force in a familiar tradition was provided by an adaptation of Charles Beaumont's short story "Perchance to Dream." Here a man with a weak heart visits a psychiatrist because his nightmares have become so horrible he is convinced that falling asleep will kill him. The session with the doctor turns out to be but another dream, for the patient falls asleep on the couch and dies from the terrors in his own mind. Perhaps the most unusual feature of "Twilight Zone" was Serling's behavior as the host. In contrast to the humorous approach that had become almost obligatory for masters of ceremonies on similar programs, Serling's demeanor was uniformly grim and earnest.

Supernatural stories of a different sort were presented on the American Broadcasting Company's "One Step Beyond." Produced, directed, and introduced by John Newland, this program was devoted exclusively to purportedly authentic accounts of uncanny events. Psychic phenomena of every sort were given a very restrained treatment which compared unfavorably with the melodramatics that audiences had come to expect in presentations of this kind, while the documentation was usually too scanty to produce a deep sense of conviction. Nevertheless there were a few interesting shows, especially one that abandoned the usual dramatic format to present a study of hallucinogenic drugs. Newland himself partook of some peyote to test its effect on extrasensory perception. This segment is especially noteworthy in retrospect, since drugs like these, although virtually unknown when the program first appeared, were to become an important factor in the occult revival of later years.

Perhaps the most ambitious of television's excursions into the unknown was the National Broadcasting Company's "Thriller." Its weekly offerings were a full hour in length, offering at least quantitatively twice as much as its rival programs, although both "Twilight Zone" and "Alfred Hitchcock Presents" made disappointing efforts to expand their time segments during their last days. "Thriller" acquired the services of the venerable Boris Karloff, already in his eighth decade but still more than able to perform as the program's host and, on occasion, its principal actor. For nearly half a century, Karloff's name had been synonymous with horror, and his presence in a production invariably added a note of dignity even though he appeared, especially in the years just before "Thriller," in some distinctly second-rate films. This program, however, maintained a solid level of quality, although it was not entirely free from clichés. As usual, crime dramas shared the screen with offerings of a more outré nature, but the macabre was represented here in greater proportion than on any previous television series. A number of the stories were drawn from the pages of the old *Weird Tales* magazine; an important contributor in this regard was veteran author Robert Bloch, whose previous credentials also included a stint as a radio dramatist. Among the most powerful of the program's productions was an adaptation of Bloch's story "The Spectacles," an episodic tale in which a pair of specially ground glasses permit the wearer to view the world as it really is. After a series of dreadful disillusionments, the protagonist glances into a mirror and, discovering the loathsomeness of his own reflection, destroys the spectacles and then himself. Another outstanding effort was a version of Robert E. Howard's improbably titled haunted-house tale, "Pigeons from Hell."

A lamentably short-lived excursion into the bizarre was provided by the CBS summer replacement series "Way Out." For a few weeks, some literate and ingenious half-hour dramas were presented by English author Roald Dahl, whose ironic tales have made him one of the modern masters of the macabre. Makeup artist Dick Smith made an important contribution to the effectiveness of the show's most striking segment, in which a photographer acquires the ability to alter the appearance of his subjects by retouching their portraits. When a drop of the enchanted liquid he uses accidentally falls on his own picture, he is horribly transformed, but not into the typical Hollywood monster. Instead, one side of his face is transformed into a flat, featureless surface, just as it had been blotted out in the photograph.

Each of these television programs had its moments, but none could compare with the old theatrical productions released to television by "Shock Theater." These films, seen by millions more than in their original appearances, established a permanent monster mythology for the mass audience. At the same time they provided a platform for dozens of new performers in the genre. The hideous host or hostess had become a staple ingredient in broadcasts of this character, and a multitude of characters found employment introducing the old movies to new audiences. Most of these "monsters of ceremonies" were crude and unimaginative, but at least one, John Zacherle, emerged as a first-rate parodist whose antics were more entertaining than all but the best of the films he introduced.

Working under the name of Roland for one season in Philadelphia, Zacherle was transferred to New York where, as Zacherley, he brought his strange profession to new heights of gory glory. Unlike many of his colleagues, Zacherley watched the movies he was presenting, and he made a specialty of building his routines around the premise of the evening's film. A "mummy" movie would find him involved in a scheme for do-it-yourself embalming, while a "mad scientist" feature would inspire him to transplant a brain (usually impersonated by a totally unconvincing cauliflower). He also injected himself directly into the films themselves, redeeming the clichés by replacing them. Confronted with the inevitable morgue scene in which a sheet would be pulled back to reveal a body for identification, Zacherley would arrange for his director to cut to a shot of Zacherley on a slab, waving at the viewers. On several occasions, he donned an Alpine hat to replace the leader of the indignant peasants out to destroy the monster in what he referred to as a "torchlight parade." As the quality of the movies declined, he became increasingly ruthless. Forced to contend with a particularly lame jungle epic, climaxed by a battle between two totally unconvincing gorillas, Zacherley killed the sound track and substituted a saccharine waltz. At the end of an interminable haunted-house mystery, the detective's elaborate explanations were drowned out by the crescendo strains of a Sousa march. One series of Zacherley's programs concluded with the gleeful ghoul being dragged away by the men in white suits; but the character has never really died, and its creator, now a comparatively subdued disc jockey, is still ready to don his white face and black coat at the drop of a head.

The shot of adrenaline provided by such video vultures encouraged motion picture producers to embark on a campaign of creature features. A solid market for such fare was indubitably present, and it seemed that any horror film could show a profit, regardless of

John Zacherle, who appeared in this guise under the names "Roland" and "Zacherley," was the best of television's horror hosts, a clever comedian whose monstrous mockery made light of dark doings.

its merits, provided that its budget was kept within certain limits. Drive-in theaters, at their peak during this era, helped to guarantee the profits on a number of films which, in all likelihood, were not even seen by their adolescent audiences. At any rate, some of the worst films ever made appeared, beside which even the poverty-row productions of the previous decade took on a certain dignity. Every connoisseur has his own favorite candidates for oblivion, but few were worse than Astor's *Frankenstein's Daughter* (1958), which disgraced a once proud name with a thoroughly inept effort about a male monster with a blonde's head attached. Equally incompetent were Allied Artists' *Attack of the Fifty-Foot Woman* (1958), featuring a disgruntled giantess knocking over papier-mâché buildings in a search for her estranged spouse while groaning "Harry! Harry!" in an overamplified monotone; and Astor's *She-Demons*, in which an unregenerated Nazi scientist conducts improbable experiments on the inhabitants of a tropical island.

One way for motion pictures to set themselves apart from this herd of monstrosities involved the use of publicity stunts. The leader in this field was producer-director William Castle, who used promotional gimmicks like heart-attack insurance policies and electric joy buzzers to keep crowds coming to see his films, providing enough ballyhoo to turn fairly ordinary flicks into sinister circuses. Strangely enough, the quality of Castle's films increased while his ingenuity kept him in business. An early outing, *Macabre* (1958), was a jumbled tale of premature burial that had little to offer except the promise that any patron dying of fright while in the theater would be eligible to collect a thousand dollars. The film's quality made this offer tolerably safe. A bit more shocking was *The Tingler* (1959), especially since Castle arranged to wire theater seats to keep his audience on the edges of them. This made about as much sense as the plot, in which a scientist discovers that fear manifests itself in the form of an oversized insect on the victim's spinal cord. The improbable was made somewhat more palatable by the presence of Vincent Price, whose brisk overplaying of the doctor helped establish him as the leading American actor in cinema shockers. Price was also on hand for Castle's prime achievement of the gadget period, *The House on Haunted Hill* (1958). This featured a process called Emergo, which consisted of a skeleton on a wire zooming over the heads of the audience, effectively disrupting the film's more authentic jolts. Still, it was a capable thriller, with some nasty ghosts explained away as the machinations of an equally nasty murderer. The Emergo device was vaguely tied into the action, since one of the killer's tricks involved the use of a marionette made out of bones; but several of his more interesting illusions went unexposed in the general rush to wind up the details of the plot.

Vincent Price also made an innocuous appearance as a well-intentioned onlooker in one of the period's most sensational science fiction shockers, *The Fly* (1958). This Twentieth Century-Fox production contravened normal expectations by not being about a giant insect. Instead, it concerned a young scientist who invents a device for transporting matter by disintegrating it in a transmitter and reintegrating it in a receiver. When he transports himself there is a fly hidden in the machine, and the result is a man with the oversized head of a fly. Most of the subsequent proceedings are devoted to his dismay at this revolting development, until he is finally put out of his misery by his wife. What rescued the film from oblivion was its grotesque climax, when the pesky fly is discovered in a spider's web, complete with a human head that screams for help in a buzzing falsetto. The story, by George Langelaan, had appeared previously in *Playboy*, a men's magazine which, against all likelihood, became an important forum for frightening fiction. Much of the responsibility for this rested with one of the editors, Ray Russell, whose own story "Sardonicus" was filmed in 1962 by William Castle.

Another science fiction effort that acquired an enduring reputation was Paramount's *The Blob* (1958). A weak script, lackadaisical direction, and bored actors could not detract from the charm of this colorful alien invader, which grew from a mere handful of goo by absorbing citizens of an all-American town. Sliding under doors, oozing through ventilators, emptying a theater at a midnight horror show, the Blob was a joy to behold, a lovable character that deserved more than its eventual destruction by the inevitable band of quick-witted teenagers, led by a slightly embarrassed Steve McQueen.

All this renewed flurry of interest in cinema and video manifestations of the macabre culminated in the emergence of a house organ for devotees of demonic drama. This was *Famous Monsters of Filmland*, an apparently inexplicable but undeniably durable magazine which, since its debut in 1958, has documented the past and present of fearsome films. Published against considerable odds by a tough-minded fantasy fancier named James Warren, *Famous Monsters* outlasted the dismay of social critics and the dissent of serious cinema scholars and eventually became something of an institution to succeeding generations of American kids. Competitors have come and gone, but the magazine's combination of wide-eyed enthusiasm and wisecracking ennui has proved unbeatable. The editor and principal writer is longtime monster lover Forrest J. Ackerman, whose credentials stretch back to the days of *Weird Tales*, when he was affectionately satirized, in a pamphlet anonymously circulated among members of the Lovecraft circle, for his unflagging devotion to the cause of fantasy fandom. Ackerman's tongue-in-cheek approach, deliberately aimed at a preadolescent audience, has contributed considerably to the concept that imaginary horrors are just good clean fun. His more serious endeavor is a gigantic collection of fantasy and science fiction material, to be housed for posterity in a Hollywood mansion.

Warren's brainchild rapidly became a rallying point and a marketplace for the fun-loving forces of fear, promoting and even inspiring not only films, but also a wide array of novelty merchandise dedicated to the proposition that every child, at heart, is a little monster. Rubber masks reproducing the features of filmland's famous fiends, glow-in-the-dark plastic vampire fangs, monster T-shirts, and similar accouterments now adorn the forms of countless children. Reportedly the Frankenstein mask alone has been worn by over a million satisfied customers. Aurora Products, a firm purveying model kits that usually ran to boats and planes, was persuaded to produce a series of scale-model monster kits, and millions of otherwise idle hands were soon employed in creating their own monsters.

No story captures this mood of monster madness more vividly than Richard Matheson's "Blood Son," even though it was written several years before the craze took hold. Originally published in an obscure 1951 pulp magazine, it surfaced in Matheson's 1957 collection *The Shores of Space*. Reprinted at the end of this chapter, this touching tale of a boy who wants to be a vampire when he grows up shifts through satire, schizophrenia, and the supernatural with telling effect. Of course, the fate of its protagonist is considerably more dramatic than that of his real-life counterparts. There may possibly be some justice in the argument that fictional crimes may inspire the impressionable to go and do likewise; but it seems reasonably clear that horror movies and similar fare do not increase the population of homicidal maniacs. Surely if a young Frankenstein fan had run amok, the media would have made the public painfully aware of it. Rather, it appears to be the repressed model of decorum who poses the real threat. Similarly, the creators of fearsome fantasies often seem to delight in depicting themselves and their fellows as dangerous lunatics, although the disappointing fact is that they are mild mannered to a fault, never inflicting tortures on anyone, occasionally excepting

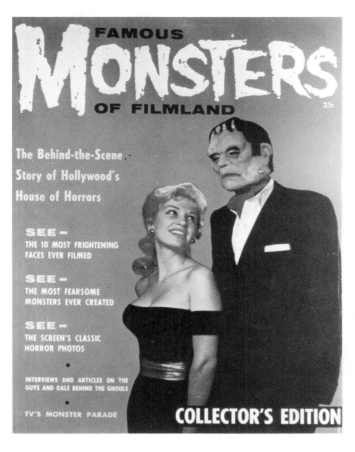

James Warren inaugurated the return of horror magazines with *Famous Monsters of Filmland* in 1958 (Warren is wearing the Frankenstein mask on the cover), and he revived horror comics a few years later with *Creepy*; the first issue's cover is by Jack Davis. *Copyright © 1958, 1964, 1975 by Warren Communications Corp. All rights reserved.*

The modern master of special effects is Ray Harryhausen, whose best techniques are demonstrated in a series of adventure epics like *The Seventh Voyage of Sinbad* (1958), in which this duel takes place between Kerwin Matthews and a skeleton who surpasses the usual oversized beasts.

themselves. All this suggests, theories to the contrary, that an interest in imaginary horrors is a sort of safety valve, creating catharsis rather than corruption.

Richard Matheson is a leader of that group of fantasy writers who, perhaps partly inspired by the indefatigable Robert Bloch, have fattened their traditionally feeble finances by finding work in films. His 1954 novel, *I Am Legend*, which offers a scientifically plausible explanation for a future plague of vampirism, was filmed twice within a decade, though neither version approached the intensity of the original. It is a grim and compelling chronicle of the last mortal on the planet, hunted by night and a hunter by day, finally eradicated by creatures who regard him as an anachronistic freak. An expert on vampire variations, Matheson is also responsible for the short story "The Funeral," a wildly comic look at an undertaker who loses his grip at the last rites of a sentimental vampire with some troublesome friends. Matheson's novel *The Shrinking Man*, about a radiation casualty who dwindles into infinity, became a tastefully low-key 1957 Universal film, *The Incredible Shrinking Man*, directed by Jack Arnold.

In contrast to this diminutive individual were the titans released with monotonous regularity by the Japanese studio Toho. After *Godzilla* came *Rodan*, an oversized prehistoric bird whose wings create cataclysmic air currents; *Gigantis, the Fire Monster*; and

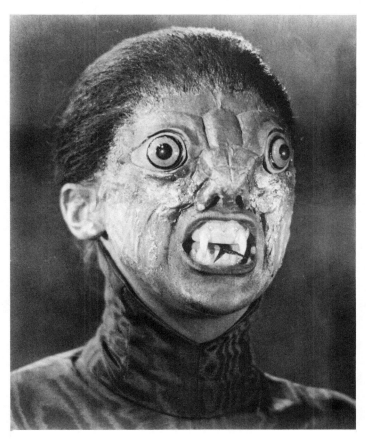

Jacqueline Pearce portrayed an unusual sort of monster, a snake woman, in the 1966 Hammer production *The Reptile*, directed by John Gilling. © *1966 Hammer Film Productions Ltd. All rights reserved. Courtesy of Twentieth Century-Fox.*

Mothra, a big, benevolent butterfly under the control of insipid twin pixies. The films became increasingly juvenile and the special effects, increasingly incompetent, and they were never aided by the atrocious dubbing they received for American release. Eventually the monsters were teamed up, often under American titles that were misleading at best. *Godzilla vs. the Thing* might have conjured up images of the famous science fiction film of an earlier day, but the "thing" turns out to be Mothra. *King Kong vs. Godzilla* particularly outraged purists by offering an actor in a shoddy ape suit as a substitute for the beautifully articulated animated model of 1933.

Other monster factories continued their onslaught with somewhat more respectable results. In 1959, Hammer Films released nicely mounted color remakes of *The Mummy* and *The Hound of the Baskervilles*, directed by Terence Fisher and costarring Peter Cushing and Christopher Lee. They slipped a bit in 1960 with *House of Fright*, an ingenious but inept variation on the Jekyll and Hyde story. In this one the doctor is rather homely, while his evil alter ego is a handsome devil; but coming up with this idea seems to have exhausted everyone connected with the project. More to the point was a sharp little fang-and-stake epic, rather deceptively entitled *Brides of Dracula* (1960). The count himself is nowhere in sight, but his old nemesis Dr. Van Helsing is on hand (Peter Cushing) to keep a crew of his followers at bay. Better yet was *Curse of the Werewolf* (1961), a relatively restrained (for Hammer) treatment of the lycanthropy legend based on a novel by Guy Endore. A surprising amount of attention was paid to the psychology of the afflicted party (Oliver Reed), who did not even show his furry face until the film's finish. On the other hand, the studio slipped in 1962 (as had Universal in 1943) by attempting to remake *The Phantom of the Opera*. The original's mythic proportions were lost when the Phantom (Herbert Lom) was explained away as a disgruntled composer with a scarred face.

The macabre motion picture gained a new aura of legitimacy in 1960 when director Alfred Hitchcock released *Psycho* on an unsuspecting public. Hitchcock's films had traditionally featured murder and mayhem of a fairly tasteful nature (with the possible exception of his 1926 silent Jack the Ripper film, *The Lodger*); but *Psycho*, perhaps inspired by the success of his intermittently morbid television show, was a thoroughgoing shocker. It also proved to be the most lucrative film produced in the genre up to the time, and it launched enough imitators to create a whole new subclassification of the horror film, one that has continued to the present day. Adapted from a novel by Robert Bloch, *Psycho* kept audiences off guard by devoting its first half to a typical Hitchcockian situation involving the adventures of a secretary (Janet Leigh) who has absconded with a small fortune. Since she serves as the sole focus for so much of the film, audiences are hardly prepared to see her brutally murdered shortly after her arrival at a seedy motel. She is ferociously stabbed to death while taking a shower, and the scene is jolting not only because of the juxtaposition of nudity and brutality, but also because of the photography and editing. The scene is a series of quick cuts from various angles, evoking a sense of frenzied violence without a direct depiction of its effects. The sequence is so revolutionary that the film is arguably among the most technically influential in the history of the medium. Hitchcock had more gore in store for his viewers, as well as the shocking revelation that the murders have not been committed by the motel keeper's mother, but rather by her crazed son (Anthony Perkins), who impersonates the old lady while keeping her mummified corpse in the cellar. Inferior variations have made this plot a trifle familiar, but in its day it was mind boggling.

A different sort of depravity reared its lovely head almost simultaneously. Virtually unnoticed by discreet students of the cinema, the glamorous English actress Barbara Steele broke new ground by emerging as the first full-time female fiend in films. Apparently regardless of writer or director, her movies display an outrageous spirit of depravity that transcends itself in self-mockery and sensible sensuality, perhaps most vividly displayed when, during the course of one obligatory love scene, she demonstrates an excess of passion by biting not her partner's but her own shoulder. A strange sort of submerged star status has enabled her to have an influence on cinema styles that far surpasses her public profile. She received star billing as an addled actress in Federico Fellini's classic *8½*, but the most clear-cut example of her work is in Mario Bava's atmospheric vampire film *Black Sunday* (1960), in which she characteristically plays the dual roles of haunter and haunted. This stylish Italian effort was one of the first European horror films to reach large American audiences since the days of the silent screen, but imports were to become increasingly common as the Hollywood studio system lost its stranglehold. Indeed, most of Barbara Steele's films have been European; the best of them include the Italian *Nightmare Castle* (1965), in which she portrayed an alternately seductive and vindictive ghost as well as her own victim; and *She-Beast* (1965), a combined Italian-Yugoslav production that juxtaposed some sinister Slavic legendry with the problems of Communist bureaucracy to produce some unexpected if not totally incongruous satire. In her only American film she was considerably overshadowed by a strong producer-director, one whose career requires separate comment.

The man in question, Roger Corman, did more than his share to upgrade the quality of the American horror film as well as that of his studio, American International. Until

1960, AI had been content with low-budget, black-and-white shockers perhaps best exemplified by the *Teenage* series. Increased capital and perhaps the example of Hammer Films led them in 1960 to a more dignified if less lively sort of production, *House of Usher*, which proved to be the first of a long series of free Poe adaptations. Corman was entrusted with this project after working wonders in the fifties with a series of inexpensive thrillers such as *It Conquered the World* (1956) and *The Wasp Woman* (1959). The best of earlier efforts were a pair of black comedies, *Bucket of Blood* (1959) and *The Little Shop of Horrors* (1960). The former concerned an ambitious if simpleminded "beatnik" who wins renown as a sculptor through the familiar device of covering corpses with clay. What made the story entertaining was the protagonist's mixture of dismay and delight as a series of accidents sets him off on a career of carnage. *The Little Shop of Horrors* featured a young florist's assistant with a prize plant that develops into a man-eater. The voracious vegetable's improbable but insistent demand "Feed me! Feed me!" seems to be firmly embedded in the minds of viewers who do not even remember the film's title.

Corman was finally rewarded with a substantial budget and a clever, accomplished actor in the person of veteran villain Vincent Price. Price created a new sort of movie "monster," a depraved mortal who struggles almost pathetically to avoid moral responsibility for past misdeeds, usually represented by a terribly tangible female corpse. In *House of Usher* he portrayed Poe's most striking character, a conception only slightly enfeebled by the inevitable elaborations on the plot which became necessary in order to turn a short tale into a full-length motion picture. Later adaptations were almost entirely original stories; but this first effort was fairly faithful to Poe's conception, although it added an improbable love affair for the doomed Madeline Usher. Still, the film did not have the proverbial Hollywood happy ending in which a pair of young lovers flee unscathed from the general disaster, and in fact almost all of Corman's Poe films have been free of this expendable cliché. This audience-identification device did not seem necessary to Corman, who has theorized that the success of his stories is based directly on the delight with which young audiences view the collapse of a corrupt establishment.

The next in the series, *The Pit and the Pendulum* (1961), retained only the title torture devices from Poe's famous tale, appending them to an original narrative by Richard Matheson (who had also adapted *House of Usher*) in which a medieval Spanish nobleman is driven mad by apparitions of his dead wife. Barbara Steele played the lady in question, who turns out to be very much alive, at least until the end of the film, and Price was in good form as the anguished aristocrat. Included in this outing, as in its predecessor, was a dream sequence in phosphorescent shades of green and blue. Such scenes were to become an inevitable part of the Corman formula. *Tales of Terror* (1962) managed to stay a bit closer to Poe by employing three of his stories; it also employed not only Vincent Price, but Peter Lorre and Basil Rathbone as well. The same year's *Premature Burial* starred Ray Milland and featured a screenplay by authors Ray Russell and Charles Beaumont. The obliquely titled *Haunted Palace* (1963) used the name of a Poe poem to disguise Beaumont's adaptation of H. P. Lovecraft's *Case of Charles Dexter Ward*. Though far from flawless, *The Haunted Palace* is not only the first but also the best filmed version of Lovecraft; Price played the possessed New Englander with characteristic aplomb, and the brief evocation of the ancient gods was appropriately awesome. This outing also included Lon Chaney, Jr., in a small role, and Corman continued his policy of hiring Hollywood's finest fiends by featuring Boris Karloff along with Price and Peter Lorre in *The Raven* (1963). Unfairly promoted as a serious shocker, this was a parody, not so much of Poe as of Corman, and not so funny as foolish, although there are some entertaining

Vincent Price loses his mind at the sight of Barbara Steele, who has convinced him of her death and will soon live to regret it, in the second of Roger Corman's Poe series, *The Pit and the Pendulum. Courtesy of American International.*

moments in a climactic magician's duel between Price and Karloff. Corman took a vacation from Poe and Price for the remainder of the year, directing Boris Karloff in an original story, *The Terror*, and casting Ray Milland as *X, the Man with the X-Ray Eyes*. The latter, written by Ray Russell and Robert Dillon, had an interesting premise and some good moments as a physician improves his vision for medical purposes and discovers that he can see through everything. Maddened by endless views of infinity, he finally tears out his glistening black eyeballs. In 1964, Corman traveled to England for his climactic endeavors, *The Masque of the Red Death* and *The Tomb of Ligeia. Masque* is his most lavish display, complete with the famous colored chambers of Prince Prospero's plague-besieged castle. It even offered Price a change of pace by allowing him to play a dedicated villain who does not spend all his time shying away from his own shadow. The film fails only in its attempts at profundity: when the Red Death appears he has Prospero's face, inspiring the dying guests to a limp and ludicrous dance, while the personified plague retreats to a

Roger Corman's spoof *The Raven* was distinguished mainly by its cast: Boris Karloff, Peter Lorre, and Vincent Price. Also present was Hazel Court, whose frequent work as a harassed heroine paralleled that of Evelyn Ankers twenty years previously. *Courtesy of American International.*

hillside to discuss the meaning of life with a group of similarly cowled figures—presumably the Yellow Death, the Green Death, and so on. All this is a long way from the petulant talking plant of *The Little Shop of Horrors*, and not necessarily in the right direction. Corman may have sensed as much himself, for *The Tomb of Ligeia* proved to be his last horror film. It was a highly polished reworking of those that had gone before, complete with perturbed Price and spectral spouse and even including fire footage from *House of Usher*. Before retiring from the field, Corman had not only made some solid films; he had also raised (at least in comparison to the previous decade) the level of competence that audiences would expect from American horror movies, and he had firmly established Vincent Price in the public's mind as the reigning master of the macabre.

A parallel development to this improvement of genre films was the increased output of what might be termed "serious" horror films—those that attempted to transcend a despised form by employing performers and attitudes generally considered too dignified for this sort of cinema. Perhaps they were inspired by *Psycho*, which had made a remarkable amount of money. *The Innocents* (1961) was an adaptation of Henry James's *Turn of the Screw*, featuring a performance by Deborah Kerr, direction by Jack Clayton, and a script by Truman Capote. The whole affair was so tasteful that it became tedious, and Capote's insistence on the psychological interpretation of the story banished the ghosts to limbo. More successful, if on a less ethereal level, was Robert Aldrich's *Whatever Happened to Baby Jane?* (1962). Bette Davis and Joan Crawford, rival queens from Hollywood's heyday, consented to appear as a pair of has-been hags who drive each other crazy in a decaying old mansion. It worked out so well that both women went on to appear in several more movies of the same type, though never together and never with the zany zest of this first encounter. In 1963 Robert Wise, who later achieved his greatest fame for directing the saccharine *Sound of Music*, served up his last morbid morsel, *The Haunting*, starring Julie Harris and Claire Bloom. Although the camera could not capture all the interior undertones of Shirley Jackson's novel, *The Haunting of Hill House*, Wise nevertheless managed to conjure up one of the most effective haunted-house atmospheres in screen history, most effective when one of the heroines realizes the hand she has been holding in the dark does not belong to anybody.

Alfred Hitchcock returned to horror of a sort in his 1963 film *The Birds*, a version of Daphne Du Maurier's enigmatic short story in which our feathered friends turn against mankind. Although much was made of the attack of the birds and its possible philosophical implications, the most shocking scene was a gratuitously introduced incident in which a carelessly dropped cigarette results in the explosion of a gas station.

At the opposite end of the spectrum from these prestige productions were the pictures released by an outfit called Box Office Spectaculars, including *Blood Feast* (1963), *2000 Maniacs* (1964), and *Color Me Blood Red* (1964). These films were truly horrible, not so much because of their renowned gruesomeness as because of their total ineptitude regarding production, performance, writing, directing, and decor. Principal responsibility for these deplorable efforts must rest with one Herschell G. Lewis, who wrote, photographed, and directed them, displaying an inordinate fondness for graphic scenes of dismemberment and disembowelment. These Box Office Spectaculars, it must be admitted, do have their adherents, if only among those who find the total lack of taste and talent to be hilarious.

Meanwhile, more orthodox producers of frightening films continued on their merry way. Hammer Films slipped a bit in 1964 with *The Evil of Frankenstein* (coming up with new titles was just one of the problems). This episode in the series retained Peter Cushing in the title role but made precious little sense as a sequel to previous films, since the plot involved the revival of a monster who had not appeared in any earlier outings. As played by Kiwi Kingston, he looked suspiciously like the old Universal monster, suggesting that this movie was an attempt to curry favor with nostalgic fans. As such, it did not succeed. Directed by Freddie Francis, this was a far cry from Don Sharp's pointed *Kiss of the Vampire* (1963), a well-mounted variation on familiar themes, featuring a whole convention of vampires and some new methods of dealing with them.

Hammer was also acquiring some British rivals, principally an organization called Amicus, which acquired the services of Peter Cushing and Christopher Lee for an anthology of short shockers called *Dr. Terror's House of Horrors* (1964). It proved to be a compendium of clichés; but Amicus stuck by its guns and in later years produced some increasingly capable chillers in the anthology style. Another outfit, Anglo-Amalgamated, revived Sax Rohmer's immortal villain in the person of Christopher Lee and came up

Dracula, Prince of Darkness continued the Hammer policy of showing horrors in gory detail. The punctured person is actress Barbara Shelley. © *1965 Hammer Film Productions Ltd. Courtesy of Twentieth Century-Fox.*

with *The Face of Fu Manchu* (1965). It worked surprisingly well under Don Sharp's capable direction, especially in its evocation of Edwardian England. Later films in the series proved to be comparatively slipshod.

Perhaps spurred on by this competition, Hammer rallied in 1965 with *Dracula, Prince of Darkness*. Christopher Lee returned in his best role, directed by Terence Fisher, and much of the excitement of *Horror of Dracula* was recaptured. A bizarre combination of history and horror was in evidence when Hammer presented *Rasputin, the Mad Monk*; it was held together entirely by Christopher Lee's dynamic performance as the hypnotic Russian. And the company attempted something like a big-budget spectacle with a version of H. Rider Haggard's *She*, with Cushing and Lee supporting Ursula Andress as the ageless Ayesha.

Still, the most interesting cinema shocker of 1965 was a black-and-white sleeper called *Dark Intruder*. Originally intended as a pilot film for an unproduced television series called "Black Cloak," it was released theatrically by Universal without creating much of a stir. Yet Barre Lyndon's Lovecraftian screenplay, involving transmigration of souls, and twins under the terrible curse of ancient gods, was unusually imaginative, and the direction by Harvey Hart was appropriately weird and compelling. Based on this small sample, the projected series would have been far superior to any of the exercises in televised terror that have actually made it onto the TV screen.

Frank Frazetta, who has since largely abandoned comics for book cover work,
did this painting for "Rock God," a story by science fiction writer Harlan Ellison.
Copyright © 1970, 1975 by Warren Communications Corp. All rights reserved.

Reed Crandall, one of the deans of comic book illustration, created this panel of medieval wizardry for the *Creepy* story "Castle Carrion," written by Archie Goodwin.

That year also saw an undeniable sign that the macabre was back in full flower: the reappearance of the horror comic book, after an enforced absence of more than a decade. The publisher was James Warren, of *Famous Monsters of Filmland* fame. He had published some one-shot comic book adaptations of films, combining motion picture stills with comic strip speech balloons to produce versions of such films as the original Hammer Frankenstein and Dracula movies, as well as such minor efforts as *Horror of Party Beach.* The success of these and various comics in the monster magazines led in 1965 to the release of *Creepy*, an oversized black-and-white comic book featuring some of the best artists in the business. Al Williamson, Reed Crandall, Frank Frazetta, and Jack Davis were among those represented in the first issue, which was written and edited by Archie Goodwin. An artistic and commercial success, *Creepy* was soon followed by more Warren horror titles and a host of imitators as well. Warren's bold move had successfully defied the industry's Comics Code Authority, all-powerful since its inception in 1954; when even the least respected of the arts was allowed to traffic in blood and thunder, it was certain that the vultures had come home to roost for good.

Yet there was more to come. The generation that had grown up insisting that death and decay were good clean fun finally reached its majority. And the artists who became spokesmen for this group began to whisper, against all common sense, that there might be something supernatural behind all this claptrap, that there might be more truth than poetry to this business of living in fear.

BLOOD SON

By Richard Matheson

The people on the block decided definitely that Jules was crazy when they heard about his composition.

There had been suspicions for a long time.

He made people shiver with his blank stare. His coarse gutteral tongue sounded unnatural in his frail body. The paleness of his skin upset many children. It seemed to hang loose around his flesh. He hated sunlight.

And his ideas were a little out of place for the people who lived on the block.

Jules wanted to be a vampire.

People declared it common knowledge that he was born on a night when winds uprooted trees. They said he was born with three teeth. They said he'd used them to fasten himself on his mother's breast drawing blood with the milk.

They said he used to cackle and bark in his crib after dark. They said he walked at two months and sat staring at the moon whenever it shone.

Those were things that people said.

His parents were always worried about him. An only child, they noticed his flaws quickly.

They thought he was blind until the doctor told them it was just a vacuous stare. He told them that Jules, with his large head, might be a genius or an idiot. It turned out he was an idiot.

He never spoke a word until he was five. Then, one night coming up to supper, he sat down at the table and said "Death."

His parents were torn between delight and disgust. They finally settled for a place in between the two feelings. They decided that Jules couldn't have realized what the word meant.

But Jules did.

From that night on, he built up such a large vocabulary that everyone who knew him was astonished. He not only acquired every word spoken to him, words from signs, magazines, books; he made up his own words.

Like—nightouch. Or—killove. They were really several words that melted into each other. They said things Jules felt but couldn't explain with other words.

He used to sit on the porch while the other children played hopscotch, stickball and other games. He sat there and stared at the sidewalk and made up words.

Until he was twelve Jules kept pretty much out of trouble.

Of course there was the time they found him undressing Olive Jones in an alley. And another time he was discovered dissecting a kitten on his bed.

But there were many years in between. Those scandals were forgotten.

In general he went through childhood merely disgusting people.

He went to school but never studied. He spent about two or three terms in each grade.

The teachers all knew him by his first name. In some subjects like reading and writing he was almost brilliant.

In others he was hopeless.

One Saturday when he was twelve, Jules went to the movies. He saw "Dracula."

When the show was over he walked, a throbbing nerve mass, through the little girl and boy ranks.

He went home and locked himself in the bathroom for two hours.

His parents pounded on the door and threatened but he wouldn't come out.

Finally he unlocked the door and sat down at the supper table. He had a bandage on his thumb and a satisfied look on his face.

The morning after he went to the library. It was Sunday. He sat on the steps all day waiting for it to open. Finally he went home.

The next morning he came back instead of going to school.

He found *Dracula* on the shelves. He couldn't borrow it because he wasn't a member and to be a member he had to bring in one of his parents.

So he stuck the book down his pants and left the library and never brought it back.

He went to the park and sat down and read the book through. It was late evening before he finished.

He started at the beginning again, reading as he ran from street light to street light, all the way home.

He didn't hear a word of the scolding he got for missing lunch and supper. He ate, went in his room and read the book to the finish. They asked him where he got the book. He said he found it.

As the days passed Jules read the story over and over. He never went to school.

Late at night, when he had fallen into an exhausted slumber, his mother used to take the book into the living room and show it to her husband.

One night they noticed that Jules had underlined certain sentences with dark shaky pencil lines.

Like: "The lips were crimson with fresh blood and the stream had trickled over her chin and stained the purity of her lawn death robe."

Or: "When the blood began to spurt out, he took my hands in one of his, holding them tight and, with the other seized my neck and pressed my mouth to the wound. . . ."

When his mother saw this, she threw the book down the garbage chute.

In the next morning when Jules found the book missing he screamed and twisted his mother's arm until she told him where the book was.

Then he ran down to the cellar and dug in the piles of garbage until he found the book.

Coffee grounds and egg yolk on his hands and wrists, he went to the park and read it again.

For a month he read the book avidly. Then he knew it so well he threw it away and just thought about it.

Absence notes were coming from school. His mother yelled. Jules decided to go back for a while.

He wanted to write a composition.

One day he wrote it in class. When everyone was finished writing, the teacher asked if anyone wanted to read their composition to the class.

Jules raised his hand.

The teacher was surprised. But she felt charity. She wanted to encourage him. She drew in her tiny jab of a chin and smiled.

"All right," she said, "Pay attention children. Jules is going to read us his composition."

Jules stood up. He was excited. The paper shook in his hands.

"My Ambition by . . ."

"Come to the front of the class, Jules, dear."

Jules went to the front of the class. The teacher smiled lovingly. Jules started again.

"My Ambition by Jules Dracula."

The smile sagged.

"When I grow up I want to be a vampire."

The teacher's smiling lips jerked down and out. Her eyes popped wide.

"I want to live forever and get even with everybody and make all the girls vampires. I want to smell of death."

"Jules!"

"I want to have a foul breath that stinks of dead earth and crypts and sweet coffins."

The teacher shuddered. Her hands twitched on her green blotter. She couldn't believe her ears. She looked at the children. They were gaping. Some of them were giggling. But not the girls.

"I want to be all cold and have rotten flesh with stolen blood in the veins."

"That will . . . hrrumph!"

The teacher cleared her throat mightily.

"That will be all Jules," she said.

Jules talked louder and desperately.

"I want to sink my terrible white teeth in my victims' necks. I want them to . . ."

"Jules! Go to your seat this instant!"

"I want them to slide like razors in the flesh and into the veins," read Jules ferociously.

The teacher jolted to her feet. Children were shivering. None of them were giggling.

"Then I want to draw my teeth out and let the blood flow easy in my mouth and run hot in my throat and . . ."

The teacher grabbed his arm. Jules tore away and ran to a corner. Barricaded behind a stool he yelled:

"And drip off my tongue and run out my lips down my victims' throats! I want to drink girls' blood!"

The teacher lunged for him. She dragged him out of the corner. He clawed at her and screamed all the way to the door and the principal's office.

"That is my ambition! That is my ambition! *That is my ambition!*"

It was grim.

Jules was locked in his room. The teacher and the principal sat with Jules' parents. They were talking in sepulchral voices.

They were recounting the scene.

All along the block parents were discussing it. Most of them didn't believe it at first. They thought their children made it up.

Then they thought what horrible children they'd raised if the children could make up such things.

So they believed it.

After that everyone watched Jules like a hawk. People avoided his touch and look. Parents pulled their children off the street when he approached. Everyone whispered tales of him.

There were more absence notes.

Jules told his mother he wasn't going to school anymore. Nothing would change his mind. He never went again.

When a truant officer came to the apartment Jules would run over the roofs until he was far away from there.

A year wasted by.

Jules wandered the streets searching for something; he didn't know what. He looked in alleys. He looked in garbage cans. He looked in lots. He looked on the east side and the west side and in the middle.

He couldn't find what he wanted.

He rarely slept. He never spoke. He stared down all the time. He forgot his special words.

Then.

One day in the park, Jules strolled through the zoo.

An electric shock passed through him when he saw the vampire bat.

His eyes grew wide and his discolored teeth shone dully in a wide smile.

From that day on, Jules went daily to the zoo and looked at the bat. He spoke to it and called it the Count. He felt in his heart it was really a man who had changed.

A rebirth of culture struck him.

He stole another book from the library. It told all about wild life.

He found the page on the vampire bat. He tore it out and threw the book away.

He learned the selection by heart.

He knew how the bat made its wound. How it lapped up the blood like a kitten drinking cream. How it walked on folded wing stalks and hind legs like a black furry spider. Why it took no nourishment but blood.

Month after month Jules stared at the bat and talked to it. It became the one comfort in his life. The one symbol of dreams come true.

One day Jules noticed that the bottom of the wire covering the cage had come loose.

He looked around, his black eyes shifting. He didn't see anyone looking. It was a cloudy day. Not many people were there.

Jules tugged at the wire.

It moved a little.

Then he saw a man come out of the monkey house. So he pulled back his hand and strolled away whistling a song he had just made up.

Late at night, when he was supposed to be asleep he would walk barefoot past his parents' room. He would hear his father and mother snoring. He would hurry out, put on his shoes and run to the zoo.

Everytime the watchman was not around, Jules would tug at the wiring.

He kept on pulling it loose.

When he was finished and had to run home, he pushed the wire in again. Then no one could tell.

All day Jules would stand in front of the cage and look at the Count and chuckle and tell him he'd soon be free again.

He told the Count all the things he knew. He told the Count he was going to practice climbing down walls head first.

He told the Count not to worry. He'd soon be out. Then, together, they could go all around and drink girls' blood.

One night Jules pulled the wire out and crawled under it into the cage.

It was very dark.

He crept on his knees to the little wooden house. He listened to see if he could hear the Count squeaking.

He stuck his arm in the black doorway. He kept whispering.

He jumped when he felt a needle jab in his finger.

With a look of great pleasure on his thin face, Jules drew the fluttering hairy bat to him.

He climbed down from the cage with it and ran out of the zoo; out of the park. He ran down the silent streets.

It was getting late in the morning. Light touched the dark skies with grey. He couldn't go home. He had to have a place.

He went down an alley and climbed over a fence. He held tight to the bat. It lapped at the dribble of blood from his finger.

He went across a yard and into a little deserted shack.

It was dark inside and damp. It was full of rubble and tin cans and soggy cardboard and excrement.

Jules made sure there was no way the bat could escape.

Then he pulled the door tight and put a stick through the metal loop.

He felt his heart beating hard and his limbs trembling. He let go of the bat. It flew to a dark corner and hung on the wood.

Jules feverishly tore off his shirt. His lips shook. He smiled a crazy smile.

He reached down into his pants pocket and took out a little pen knife he had stolen from his mother.

He opened it and ran a finger over the blade. It sliced through the flesh.

With shaking fingers he jabbed at his throat. He hacked. The blood ran through his fingers.

"Count! Count!" he cried in frenzied joy. "Drink my red blood! Drink me! Drink me!"

He stumbled over the tin cans and slipped and felt for the bat. It sprang from the wood and soared across the shack and fastened itself on the other side.

Tears ran down Jules' cheeks.

He gritted his teeth. The blood ran across his shoulders and across his thin hairless chest.

His body shook in fever. He staggered back toward the other side. He tripped and felt his side torn open on the sharp edge of a tin can.

His hands went out. They clutched the bat. He placed it against his throat. He sank on his back on the cool wet earth. He sighed.

He started to moan and clutch at his chest. His stomach heaved. The black bat on his neck silently lapped his blood.

Jules felt his life seeping away.

He thought of all the years past. The waiting. His parents. School. Dracula. Dreams. For this. This sudden glory.

Jules' eyes flickered open.

The inside of the reeking shack swam about him.

It was hard to breathe. He opened his mouth to gasp in the air. He sucked it in. It was foul. It made him cough. His skinny body lurched on the cold ground.

Mists crept away in his brain.

One by one like drawn veils.

Suddenly his mind was filled with terrible clarity.

He felt the aching pain in his side.

He knew he was lying half naked on garbage and letting a flying bat drink his blood.

With a strangled cry, he reached up and tore away the furry throbbing bat. He flung it away from him. It came back, fanning his face with its vibrating wings.

Jules staggered to his feet.

He felt for the door. He could hardly see. He tried to stop his throat from bleeding so.

He managed to get the door open.

Then, lurching into the dark yard, he fell on his face in the long grass blades.

He tried to call out for help.

But no sounds save a bubbling mockery of words came from his lips.

He heard the fluttering wings.

Then, suddenly they were gone.

Strong fingers lifted him gently. Through dying eyes Jules saw the tall dark man whose eyes shone like rubies.

"My son," the man said.

·10·

HEAVEN AND HELL: INNER SPACE

The late 1960s proved to be an extraordinary period for the promulgation of fearsome fantasies. The monstrous movement of the preceding years continued to gain momentum, and it was augmented by a new wave of mysticism which, while ostensibly directed toward sweetness and light, displayed a darker side as well. The extreme intensity of this new belief in the supernatural proved to be comparatively short-lived, but it left in its wake an atmosphere more favorable to occultism than there had been for two centuries. Ironically, if not too surprisingly, subsequent disillusionment with dabblings in the divine did not dramatically diminish the plausibility of the demonic, and many who had trouble believing in heaven found hell comparatively credible.

The cultural tone of this era was largely the product of the young people who were just coming of age. What happened to this generation has been described in many terms, some positive and some negative but all inadequate. To some observers (and participants) they were a "psychedelic" generation, and certainly the fascination with hallucinogens provided much of the imagery employed by emerging artists; but there was a simultaneous increase in the use of narcotics and depressants that produce a diametrically opposed effect. Such extremism was the order of the day, producing as many bright-eyed "Jesus freaks" as bleary-orbed devil worshipers. Those inclined toward the rediscovered art of astrology attribute such unorthodox behavior to the presence of Pluto in Leo and the reversals in mentality and morality, to the coming "Age of Aquarius," expected momentarily to replace the Piscean or Christian bimillennium that has occupied human attention since the year one. Searching for heights and depths beyond the range of more earthbound mortals, those creators who attempted to express the new consciousness often referred to themselves as members of the "Underground" or as advocates of the "Revolution," which might not be a war and might not even happen at all. For the most part, they were attempting to alter the human condition by burrowing from within, not from within the established system—that would be too traditional—but from within the individual's mind and, if there is one, from within the soul.

The well-received black music of the period is in fact described as "soul music," but this seems to define its level of sincerity rather than its spirituality. Yet there certainly is a search for some sorts of spirits being conducted in today's popular songs, especially among the British composers and performers whose translation of American "rock and roll" has led some observers to suspect that the combination of electric tone and lyric poetry is the most significant art form of the sixties and seventies. The range of expression employed proved wide enough to make horrors right at home.

There had been a few foreshadowings of such monstrous music, but only in burlesque form. In 1958, television horror host John Zacherle had moderate success with "Dinner with Drac," a spoken recitation delivered over a rock-and-roll background. Considerably more successful was "The Monster Mash," recorded a few years later by Bobby Pickett, imitating the inflections of Boris Karloff. This song broke some sort of precedent when it was released in the original version for the second time in 1973; it proved even more popular than in its first outing, and was for a time the most popular record in the United States.

A more serious sort of sinister strain made its appearance in the works of the London-based band the Rolling Stones, whose stance, generally hostile and antisocial, became positively morbid with the song "Paint It Black" (1966), a minor-key tribute to death and despair with a droning sitar accompaniment. It was very well received, and subsequent Stones albums have usually included at least one song with a similarly sinister theme. Lyricist and lead singer Mick Jagger has frequently indicated an interest in occult subjects; he is, for instance, an Arthur Machen enthusiast who cites "Novel of the White Powder" in arguing that no drug should be consumed unless its ingredients are ascertained. The 1967 album *Their Satanic Majesties Request* was indicative in its title alone, and the impression was intensified by the cover photograph, depicting the Rolling Stones in the costumes of medieval magicians. Most of the songs on the album had science fiction or supernatural subjects, and there is a long passage of primitive chanting that seems to suggest some unholy ritual. The 1968 album *Beggar's Banquet* contained a number that crystallized the band's image as spokesmen for the supernatural: "Sympathy for the Devil." Complex, hypnotic rhythms accompanied this dramatic monologue by no less a personage than Lucifer himself, recounting his triumphs and soliciting souls with a mixture of charm and threats. This powerful piece also provided the basis for a Jean-Luc Godard film, originally titled *One Plus One* but generally released in the United States under the more marketable *Sympathy for the Devil* (1970). Pieces like "Let It Bleed" (1969) and "Sister Morphine" continued in the same vicious vein, and 1973 found the Rolling Stones doing a duet with death in "Dancing with Mr. D."

The only English group whose reputation exceeded that of the Stones was the Beatles (John Lennon, Paul McCartney, George Harrison, and Ringo Starr). Their early image defined them as lovable moppets, but a few years after their debut in 1964 they began to pen some psychically suggestive songs like "Tomorrow Never Knows" (1966), "Strawberry Fields" (1967), "I Am the Walrus" (1967), and "Glass Onion." Harrison's increasingly frequent compositions revealed him as a melancholy mystic, while Lennon displayed the greatest fondness for the grotesque.

No pop group has done more to explore bizarre states of mind than The Who, whose full-length and coherent but barely comprehensible "rock opera" *Tommy* (1969) has even been performed at the Metropolitan Opera. *Tommy* is very likely the magnum opus of electric music. The plot, involving the private regeneration and public rejection of a modern messiah, is indicative of the hard-nosed and probing mysticism of its composer, Peter Townshend. More immediately macabre are the songs of his colleague, bassist John Entwistle, whose "Boris the Spider" was the first authentically frightening rock tune, a combination of throbbing bass and quavering treble which achieved a hair-raising sonic range. Entwistle's first solo album, *Smash Your Head against the Wall* (1970), is an unadulterated horror show, with songs like "External Youth" and "Heaven and Hell" exposing the simplemindedness of traditional dualistic morality in a manner that can only be described as Mephistophelean. His second album, *Whistle Rhymes* (1972), is equally morbid in a slightly more mortal manner, although the disconcerting sounds of "Nightmare" are as effective as anything he has accomplished. Followed by bands like Procul Harum, Pink Floyd, and King Crimson, these British rock revisionists have made fearful fantasy a permanent part of the music market.

The only American artist of comparable stature is singer-songwriter Bob Dylan, whose lyrics come closest of all to the standards of traditional poetry. His middle and most powerful period (postprotest and preprettification) contained some shattering images of urban despair, complete with characters like Jack the Ripper, Captain Ahab, and the Phantom of the Opera. His nerve-racking nihilism is perhaps most impressive in songs like "It's All Right Ma, I'm Only Bleeding" and "Desolation Row." The same sickness of the soul pervades his three best albums, *Highway 61 Revisited* (1965), *Blonde on Blonde* (1966), and *John Wesley Harding* (1967). Dylan's influence is most obvious on such fine American performers as the Byrds and the Band, and his negativism had its West Coast counterpart in the apocalyptic visions of "psychedelic" groups like the Grateful Dead, the Jefferson Airplane, the Mothers, and the Doors. The last of these, under the leadership of Jim Morrison, showed a special fondness for psychological melodrama.

Some bands have attempted to make horrors the sole focus of their performances. There was, for instance, a short-lived outfit that named itself H. P. Lovecraft, but it failed to live up to its namesake's standards. The most popular group of this type, in fact one of the most successful in recent years, is Alice Cooper. Not only do they specialize in sinister songs like "Halo of Flies," "Dead Babies," and "Dwight Frye" (a tribute to the character actor who appeared in *Dracula* and *Frankenstein*), but they also incorporate various forms of visual nastiness into their stage act. Starting with minor atrocities like dismembering dolls, they have worked up to the point where Alice (the lead vocalist) has, with the aid of professional conjurers, arranged to hang himself on stage and to be decapitated by a trick guillotine.

A radical crew with similar sentiments has also invaded the comics. By working with a despised and therefore accessible medium, a dedicated band of young cartoonists has altered the values of an art form, just as their more richly rewarded brothers have polarized popular music. The subject matter of "underground comix" is deliberately shocking, graphically depicting taboo forms of sex, of violence, and of political opinion, the last of which is presented as being inextricably bound up with the other two subjects. The most prominent artist in underground comics is Robert Crumb, whose *Zap* comic books began to appear in 1968. Crumb is conducting an all-out assault on our culture in which horrors are only part of the picture; but everything he portrays is grotesque, and some of his subjects are quite gruesome. All of his characters are mad, either by society's standards or those of the creator, who has described himself as a purveyor of "psychological sadism, with you, the reader, as the victim." Several of his heroes, like Nuts Boy and Forky McDonald, are psychopathic killers. Even more outlandish are the frantic figures of Crumb's cohort S. Clay Wilson, who are all practicing sadists or masochists, often members of cult groups; they are not much surprised to find demons in their midst. Wilson specializes in vivid renderings of appalling acts of perverted violence. The science-fantasy strip *Trashman* by Spain depicts the struggle of urban guerrillas against authorities who practice cannibalism and human sacrifice. Underground horror comic books were formalized by Rory Hayes and Gary Arlington with *Bogeyman* (1969), and since then almost every artist in this field has worked in the genre, acknowledging the inspiration of E.C. comics such as *Tales from the Crypt*. Some of the better titles in the

This knife-wielding, leather-jacketed, two-headed monster is actually Peter Townshend and Keith Moon of The Who. Not shown is their colleague, John Entwistle, who composes the band's most morbid material. *Photo by Roswell Angier.*

Rock star Alice Cooper hanging around as part of an elaborate stage show that included scenes of sin, retribution, and resurrection. The singer invariably returns from beyond in a shiny white suit. *Courtesy of Alive Enterprises.*

field include *Skull, Death Rattle,* and *Slow Death,* the latter specializing in terror tales with ecological overtones. Among the most accomplished practitioners of underground gore are Greg Irons, J. Osborne, and Richard Corben.

These outrageous comics originated in the radical newspapers that constitute the worldwide Underground Press Syndicate. Virtually all of these papers have featured sincere promotion of various occult studies, including astrology, card reading, and witchcraft. Astrology enjoyed an especially widespread revival, perhaps because its appeal is more immediately egocentric; but almost every sort of lost magical art acquired its adherents, and disciples in varying numbers crowded around almost any individual with the audacity to claim supernatural powers.

The most notorious of these proved to be one Charles Manson, a Californian who mesmerized a small army of mindless followers with a combination of powerful drugs, political propaganda, and purported occultism. They became the most notorious Satanist group in the world when Manson and several members of his cultish clan were arrested in 1969 for mass murder. Widespread publicity and the gang's ultimate conviction did much to discredit the whole underground movement; minds served by the mass media were inclined to identify them as typical of the counterculture, despite the obvious fact that most "hippies" were mild-mannered misfits rather than murderous maniacs.

Much of the public interest in the Manson case derived from the fact that one of the murder victims was motion picture actress Sharon Tate. Ironically, she had recently played a vampire victim in a film directed by her husband, Roman Polanski, a Polish expatriate who had made a specialty of macabre motion pictures. His peripheral connection with the gruesome crimes (he was abroad when the murders occurred) represents the closest connection ever between a major creator of imaginary terrors and actual atrocities. In fact, Polanski had made an amazingly popular movie about actors and Satanists and an earlier one about a deranged killer. The latter was *Repulsion* (1965), an exceptionally grim study of a muddled manicurist who slips into madness and murders two men. Although cast in the same mold as Hitchcock's *Psycho, Repulsion* lacked the elements of mystery and suspense, offering instead a clinical approach that made it seem more like a case history than a horror film. Still, it was an extremely capable effort; the obvious shock value of the killings was almost totally eclipsed by the bizarre visions that accompany the breakdown of the heroine (Catherine Deneuve). A completely different vein was tapped in Polanski's 1967 spoof *The Fearless Vampire Killers,* which featured the director as one of the title characters and Sharon Tate as a village maiden who is transformed into one of the undead. This film, subtitled *Pardon Me, but Your Teeth Are in My Neck,* contained a number of amusing gags, some of them part of fan folklore (a Jewish vampire displaying indifference when confronted with a cross), and some of them original (a fiend pursues his victims across snow-covered mountains, using his coffin as a sled). There were also just enough scenes of picturesque atmosphere to produce a lingering regret that Polanski did not make a serious attempt to come to grips with the subject. This entertaining effort made little impression on the public, but Polanski's next project proved to be the most profitable horror film to date.

This was *Rosemary's Baby* (1968), produced by veteran menace merchandiser William Castle. It impressed some critics and most customers by avoiding many of the stylized trappings of the traditional monster movie, but what it substituted for them were the equally conventional clichés of a slick, vacant soap opera. An inane young couple, who might normally have been employed as the background for the more entertaining antics of assorted fiends, were here presented as the focal point of the film. As the principal character, Mia Farrow gave a performance as hollow as her role, while better actors like John Cassavetes and Maurice Evans were obliged to stand in her shadow trying to avoid looking embarrassed. The story was derived from Ira Levin's best-selling 1967 novel, which utilized long passages about the tragic state of current events to add credence to the idea that Satan was up and about. Yet even granting the premise that the father of evil was ready to unleash a half-human offspring on the world, it still seems implausible that he would choose the neurotic and reluctant Rosemary to be the mother, especially considering the number of followers he had in her apartment building alone. The devil worshipers were portrayed against type as individuals both normal and boring; Ruth Gordon won an Oscar for enacting one of them as a perfectly lovable old lady.

Rosemary's Baby is just one of a number of novels with bizarre themes to enjoy wide popularity during this era, the first such literary period since the heyday of the Gothic novel almost two centuries ago. Perhaps the most talented author to mix the macabre with mass appeal was John Fowles, whose suspenseful debut *The Collector* appeared in 1963 and was capably adapted for the screen in 1965 by veteran director William Wyler. The story concerns a repressed young clerk who buys an isolated house with his huge lottery winnings, then kidnaps a young woman he has admired with the hope that she will fall in love with him. Avoiding the obvious melodramatics, Fowles paints an exquisite portrait of the butterfly-collecting psychopath, whose plan idealistically eschews such predictable devices as rape or murder. The result is a terrific tension concerning whether or not he will completely lose control, only intensified by the realization that the character is not entirely unsympathetic and that a disaster for his victim will be one for him as well. The conflict degenerates into sickening horror as the girl contracts pneumonia and the collector, torn between pity and paranoia, allows her to die before he can bring himself to seek medical help. The motion picture version, although unable to reproduce all the insight of the original, was one of the most accurate film adaptations of high-quality terror tales, and best acting awards at the Cannes Film Festival went to the principal performers, Terence Stamp and Samantha Eggar.

In 1966 Fowles followed *The Collector* with a more ambitious if less perfectly controlled novel, *The Magus.* The plot involved a visitor to a Greek island who comes half-voluntarily under the power of its mysterious proprietor, a man whose odd behavior and odder entourage suggest that he is a magician who has mastered the secrets of life and death. Illusion and reality become hopelessly scrambled for the hero, who sometimes suspects that he is the victim of an elaborate hoax but sometimes toys with the conviction that he is in the presence of the supernatural. The puzzle is never perfectly solved; while some of the bizarre manifestations are explained away as theatrical trickery, a tantalizing residue of doubt remains. The question is not only whether the "magus" is a magician or a fraud but, regardless, whether he should be considered a sadistic madman or a profound teacher. All of this proved a little too subtle and complex for the 1968 film version, which was nonetheless handsomely mounted and well played by a cast including Michael Caine and Anthony Quinn.

A moderately successful actor named Tom Tryon managed to become a popular author with nerve-racking novels like *The Other* (1971) and *Harvest Home* (1973). *The Other* was almost immediately adapted into a motion picture; its narrative of children involved in murder and possession is another embodiment of the almost obligatory theme (as in *Rosemary's Baby* and later *The Exorcist*) which, by outraging maternal instincts, appeals to the predominantly matronly audience for best-selling novels.

A different sort of audience, predominantly students, constituted a considerable market for fantasy novels in inexpensive paperback editions. Wonders of the most unpredictable nature appear in the works of Kurt Vonnegut, Jr., whose sarcastic despair somehow brought hope to a vast throng of young science fiction readers. His novel *Cat's Cradle*, originally published in 1963 but increasingly popular in later years, might qualify as a tale of terror, since its subject was the destruction of the planet by a chemical that solidifies the water supply; but the book is so fashioned that its tone implies no more than a wry dismay over human stupidity. Many of Vonnegut's adherents also read J. R. R. Tolkien's elfin epic *The Lord of the Rings*, a revived trilogy from an earlier era which, although it was devoid of the dreadful, did at least demonstrate the continued growth of a market for the literature of fantasy. A somewhat grimmer picture was provided by science fiction author Robert Heinlein's *Stranger in a Strange Land*, about an extraterrestrial messiah executed for excessive humanism. More to the point were at least some of the tales collected in Harlan Ellison's anthology of original science fiction stories, *Dangerous Visions* (1967). Fascinated by Robert Bloch's famous story "Yours Truly, Jack the Ripper," Ellison solicited a story from Bloch in which that tale's immortal protagonist would be transported into the future. The result, "A Toy for Juliette," was good enough, but Ellison had ideas of his own that led to a sequel to the sequel entitled "The Prowler in the City at the Edge of the World." This immensely powerful picture of a maniac's mental processes also provided some wrenchingly realistic descriptions of his unsavory behavior, but it was most effective in its vision of a degenerate postatomic society so cold-bloodedly degenerate that even the Ripper finds it unbearable.

Less widely known, but more accomplished than many modern books in the genre, were two fine novels by James Blish and Brock Brower. Blish, renowned for his science fiction, created an impressive picture of satanism in *Black Easter* (1968). This tale of an attempt to unleash all the forces of evil upon an unsuspecting world includes some convincing demonology, and a pessimistic conclusion which is likely to rattle even the most hardened reader. Brower's *The Late Great Creature* (1971) is the story of an imaginary horror movie star who slips into madness with a bit of method to it. This piece of frightening fun contains interesting background on the preparation of monstrous motion pictures, as well as some unflattering portraits of slightly disguised celebrities in the field.

Of course no literary effort enjoyed the vast audiences that were commonplace for television, where programs with a sinister slant were spreading like plague. Not too surprisingly, the early symptoms included a pair of shows with a parody flavor. Televised terror remained a tricky problem, because the medium is subjected to heavy censorship and because commercial and household interruptions are not conducive to a sustained mood. A comedy treatment appeared to be a painless way for video producers to get in on the burgeoning monster boom, and Universal studios, by now heavily involved in television film work, revived its heavily copyrighted Frankenstein makeup and unleashed "The Munsters." This was a typical television situation comedy series, expressed through the clichés of the old-school horror film. The basic gag was that a family of monsters could be completely sociable and totally unaware of the effect they have on the public at large. As the head of the family, Herman Munster (Fred Gwynne) was a dead ringer for Universal's Frankenstein monster; his son was a budding werewolf, his father-in-law a vampire, and his wife Lily (Yvonne De Carlo) some sort of undifferentiated zombie. The show was pretty predictable, but it managed to survive for more than one season, and it even spawned a lackluster theatrical feature, *Munster Go Home*, in 1966.

"The Munsters" of 1964 spawned "The Addams Family" of 1965, although the new program had another origin a quarter of a century older, which may in fact have been an inspiration to the producers of "The Munsters." "The Addams Family" was derived from the cartoons of Charles Addams, which had been for years a popular feature of the

A holiday scene at the home of the fiendish family created by Charles Addams, whose work delighted readers of *The New Yorker* for years before getting a wider, if weaker, exposure through a television series. *Drawing by Chas. Addams. Copyright 1946, 1974 The New Yorker Magazine, Inc.*

New Yorker magazine. Virtually every cartoon Addams has done derives its humor from a macabre premise, and many of them have featured a household of nameless ghouls residing in a decrepit mansion, complete with a butler who bears a striking resemblance to Boris Karloff, as the actor himself noticed in his introduction to a collection of Addams drawings, *Drawn and Quartered* (1942). Although the television version was somewhat restrained (there was never anything approaching the Addams cartoon in which the family prepared to pour boiling oil on a crew of Christmas carolers), the series improved somewhat on "The Munsters" by offering a group, portrayed by John Astin, Carolyn Jones, and Jackie Coogan among others, that was, if not actually fiendish, at least entertainingly depraved.

Science fiction also provided a share of rather oblique televised terror. The ABC network offered a variety of programs in this vein; the longest run was enjoyed by producer Irwin Allen's "Voyage to the Bottom of the Sea," the saga of a futuristic atomic submarine crew who encounter monstrous menaces as regularly as clockwork. "The Time Tunnel" featured a group of scientists experiencing anxiety on journeys to the past which seemed to be made up of old feature film footage, and "Land of the Giants" portrayed the adventures of a group of space travelers in a place where the people are ten times their size. "The Invaders" pitted actor Roy Thinnes against a horde of aliens who, disguised as human beings, contemplated the conquest of our planet in what appeared to

One of the unearthly beings that slithered through Gene Roddenberry's science fiction television series "The Outer Limits." Perhaps the best episode is "Demon with the Glass Hand," by Harlan Ellison.

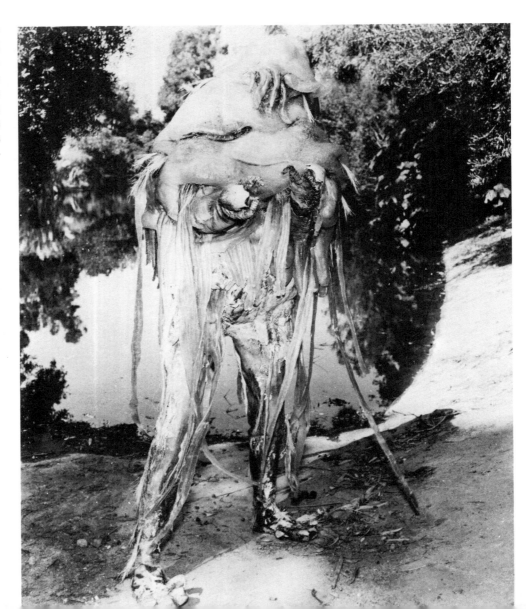

Peering through the cobwebs is Jonathan Frid, who portrayed the vampire on the daytime television serial "Dark Shadows."

be a singularly uninspired fashion. The program did not last long enough for them to inflict any serious damage.

The best work in this video vein was done by producer Gene Roddenberry, whose science fiction anthology series "The Outer Limits" enjoyed a respectable run in the early sixties. It was perhaps most noteworthy for the variety of outlandish creatures from outer space who paraded through its episodes. In 1966 Roddenberry and the NBC network launched what must be considered as the most successful science fiction program, "Star Trek." This saga of an exploratory mission through space lasted for three years, its life extended by an unprecedented viewer demand for its continuation. Even its eventual demise did nothing to discourage its fanatical followers, who even have annual conventions to celebrate their favorite TV fare. The program had, not surprisingly, its share of unearthly incidents and individuals, not the least of which was Mr. Spock (Leonard Nimoy), a half-human, half-alien member of the spaceship's crew whose pointed logic and pointed ears endeared him to millions.

A similar cult following was enjoyed by Jonathan Frid, who portrayed Barnabas Collins on that most improbable of television shows "Dark Shadows." It was ostensibly a soap opera, one of those sentimental daytime dramas with which networks hope to entertain housewives; but "Dark Shadows" soon developed into something quite different. Producer Dan Curtis hit upon the idea of a soap opera in the mode of the so-called Gothic novels that are enjoying current popularity; but the show rapidly became a frankly supernatural melodrama, complete with a werewolf named Quentin and Barnabas, the reluctant vampire. The program was broadcast by ABC late enough in the day to acquire an after-school juvenile audience, and it experienced several years of wild popularity, giving rise to such spin-offs as a series of novels and bubble-gum cards.

The horror content was somewhat subdued, but there was some compensation for bloodthirsty fans in the MGM motion picture version, the gory *House of Dark Shadows* (1970).

Writer Rod Serling, whose "Twilight Zone" had etherealized the airwaves a decade earlier, returned in 1970 as the host of "Night Gallery," a program that abandoned science fiction and fantasy to concentrate on hard-core chills. "Night Gallery" had a unique origin, beginning experimentally as one of a group of four rotating programs and becoming a full-fledged series in the next season. This NBC offering was perhaps the first network show to commit itself completely to the macabre, rather than gingerly introducing that element into a format built around a more general theme such as mystery or imagination. As such, it had its ups and downs, sometimes coming up with a good moment but usually falling victim to its own heavy-handedness, attempting to maintain suspense with a plot whose outcome was obvious before the exposition was over. Serling was no longer writing most of the scripts; a number of stories were adapted from writers like H. P. Lovecraft and Richard Matheson. The best effort was "They're Tearing Down Tim Riley's Bar," a tale involving the nostalgic hallucinations of a middle-aged man (William Windom) which was more poignant than petrifying.

Less sincere and less successful were such short-lived shows as "The Sixth Sense" and "Ghost Story." The former featured Gary Rhodes as a colorless psychic investigator; the latter was an anthology with Sebastian Cabot as the inevitable host. The failure of "Ghost Story" was especially surprising in that its producer was William Castle, whose motion pictures usually displayed expertise and enthusiasm. As it was, the series evidenced little more than someone's inexplicable enthusiasm for stories about animal ghosts. An attempt was made to stir up interest by changing the title to "Circle of Fear," but no other alterations were apparent. In 1973 the three major networks had abandoned this sort of programming, although syndicated shows included revivals of many of these morbid moments. There were also two British productions, "Touch of Evil" and "Great Mysteries," which occasionally touched on the terrifying, usually without much effect.

Television has hardly abandoned horror, however. Instead, the networks have promoted the genre with what would appear to be an ever increasing number of special one-shot productions. The demand for televised theatrical feature films has become so great that the supply is in danger of being exhausted; as a result several companies, notably Universal, have begun production of made-for-TV "movies," which have since become a network staple, especially on ABC. Inevitably there have been a few stabs at the supernatural, and a trend was inaugurated when one of them broke the ratings record for television movies. This was *The Night Stalker*, a contemporary vampire tale made for ABC's "Movie of the Week." It was, in its modest way, a clever and capable production. Produced by Dan Curtis of "Dark Shadows" fame, with a script by Richard Matheson based on a story by Jeff Rice, *The Night Stalker* featured Darren McGavin as a Las Vegas reporter who deduces that a series of murders are the work of a vampire (Barry Atwater). The supernatural menace is equated with the corruption and commercialization of the city, where the authorities refuse to accept even the most powerful proof of the vampire's existence, apparently less awed by the unholy than by the business reversals that publicity might produce. The newspaper stories are killed along with the vampire, and the reporter is run out of town. The film was popular enough to spawn a sequel and, in 1974, a weekly ABC series featuring McGavin as the occult investigator Kolchak. The wave of films that have followed in the wake of *The Night Stalker* have generally ranged from the dull to the deplorable; but there has been at least one exception: another Richard Matheson brainchild entitled *Duel*. This unnerving little film depicted the ordeal of a motorist who is pursued by a huge truck. The truck driver is never seen, and the persecution takes on occult or allegorical overtones while remaining a tangible threat. This TV movie, starring Dennis Weaver, was good enough to be released as a theatrical feature in Europe.

ABC has also employed another format for televised thrillers, ninety-minute taped dramas produced (sometimes in England) for their late-night grab bag, "Wide World of Entertainment." The originals have largely been a lame lot based on the premise that nothing is as chilling as watching a starlet age suddenly; but there have been a few more ambitious projects based on the classics. The man behind these is Dan Curtis, certainly the past decade's busiest perpetrator of video villainy. His taped version of *Frankenstein* in 1972 ran on two successive nights for a total of three hours. Like all previous adaptations, it altered the original story; more to the point, it was a disappointingly lackluster production, slow and shoddy with a monster whose appearance and behavior suggested a village idiot rather than an uncanny creation. Curtis did far better with his two-part adaptation of Oscar Wilde's *Picture of Dorian Gray*; it was in fact comparable to the 1945 MGM treatment which had featured Hurd Hatfield and George Sanders. Much of the credit for the TV version belongs to Wilde, whose dandified dialogue makes the scriptwriter's job enviable and easy; but the direction and acting were more than capable, with unknown Shane Briant quite effective in the title role.

Curtis also concocted a two-hour TV film version of *Dracula* for CBS in 1974, but it was something less than a triumph. Richard Matheson's script surprisingly failed to draw new blood from the old chestnut; the innovations he did present were frequently embarrassing (for instance, the soft-focus flashbacks representing the prevampire count as a great lover). Veteran villain Jack Palance was a disappointing Dracula, his performance an uneasy cross between Bela Lugosi and Christopher Lee that never got off the ground. As a director, Curtis failed to provide much atmosphere, and the rigid CBS censor left little opportunity for scenes of physical horror. This network, in fact, has displayed a strangely schizophrenic attitude regarding the whole genre: it has purchased and shown innumerable theatrical features of recent vintage, but it has cut them mercilessly. The current trend in horror films, for better or worse, is to structure them around sequences leading up to scenes of a shocking nature. To cut these, as CBS invariably does, is to create a series of anticlimaxes, often incoherent and occasionally incomprehensible. If the network finds the movies tasteless, it would surely be preferable not to show them at all.

NBC surpassed its rival in prestige if not productivity by presenting two elaborately mounted and well-publicized revivals; the first featured Kirk Douglas in, of all things, a musical version of *Dr. Jekyll and Mr. Hyde*, conceived and directed by David Winters. The combination of music and the macabre proved less incongruous than might have been anticipated. The songs were hardly memorable, but neither were they intrusive, and the result was something more than a spoof, not really a bad treatment of a once frightening story that had been done to death. Douglas's enthusiasm carried the show through some shaky transitions in tone, and there was one memorably macabre if essentially silly scene: Mr. Hyde seated at a piano in a graveyard, contemplating mayhem while sardonically serenading his masochistic mistress. Almost a year later, toward the end of 1973, NBC presented the most ambitious TV horror show to date, a two-part, four-hour version of Mary Shelley's story, entitled, with more arrogance than accuracy, *Frankenstein: The True Story*. It was, in fact, no more faithful to the novel than other adaptations and perhaps violated the spirit of the original more than less elaborate versions. Scriptwriters seem to find the theme so fascinating that they cannot resist attempts to improve on its treatment. The principal conceit of this version by Christopher Isherwood and Don Bachardy was to make the monster a handsome and charming young man who even makes a debut in high society before he begins to deteriorate with what looks like a case of terminal acne. Frankenstein himself is depicted as the unwilling tool of a sinister scientist named, in tribute to the original author's acquaintance, Dr. Polidori. Since yet another experimenter is given credit for the life-giving technique, Frankenstein (Leonard Whiting) emerges as a cipher, devoid of both immorality and ingenuity. A female "monster" is duly created and proves to be a presentable if unscrupulous young lady who is destroyed by her degenerated male counterpart (Michael Sarrazin) in a fit of jealous rage. The film also suffered from pedestrian direction by Jack Smight; but on the bright side of the coin, there was an outstanding supporting cast (James Mason, John Gielgud, Ralph Richardson, Michael Wilding, Margaret Leighton, and Agnes Moorehead), and an expensive series of period costumes and settings, including the climactic ocean voyage to the Arctic (characteristically mismanaged so that Frankenstein is fleeing the monster rather than pursuing). Despite its glaring faults, this sincere and serious effort, obviously involving large expenditures of time, talent, and cash, indicated the growing respectability of the genre, and devotees considered it a good sign. It was certainly a silk purse, albeit an empty one.

Television's acceptance of macabre material has been paralleled by developments in publishing. Not only are nerve-racking novels becoming increasingly popular, but pulse-pounding periodicals are on the upswing. Still the leader in the field is publisher James Warren, whose *Famous Monsters of Filmland* revived the morbid magazine in 1958 and whose *Creepy* resurrected the horror comic book in 1965. The latter was almost immediately joined by a second title, *Eerie*, followed in 1969 by *Vampirella*, which in addition to the usual variety of stories launched the adventures of the first sustained spectral character in comic books for many years. The beautiful bloodsucker Vampirella, as conceived by *Famous Monsters* editor Forrest J. Ackerman, is a refugee from outer space. The idea that her behavior is normal on her home planet makes her something less of a villainess, if no less a vampire, and most of her adventures have found her fighting temptation and a variety of menaces less moderate than herself. The striking portrait of "Vampi" on the cover of the first issue was by Frank Frazetta; Tom Sutton illustrated the early stories, and was later succeeded by José Gonzales, and then Leopold Sanchez. The first years of Warren's horror comics were distinguished by the work of artists like Wallace Wood and Johnny Craig, who had originally made their mark in the E.C. comics of an earlier era; later issues have introduced a variety of new artists, including many who live and work in Europe. Among the most talented of the young American contributors are Berni Wrightson, a master of mood whose style is reminiscent of E.C.'s Graham Ingels; and Richard Corben, recruited from the ranks of the underground horror comic books. All of these publications are edited by William DuBay, who is also at the helm of Warren's latest publication, a revival of Will Eisner's spectral sleuth the Spirit, who delighted aficionados by returning from the dead in 1974.

There may be no way to duplicate Eisner's unique talents, but all of Warren's earlier efforts inspired a rash of imitators. Dozens of horror film magazines appeared in the wake of *Famous Monsters*, most of them halfhearted efforts that collapsed after a few issues. An exception of sorts is Calvin T. Beck's *Castle of Frankenstein*, which has managed to hang on despite an extremely erratic schedule that has yielded only twenty issues in almost as many years. It can hardly be considered an economic rival to its more popular predecessor, but it is worth noting as the one magazine in the field that has not

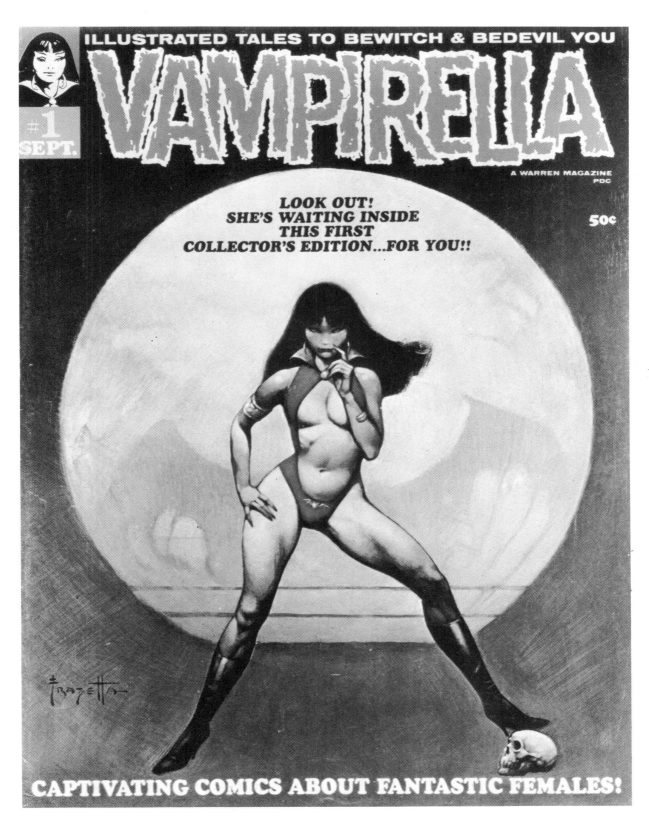

Frank Frazetta's version of the exotic Vampirella, an extraterrestrial, glamorous
bloodsucker. *Copyright © 1969, 1975 by Warren Communications Corp. All rights reserved.*

Will Eisner's spectral comic book character the Spirit was recently revived for a new generation by Warren Publishing. *Copyright © 1974, 1975 by Warren Communications Corp. All rights reserved.*

Barry Smith illustrated the Conan saga "Red Nails" in this striking panel from the pages of *Savage Tales. Copyright* © *1973, 1974. Courtesy of the Marvel Comics Group. All rights reserved.*

attempted to follow in Ackerman's jocular footsteps, offering instead a more serious treatment that makes it an alternative instead of just an imitation. As for horror comics, they have proliferated without much success, the longest run inexplicably achieved by an outfit specializing in reprinting second-rate stories from an earlier era and, when these have been run into the ground from constant overexposure, hiring an even less capable artist to redraw them. That this miserable line has continued to perpetuate itself for over a decade is a tribute to the popularity of the genre.

Warren's horror comics (and their imitators) defied the Comics Code ban on such material by using a new format: larger, premium-priced magazines printed without color. The mainstream comics publishers have approached the genre gingerly. Marvel Comics, the best-known line of the last decade, specializes in atomically mutated heroes like Jack Kirby's *Fantastic Four* and Steve Ditko's *Amazing Spider-Man*; but editor and writer Stan Lee has featured some occult characters like the psychic investigator Dr. Strange, who bowed in 1963. Lee's successor Roy Thomas has amplified this impulse, especially since Comics Code taboos regarding the macabre were modified in early 1971. The most impressive result was an adaptation of Robert E. Howard's *Weird Tales* stories, increasingly popular through paperback book revival, which began in 1970 under the title *Conan the Barbarian.* Much of the critical and popular success of this effort was due to the young English artist Barry Smith, whose increasingly capable renderings were vividly detailed and unusually imaginative. Perhaps sensing that their adaptations seem a bit tame beside their gory, sexy source, Marvel has moved into the black-and-white uncensored format with a Conan showcase called *Savage Tales*. It was a tentative venture, with more than a year between the first and second issues; but the company eventually moved into the field with several terror titles, although only the Conan stories display suitable enthusiasm. And since Barry Smith's departure to publish his own work, even the Conan series has shown a marked decline. Marvel also made Dracula and the Frankenstein monster the heroes of their own color comic books, with mixed results, and attempted to revive the horror fiction pulp magazine with *The Haunt of Horror*, which lasted for only two issues before it was transformed into a comic book.

A much more commendable move in the same direction was made in 1973 when publisher Leo Margulies and veteran editor Sam Moskowitz revived the legendary *Weird Tales*, half a century after its original appearance and nineteen years after it had folded. The magazine has presented fiction of the highest quality, concentrating on reprints not only from its earlier incarnation but also from a variety of sources uncovered by the editor's remarkable research. A labor of love that appears to be growing in circulation, the new *Weird Tales* is a signal that the morbid imagination is experiencing its finest hour.

Nothing shows this more clearly, though, than the incredible proliferation of horror films, climaxed by the appearance of one that seems likely to become one of the most lucrative movies in motion picture history, *The Exorcist* (1973). This major production was a far cry from the growing number of cheap and lurid "exploitation" films loosely based on horror themes. Television had produced a jaded audience, and thus movies with vaguely *verboten* contents came into vogue, often making profits without showing the slightest sign of artistic achievement or even intention. While most of these deplorable grade "Z" quickies tended toward pornography, a few found financial rewards in depicting the crudest of tortures and mutations, generally rendered totally unbelievable by lack of technical ability. Occasionally sex and the supernatural were combined, as in the feeble *Orgy of the Dead* (1966). No film in this category was more thoroughly repulsive than the German export *Mark of the Devil* (1972). This catalog of the atrocities perpetrated by witch-hunters featured, at least for American audiences, the offer of a free vomit bag to anyone bored enough to attend. Thus the worst hacks of the previous generation, motivated by materialism, pursued the same extremism the young underground artists embraced in their search for artistic freedom.

Still, many of the most effective motion pictures in the genre continue to be produced not by the officially sanctioned studios on slumming expeditions, nor by their equally insincere counterparts in the lower depths of technical poverty. Most of the important work has been done, as it usually is, by those with an authentic commitment to their product. This category consists, as it has for the past decade, of American International in the United States and Hammer Films in England, although the latter has considerable competition from the newer company, Amicus, which continues to specialize in films combining several short episodes.

Some of the Amicus productions, including *Torture Garden* (1968), *The House That Dripped Blood* (1971), and *Asylum* (1972), were written by the prolific Robert Bloch, adapted from his stories. The latter two especially were well received by reviewers, presumably because they were well mounted and capably performed; but not even a Bloch screenplay could capture the wry quality of his fiction. Amicus encountered much the same problem with *Tales from the Crypt* (1972) and *The Vault of Horror* (1973), two collections from the old but increasingly reputable E.C. comic books. Screenwriter

Peter Cushing, an actor who usually plays his parts with minimal makeup,
portrayed this vengeful corpse in the film adaptation of the
comic book series *Tales from the Crypt. Courtesy of Cinerama Releasing.*

Milton Subotsky failed to convey the tone of the originals, a fact that was only
underscored by the decision to have the staid English actor Ralph Richardson portray
the formerly leering, jeering Crypt-Keeper. The only episode in either film that was
really effective was "Poetic Justice," a tale from *Crypt* starring Peter Cushing, adapted
from drawings by Graham Ingels. Still, the mixing of the media in these two films was an
irresistible lure for horror fans.

Meanwhile, Hammer Films seems to have been experiencing some fluctuation in the
quality of its production, although the quantity has remained consistently high. Most of
the newer movies from Hammer have not enjoyed the services of writer Jimmy Sangster
or director Terence Fisher, whose efforts made the studio's early efforts so impressive; yet
it seems fair to suggest that the more recent efforts are not so much markedly inferior as
overly familiar. Perhaps the outstanding production, at least partly because it was the
most unusual, was *Five Million Years to Earth* (1968). This sedate yet suspenseful science
fiction story, directed by Roy Ward Baker from a script by Nigel Kneale, bypassed
Hammer's beloved Victorian setting to depict excavations in modern London which
reveal evidence of an ancient alien invasion. The hypothesis of the story is that these
visitors from space inspired the legends of demonology and altered the history of the
human race.

Hammer's series characters were not on their best behavior. Christopher Lee returned
in *Dracula Has Risen from the Grave* (1968), *Taste the Blood of Dracula* (1969), *Scars of Dracula*
(1970), *Dracula A.D. '72* (1972), and *The Satanic Rites of Dracula* (1974). The titles alone
give some indication of the increasing desperation of the writers, who found it difficult to
concoct new tricks for the count and began structuring their stories so that he was more

and more of a minor character. Lee, whose commanding presence gave each of these films at least a few good moments, finally announced in 1974 that he was through with the part for good, although there remains the possibility that a suitable script might tempt him. As it happened, Lee's best recent film for Hammer was *The Devil's Bride* (1967), directed by Terence Fisher with a screenplay by the busy Richard Matheson. The source was Dennis Wheatley's novel *The Devil Rides Out*, and Lee, strange as it seems, played the hero, psychic investigator de Richleau. This movie was just a bit too early to benefit from the trendy interest in Satanism, but it was superior to most of its successors; the scene in which the protagonists huddle within a pentacle while the forces of evil rage around them is authentically awesome.

Peter Cushing has carried on as Dr. Frankenstein in *Frankenstein Created Woman* (1966), *Frankenstein Must Be Destroyed* (1969), and *Frankenstein and the Monster from Hell* (1974)—none of them exactly classics, but all preferable to some of the sleazy American products that were beginning to appear using Frankenstein and Dracula. The most astounding of these were combined on a double bill in 1966: Embassy's *Jesse James Meets Frankenstein's Daughter* and *Billy the Kid vs. Dracula*, which unfortunately were not as hilarious as their titles might suggest. Hammer may have been reacting to this sort of product when it released *Horror of Frankenstein* (1970), in appearance and apparently in intention a parody of the company's germinal 1957 offering, *The Curse of Frankenstein*. Ralph Bates played the demented doctor in the 1970 film, sparing Cushing the task of burlesquing his most famous role.

The best Hammer productions of recent years, as has been indicated, were not bound by the restrictions of the series format. The vampire theme proved most durable. *The Vampire Lovers* (1970), directed by Roy Ward Baker, was a capable version of Le Fanu's "Carmilla," with the erotic elements emphasized, particularly by the performance of the star, voluptuous Ingrid Pitt. This story was rehashed a scant year later in *Lust for a Vampire*, an inferior sequel that looked like a regrettable remake. The most interesting treatment of the bloodsucking breed was *Vampire Circus* (1972), an uneven but extremely eerie effort that recaptured some of the air of mystery absent from the era's busier films. Robert Young directed this tale of a traveling troupe of terrors who descend on an isolated village, using their supernatural powers to put on a dazzling show that is also devilishly seductive.

In other areas, Hammer has offered a glut of ghouls that includes a few interesting variations on familiar themes. Ralph Bates and Martine Beswick (in appearance if not intensity a latter-day Barbara Steele) portrayed *Dr. Jekyll and Sister Hyde* (1972). The title tells the whole story; the details of the scientist's transformation were not as interesting as the concept. Hammer's lackluster mummy series was invigorated after several dull entries by *Blood from the Mummy's Tomb* (1972), which was not the usual ambulatory bandage saga but a version of Bram Stoker's novel of reincarnation, *The Jewel of the Seven Stars*. Despite the tasteless title (perhaps the inevitable result of too many movies with the same subject), the film, directed by Seth Holt, was subtle and imaginative.

American International has continued its dominance of macabre movies in the United States, even distributing many of Hammer's offerings. Although Roger Corman has abandoned the genre, his influence lingers on in the comparatively polished color productions that have replaced the black-and-white quickies of the company's earliest days. More attempts have been made to adapt the works of H. P. Lovecraft, with depressing results; *Die, Monster, Die!* (1965), directed by Daniel Haller, turned "The Colour Out of Space" into a pedestrian "mad doctor" muddle, unredeemed even by the presence of Boris Karloff. *The Dunwich Horror* (1970) was duller still, with the perennial juvenile Dean Stockwell totally miscast as the demented, demon-spawned Wilbur Whately, and Sandra Dee, unbelievable as the inevitable Hollywood heroine. Haller muddled through again, making no attempt to depict the monstrosities of the author's imagination, opting instead for a feeble attempt to turn the tale into *Rosemary's Baby*.

The studio's Poe series has continued in fits and starts; for a while it seemed that every Vincent Price film would be credited to that author. Such was the case with *The Conqueror Worm* (1968), shown in England under the more appropriate title *The Witchfinder General*. This account of the inquisitorial tactics of the historical figure Matthew Hopkins had nothing to do with Poe; but it was effectively directed by Michael Reeves, and it received high praise in some quarters, although it was a bit grim and realistic for the average "monster movie" buff. *The Cry of the Banshee* (1970), a crude elaboration of an Irish legend, was attributed to Poe without even the courtesy gesture of naming it after one of his works.

The ultimate abandonment of literary adaptations led, on the whole, to preferable productions. Vincent Price got one of his juiciest roles as *The Abominable Dr. Phibes*, playing a crazed physician who takes revenge against the colleagues who have allowed his wife to die. Presumably deceased, Phibes keeps himself in action with a quaint clockwork conglomeration, part of the art deco decor that made the film charming as well as chilling. Beneath his suspiciously stiff Vincent Price mask, the face of Phibes was foul and fearsome, giving Price one of his rare chances to play a monster instead of just a malevolent mortal. This 1971 film, directed by Robert Fuest, was so successful that it led to a sequel a year later, giving Price his first continuing character—remarkable in that few actors have received star status in the genre, as he had already done, without this kind of audience identification. Still, Price was perhaps better served by *Theater of Blood* (1973), in which he was cast as a crazed Shakespearean actor who reacts to a bad press by murdering the critics. Price's essentially comic portrayal, matched by that of Diana Rigg as his helpful daughter, was contrasted with scenes of explicit horror. Possibly fearing for their own safety, real reviewers were generous with their praise for this film, which, although released by United Artists, maintained the tone and the plot structure of American International's Dr. Phibes movies.

Featured with Price in *Dr. Phibes Rises Again* was Robert Quarry, an actor who gained some following in *Count Yorga—Vampire* (1970) and *The Return of Count Yorga* (1971). Quarry was a bit heavy-set for a hungry horror, but he looked good in contrast to the ragged production and intermittently inept performers around him. Considerably more interesting (if not entirely for artistic reasons) was the vampire series American International inaugurated in 1972 with *Blacula*. William Marshall portrayed an African prince, corrupted by Count Dracula, who is revived unexpectedly in modern Los Angeles. The racial switch was startling if not inherently implausible, and there were some political implications in the action, as "Blacula" (fortunately never addressed by this title during the course of the film) wipes out a platoon of police to express his indignation over the destruction of his mistress. The protagonist also breaks precedent when, having done his worst, he commits suicide, disdainfully exposing himself to sunlight in what appears to be a commentary upon the efforts of his opponents. Marshall had sufficient dignity and energy to keep the project afloat, resulting in plans for a number of movies in the same vein. The only one to appear, however, was *Scream, Blacula, Scream* (1973), an inferior sequel.

Although Amicus, Hammer, and American International have been manufacturing the majority of movie menaces in recent years, less sinister studios have done their worst as well. The field of fantasy films received a boost from the release of some expensive and profitable science fiction films, notably Stanley Kubrick's massive *2001: A Space Odyssey* (1968). This ambitious MGM release, presented on the huge Cinerama screen, explored the theme, by now familiar in fiction, that our planet has been under the influence of omniscient extraterrestrial forces since the dawn of time. Although the treatment was occasionally awesome, the result could hardly be classified as a "horror film." The same was true of the less impressive but more accessible *Planet of the Apes* (1968). Scripted by Rod Serling from a novel by Pierre Boulle, this depicted a voyage to a world where intelligent simians rule primitive humans, revealing in the climax that this is the earth as it will be in the future. As indicated by the presence of heroic star Charlton Heston, the movie was basically an adventure, with some small touches of social satire. It was pretty well divorced from the mood of terror, but it nevertheless appealed to the many monster lovers who seem to have an inordinate fondness for apes and were justifiably impressed with the ingenious monkey makeup. Twentieth Century-Fox did well enough in this monkey business to follow it up with four sequels in as many years, and the simian saga became, briefly, a CBS television series in 1974. Heston avoided the sequels, but he went on to appear in *The Omega Man* (1971), a slick version of Matheson's *I Am Legend* which turned the novel's vampires into presumably more respectable "mutants"; and *Soylent Green* (1973), a view of an overpopulated future in which industry provides protein for people by using the previous population. These efforts proved to be more earnest than effective, but their big budgets and intermittent moralizing created the impression that films with bizarre subjects were being taken seriously.

Of course, events such as the recent moon landing gave science fiction a sort of status with which more frankly fearsome fantasies could hardly compete, despite the burgeoning interest in the occult. Still, there were some interesting developments from unexpected sources, as producers and studios not usually associated with the macabre ventured into the domain of dread. Cinerama, usually identified with elaborate spectacles, released a small shocker called *Willard* in 1971. Much to their amazement, it proved to be a box office bonanza and even inaugurated a small cycle of imitations. Willard was a young man with a trained pack of murderous rats, and his unlikely popularity inspired a number of films featuring not overgrown monsters, but lots of little ones. There was even a sequel, *Ben*, named for the lead rodent. MGM followed the trend off the deep end with *Night of the Lepus*, about a plague of rabbits. Nobody was capable of taking this too seriously.

On the brighter side, two outstanding directorial debuts resulted in films with impressive new perspectives. *Targets* (1968) was written, directed, and produced by Peter Bogdanovich, who has since acquired an enviable reputation for work of considerably less ingenuity. *Targets* also provided an admirable swan song for Boris Karloff, who died shortly after its release. His role was virtually a self-portrait, that of an elderly horror movie star who wishes to retire, convinced that his roles are irrelevant when contrasted with the less romantic terrors of contemporary civilization. As the film progresses, his preparations for his last premiere, at a drive-in theater, are juxtaposed with adventures of an apparently normal young man who goes berserk, first murdering his family and then setting out on a career of aimless sniping. The paths of the two characters cross at the climax of the film, as Karloff arrives at the drive-in where the sniper, hidden behind the silver screen, is picking off thrill-seeking patrons in their cars. The aged actor, furious when his secretary is shot, marches mechanically toward the killer, who panics at the sight of the man whose gigantic image is also menacing him from the screen. Thus, in a contrived but powerful scene, the imaginary monster defeats a genuine menace. Although a trifle self-conscious, *Targets* is an impressive tour de force, Karloff's best film in decades, and an important landmark in the genre. Unfortunately the film was badly handled by Paramount, receiving less promotion and distribution than the most pedestrian product might be expected to deserve.

Much the same problem affected the success of *Night of the Living Dead* (1968), an independent production that got no attention at the time of its release but eventually acquired an underground reputation that kept it in circulation for years. Made on a minuscule budget, it ultimately earned millions. Directed and photographed by George Romero from a script by John Russo, *Night of the Living Dead* was the work of a television crew from Pittsburgh, Pennsylvania. Working with a cast of unknowns and limited technical facilities, they created a harrowing film, all the more effective because of its naturalistic documentary quality. The premise is that the dead have risen to devour the living (the cause, that old devil radiation, is passed over without much interest by author and audience); the plot involves a group of people besieged in an isolated house. Many effects are dependent on irony and reversed clichés: an attractive young couple who seem most likely to survive are destroyed in a rash attempt to escape. Even the film's apparent hero, a black veteran who plots strategy against the ungodly invaders, is in for his share of surprises. This man of action (Duane Jones), is opposed by a blustering, cowardly businessman (played by the film's coproducer, Karl Hardman) who argues impotently that everyone would be safe barricaded in the cellar. Finally, after all his companions have been slaughtered, Jones manages to save himself—by hiding in the cellar. He emerges when he realizes that the authorities have cleared the area of the awful army and, dazed and bedraggled, he is taken for a walking corpse; his rescuers kill him. One of the most brilliant sequences shows the group gathered around the house's television set. At first eager for information, they are gradually lulled by their role as observers, nearly oblivious to the horrors around them until the electricity suddenly fails and reality rears its ugly head. Uncompromisingly realistic, perhaps all the more so for its almost archaic use of black-and-white film, *Night of the Living Dead* generates so much clammy claustrophobia that it has become the center of a cult.

But this and all other recent frightening films have been overshadowed by the monumental impact of *The Exorcist* (1973), at once the most expensive and the most profitable production of its kind. Based on the best-selling 1971 novel by William Peter Blatty, it deals with the theme of demonic possession. What distinguishes both versions of *The Exorcist* from less popular works in the genre is, among other things, its air of conviction. Most fearsome fantasies for the past two centuries have at least indirectly

Linda Blair, as a child possessed by a demon, gives her movie star mother (Ellen Burstyn) a hard time in the controversial but undeniably effective film *The Exorcist. From the motion picture* The Exorcist *courtesy of Warner Bros. Inc. Copyright © 1974.*

acknowledged the skepticism of their audiences, making an almost playful appeal to archaic beliefs. Blatty's story is based on a sort of psychic phenomenon that major religious institutions are still inclined to take seriously, and reports of presumably authentic cases of possession and exorcism were used as part of a publicity campaign. Critics who were dumbfounded by the appeal of *The Exorcist* attempted to attribute its success to the era's renewed interest in the occult; Blatty replied with some indignation that numerous works with comparable subjects had not done nearly as well. He was better at refuting other people's suggestions than at providing his own, for there seems little doubt that what attracted sensation seekers to the book and especially to the movie was the scurrilous nature of its incidents. Blatty employed what Henry James called "the turn of the screw," the twist of having evil wreak its havoc upon an innocent child, a ploy that by now seems almost obligatory for those who wish their horrors to reach a public usually immune to them. But *The Exorcist* was not content to depict innocence threatened by death and decay; instead, it showed the possessed young girl urinating on a carpet, masturbating with a crucifix, and vomiting on a priest. These are the scenes that patrons of the film seem to find the most memorable, and they are fairly obviously distinguishable from the graphic gruesomeness that might be expected of a horror movie. In this sense at least, *The Exorcist* is more shocking than frightening. On the other hand, director William Friedkin did succeed in conjuring up some uncanny atmosphere, aided and abetted by elaborate work with the sound track, makeup, and special effects. Still, with all this effort, and with all the offensive details, it is ironic that many viewers should report themselves most disturbed by the coldly clinical scenes in which the child Regan undergoes a series of exhaustive medical tests.

A work like *The Exorcist*, with its scandalous incidents and its insistence that its subject is plausible, only serves to emphasize the essentially playful nature of most work in the field. While the new credibility of the occult has inspired a few fantasies, there is an apparently permanent audience, gleefully living in fear, who recognize imaginary terrors as projections of sublimated emotions. For this audience, an air of conviction is sufficient. The demons of the unconscious serve social purposes by expressing antisocial attitudes, and in time they become so acceptable that they can be employed in extraordinary ways. It has already been noted that these presumably frightening figures are regarded with considerable affection by children; while Blatty titillates adults with his tale of corrupted youth, the average kid finds Dracula about as disturbing as Donald Duck. In fact, the Count and his colleague the Frankenstein monster have recently been used by a large cereal concern, General Mills, to make its products more attractive to prepubescent palates. The pair appear in animated form on television, endorsing breakfast foods called Count Chocula and Frankenberry, and their pictures appear on the boxes on supermarket shelves. The monsters are among us, sugarcoated and vitamin enriched. Such a situation might be viewed with alarm; but it is really a demonstration that we have nothing to fear from these creatures, that the slight shudder they may evoke and the minor misanthropy they may express are simply safety valves that make our often grim world, if anything, a little less monstrous.

INDEX

Note: Films, television and radio programs, and comics are listed by title. Literary works appear under their authors' names.

243